Bodies and Other Objects

Bodies and Other Objects is written for students, scholars and anyone with an interest in embodied cognition – the claim that the human mind cannot be understood without regard for the actions and capacities of the body. The impulse to write this book was a dissatisfaction with the inconsistent and often shallow use of the term 'embodied cognition'. This text attempts to reframe cognitive science with a unified theory of embodied cognition in which sensorimotor elements provide the basis for cognition, including symbolic exchanges that arise within a society of agents. It draws on ideas and evidence from experimental psychology, neuroscience, philosophy and anthropology in reaching the conclusion that human cognition is best understood as the means by which exchanges within a constantly evolving network of skilful bodies and objects are regulated so as to further human interests.

Rob Ellis is Emeritus Professor of Psychology within the School of Psychology at the University of Plymouth.

Bodies and Other Objects

The Sensorimotor Foundations of Cognition

Rob Ellis

University of Plymouth

CAMBRIDGE
UNIVERSITY PRESS

CAMBRIDGE
UNIVERSITY PRESS

University Printing House, Cambridge CB2 8BS, United Kingdom

One Liberty Plaza, 20th Floor, New York, NY 10006, USA

477 Williamstown Road, Port Melbourne, VIC 3207, Australia

314-321, 3rd Floor, Plot 3, Splendor Forum, Jasola District Centre, New Delhi - 110025, India

79 Anson Road, #06-04/06, Singapore 079906

Cambridge University Press is part of the University of Cambridge.

It furthers the University's mission by disseminating knowledge in the pursuit of education, learning and research at the highest international levels of excellence.

www.cambridge.org
Information on this title: www.cambridge.org/9781107629806
DOI: 10.1017/9781107446809

First published 2018
First paperback edition 2020

A catalogue record for this publication is available from the British Library

Library of Congress Cataloging in Publication data
Names: Ellis, Rob (Psychologist), author.
Title: Bodies and other objects : the sensorimotor foundations of cognition /
by Rob Ellis, University of Plymouth.
Description: Cambridge, United Kingdom ; New York, NY : Cambridge
University Press, 2019. | Includes bibliographical references and index.
Identifiers: LCCN 2018019759 | ISBN 9781107060289
Subjects: LCSH: Cognition. | Cognition and culture.
Classification: LCC BF311 .E485135 2019 | DDC 153–dc23
LC record available at https://lccn.loc.gov/2018019759

ISBN 978-1-107-06028-9 Hardback
ISBN 978-1-107-62980-6 Paperback

For Clare, Joe and Tom

Contents

Illustrations

Acknowledgements

This text, like all other artefacts, is the product of an almost unbounded set of influences and collaborative encounters, most of which are invisible or forgotten. Among the most salient examples are three years in the Department of Experimental Psychology at Oxford, where I was meant to be busy with behavioural investigations of computational theories of vision. In fact, I learned that nothing was that neat, guided by the superb iconoclast, and my thesis supervisor, Alan Allport. There then followed several decades in the School of Psychology in the University of Plymouth, where I was meant to be busy with, among other things, research in artificial intelligence. I was saved again by encounters with a group of very talented experimentalists who became the Vision and Action research group at Plymouth: Mike Tucker, Ed Symes, Noreen Derbyshire and Lari Vainio. More recent guides have been Patric Bach, who forced me to think harder about other agents in the dynamics of affordance, and Joe Ellis, who broadened my gaze to include the role of material culture in shaping human behaviours. Many people helped directly with the text. Jon Silas read the original manuscript and provided comments which have improved the final version. Hetty Marx and Janka Romero, editors at Cambridge University Press, provided the patient encouragement needed to complete the project.

Introduction

This monograph seeks a unified theory of embodied cognition by gathering together work in cognitive science, experimental psychology, neuroscience, anthropology and philosophy of mind. It will attempt to persuade the reader that human cognition is not a biological given, but in large part a cultural artefact, invented by successive generations of especially dexterous primates.

The bulk of the text will be concerned with the mundane. Buried within the everyday bodily actions of humans is the key to understanding their more celebrated achievements. We tend to take much of what we do in the world for granted. This is not surprising because we just do most of it, seemingly without any great effort. Consider this typical scene from a – typical day in a typical metropolitan culture. A mother, father and three children are gathered together for breakfast. All have a busy day ahead of them. The parents both work and the children attend school. Breakfast is a rushed affair, and everyone is helping with its preparation, except the eldest child, a teenage boy who is seated at a table sending a text message with a flurry of thumbs on his smartphone screen. The father is standing behind the boy and passes a jug of milk over the boy's head to his daughter standing on the opposite side of the table. He holds the jug around its base so that his daughter can securely grasp it by the handle. She places the jug at the centre of the table. Her sister, who has been preparing a pot of coffee, arrives at the table and places it alongside the milk jug. The mother adds a basket of bread and pastries. They all now sit and begin a seemingly orchestrated exchange of bowls, cups and food stuffs. Liquids are poured, and bread is cut. Conversations begin. The father asks the boy if he finished his homework the previous evening. The boy simply smiles in response. The mother, witnessing this exchange, raises her eyebrows, but changes the theme of the conversation. She asks her husband to call into the shops on his way home that evening to buy the ingredients for the evening meal, telling him she has left a list on the table by the front door.

The music that has been playing in the background now switches to a weather forecast. It will rain heavily in the afternoon. There are hurried conversations about changing their plans as a consequence. The mother decides to collect her daughters from school by car, rather than their usual routine of walking home. And so, it goes on; this routine and familiar coping in the world. We tend to think that there are no great accomplishments here; no acts of creative genius. But if we delve just a little into these routine exchanges between humans and the objects in their world it becomes clear that they depend on quite remarkable abilities, many unique to our species.

Probably the most immediately striking in this regard is the extensive use of symbolic exchanges. Much of the activity is immersed within, and depends, on spoken language: requests for objects to be passed, enquiries about past events and dialogues about plans for future events. But there also other symbolic 'props'. The written shopping list placed by the front door is an augmentation of unreliable human memory. The radio provides information about events distant in time and space, as does the smartphone, which in addition allows communication, using written or spoken language, with people not currently present. There are other types of communication too. The meaning of the son's wry smile and the mother's raised eyebrow in response is transparent. The two humans appear to have an almost direct access to the other's state of mind as a consequence of the merest facial expression. Look a little closer and there appear to be many other cases of 'mind reading'.

The simple act of passing an object, such as the milk jug, from one person to another involves precise coordination between the two agents, which depends on an element of prediction. The grasping hand of each person must arrive at a position in space and be oriented so as allow the one to maintain an effective grip until the moment of exchange, and the other to find a place to grasp at the same moment. The degree of dexterity and coordination of such actions is almost certainly unique to humans. As is, of course, the making of artefacts that facilitate this joint activity, such as the handled milk jug which allows a precision grip to secure the object and use it effectively or to take it from another person who offers it by grasping it with a power grip around its body with the handle orientated towards the recipient. Or the smartphone which allows the very mobile human thumb to dance across its screen.

Other important aspects of the scenario are entirely hidden from view. Our observations and description of an unfolding scenario such as this is likely to be highly anthropocentric: we tend to notice what the humans are doing or saying, and mostly ignore the other entities. The people are the actors and prime movers of events. In fact, as will be made clear as we proceed, the objects on which the humans act are not passive. They summon behavioural responses from the actors and are active participants in the acts of object exchange for example. The precise posture of a hand as it closes on a three-dimensional object is potentiated by the visual properties of the to-be-grasped object, its shape and orientation. The objects in the scene assist human activities in other ways. Objects in the world are arranged so as to facilitate actions, for example jugs and pots and cups are placed on the table within the reaching space of those sitting around it. The placing of the shopping list by the front door, so as to draw attention to it as the father leaves the house, is another example, but now its placement is an external support for an act of remembering, rather than reaching. Both are illustrations of external scaffolding, a term widely used in embodied accounts of cognition. That is, they serve to augment the mental and physical activities of an individual. Moreover, much of what we do depends on external scaffolding of some sort, so, and this is very important for what follows in the main text, the essential processes and mechanisms of cognition are not confined to those internal to the person. They extend beyond the body.

The text that follows has the aim of illuminating the connections between these various and, seemingly, very different human behaviours. The central argument is that they are intrinsically interwoven. Human dexterity and sociality are the foundations on which human cognition has been built. At some point in the evolution of the ancestors of *Homo sapiens* it became possible for them to fabricate and use stone tools. With these technical skills, it was possible to constantly reconstruct and enrich their environmental niche which forced adaptations in subsequent generations, allowing an expansion in group size and thereby placing increasing demands on coordination among the members of the group. The need to predict the actions of others when engaged in joint actions, to read their minds, became important. Simultaneously or subsequently explicit communication augmented this implicit dialogue, with, again, their dexterity making it possible for them to use gesture in a prototype language, which with subsequent elaborations became a spoken language. Such refinements in, now, our social and *material* cultural provided novel forms of scaffolding and formed the basis of the paradoxical explosion in human capacities that *came after* the fixing of the human genome. In particular symbol systems, including written language, took us from the late Palaeolithic to the space age.

In abstracting from mundane joint activity in a world of objects, cognitive science has tended to neglect the essential mutual dependencies of the sort just sketched. It is perhaps guilty of an excessively individualistic approach, in that its centre of attention has been the capacities of the lone agent responding to, rather than acting on, very impoverished fragments of their world. It might be argued, in its defence, that such abstractions are essential to the process of scientific analysis. To understand the psychophysical properties of the human visual system, say, it is necessary to methodically investigate its capacities and properties, in isolated, empty handed and largely immobile individuals. Yet this way of understanding vision misses much that is important. For example, we humans are fairly good at judging middle-range distances, say, seeing whether the coffee pot is reachable from where you sit at the breakfast table. This 'seeing' of a distance is not the outcome of purely visual processes. Rather it also depends on the potential for acting on the object: whether you can actually reach the pot and whether you intend to. This was demonstrated by Witt, Proffitt and Epstein (2005) who had participants judge the distance of targets while either holding a tool or not. Their estimates of distance were reduced while holding the tool, but only if they intended to reach towards the target. This dependence of a perceptual judgement on a bodily capacity and an intention to act on the world illustrates the way our understanding of cognition is incomplete if it is considered independent of bodily activity in the world.

There are many, many similar demonstrations of a close link between action and perception. Also, between action and higher-level cognition. These observations have tended to form the core of what might be termed a school of embodied cognition, within which various ideas on how to account for the data contend. This, rather loose, coalition tends to draw on particular modern philosophical traditions. Chapter 1 attempts to make sense of these diverse ideas and their, as it turns out, rather awkward philosophical bedfellows. Chapter 2 discusses the human visual system so as to illustrate an embodied understanding of perception in which the detection of behavioural possibilities is central, and thus contrast this with an orthodoxy that treats the perceiver as a passive recipient of sense data from which descriptions of the external world are derived. Chapter 3 focuses on tool use and its role in sculpting the human perceptual-motor system during evolution and individual lifespans, noting that skilled tool use results in an extension of the agent's effective body. Chapter 4 places the agent in their social context and discusses the implications of recent work investigating the human mirror neurone system. It will be claimed that joint action on objects is the key to understanding its function. Chapter 5 attends to the role of physical objects in shaping human societies and human brains. It will argue that the neglect of human material culture within cognitive science has led it to underestimate the degree to which human cognition is a cultural artefact. Chapter 6 treats language as a special case of a cultural artefact and speculates that it arose as an elaboration of the skills needed to cooperate with others in joint actions. The seventh, and final chapter attempts to synthesise the arguments to form a unified framework for cognition and an associated research programme.

1   Reframing Cognition

Cognitive science is immature. A symptom of its immaturity is the flux of contending theoretical schools or, to use the term favoured here, conceptual frameworks. Right now, one of its periodic shifts may be in progress, with so-called embodied accounts of mind challenging the decades old dominance of, so-called, symbolic or computational approaches. In this first chapter we will attempt to trace the gross outlines of the embodied school and then suggest how it might be elaborated and refined so as to provide a coherent conceptual framework for cognitive science. A consequence of this project is a broadening of the notion of 'cognitive science'. The remainder of the book will dig deeper, examining the elements of the argument in more detail and considering the evidence in each case. The aim is to present, finally, a unified framework for embodied cognitive science, alongside the existing empirical support for it and a research programme that the framework entails.

Competing Conceptual Frameworks

Embodied cognition, or an embodied account of mind, to be characterised in this chapter, is a major growth point in cognitive science. Undoubtedly. What is less certain is its coherence. At this point it appears to be a very loose alliance of fragmented, empirical demonstrations of close links between some aspects of cognition and the human body (as in the example of a perceptual judgement of distance in the introduction), combined with some aspects of a, roughly, phenomenological philosophy of mind. It is also often portrayed as hostile to 'symbolic' accounts of human behaviour. This text is an attempt to move towards a unified theory of embodied cognition, in which sensorimotor elements provide the basis for cognition, including symbolic exchanges that arise within a society of agents.

Let us begin with a crude caricature of the two positions: embodied and symbolic accounts of mind. Two very different depictions of the human body are shown in Figure 1. The first is both beautiful and well known: Rodin's sculpture of the *Le Penseur* (*The Thinker*). It is usually taken to represent a person (perhaps a philosopher) in deep thought. This is suggested by the very pose. It depicts a man who has stilled his body by sitting, braced on a rock, his head held steady by resting his chin on the back of one of his empty hands. His eyes are half-closed and directed towards the ground to better shield his thoughts from sensory interruptions. Perhaps. The fact that it suggests this so directly reveals our pre-conceptions about what it is to think. We tend to share the idea that thinking is something occurring in the head of an individual and not dependent on either sensory or body activity, both of which get in the way of really serious thought. These preconceptions are so powerful that the sculpture was actually renamed 'Le Penseur' by the foundry workers casting early versions in bronze. Its original title had been 'Le poète'. Now contrast this image of thought with the second depiction of the human body in Figure 1. This slightly unsettling image, it will be contended, better captures the essence of human mental activity.

The troll-like figure is in fact a three-dimensional version of Penfield's sensory cortical homunculus, with the body scaled to the proportion of sensory cortex devoted to its various parts (Penfield and Boldrey, 1937). Penfield, a neurosurgeon, investigated the brains of patients with epilepsy prior to surgical treatments. He applied mild electrical stimulation to the motor and sensory cortex of the brains of conscious patients, noting how this affected their speech and other bodily responses so as to minimise speech and movement losses after surgery. Data from many such proce-dures revealed that human motor cortex and sensory cortex were both organised as if they were a map of the body, with adjacent regions related to (roughly) adjacent regions of the body. Two aspects of these map are of concern to the development of the argument here. First, the distortions: our troll clearly shows that the hands, mouth and tongue have a disproportionate amount of cortical surface devoted to them.[1] Second, the fact that these sensorimotor 'maps' are found in the cortex at all. That such extensive *cortical* mechanisms for the control of hand, and other, movements, exist should be surprising given their lowly posi-tion in current theories in cognitive science in which symbols and trans-formations of symbols constitute the primary currency of mental processes and cognition generally.

---

[1] It will slowly become apparent as we proceed here how these three body parts might be linked and why they are so important in understanding human cognition.

Figure 1a and 1b Two images of a human, which seem to capture a very difference essence.

The first is an image of Sharon Price-James's sculpture depicting Penfield's *Sensory homunculus* and the second shows August Rodin's *Le Penseur*.

The early investigators of cortical function in non-human primates, using similar electrical simulation techniques to Penfield, questioned why such basic, motor functions did not have purely spinal and subcortical origins. Leyton and Sherrington (1917) provided a possible answer. The motor responses they elicited by the electrical stimulation of cortex of apes were 'fractional', that is, they appeared to be an element of a number of higher-order combinations of such elemental parts. Examples were the extension of an index finger, lip closure, retraction of the tongue and flexion of an ankle. They concluded that:

It would seem that in order to preserve the possibility of being interchangeably compounded in a variety of ways, successive or simultaneous, these movements must lie, as more or less discrete and separable elements, within the grasp of the organ which has the varied compounding of them. (ibid.: 178)

Thus, it was possible, the argument goes, to construct a large number of movement sequences by combining elemental parts in different ways. Importantly it also provides the basis of skill acquisition allowing the construction of entirely, for the actor, novel sequences. It will become clear, as we proceed here, that these early insights support some of the central claims that will be elaborated in subsequent chapters of this book. That is, they place sensorimotor coordination closer to the pinnacle of brain and mental processes, and the combinatorial organisation of behaviour has profound consequences for cognition.

For now, though, return to the contrast between the two images in the figure, which can be summarised thus. In one we have a lone and physically passive thinker. That is a person who's mental life is internal, solely depending on processes within their brain which necessarily intercede on events in the world and are independent of the rest of their body. It matters little to their experiences of the world that their brain is in a body, in a world, rather than one of those famous vats![2] In the other we have an agent seemingly built primarily for acting on the external world, with much of their brain activity devoted to the control and monitoring of their body, particularly, note, their hands. This second image or metaphor captures many of the core ideas of embodied cognition, the elaboration of which is the work of this text. It is deficient as a metaphor in one important aspect however: the agent is alone. A better illustration would

---

[2] This is glib of course. The brain in a vat could be fed with a simulation of whatever an embodied cognitive science deems to be authentic human experience. Perhaps the better way of expressing this point is to note that embodiment simply rejects Cartesian notions of the world being passively *presented* to us by our senses, and that we actually enjoy unmediated access to, at least, some elements of the world as a consequence of our activity within it. The point is how to make sense of that sort of engagement and thereby escape the Cartesian trap.

depict a community of such creatures, busy in moving around and acting on their world: grasping objects, assembling artefacts, passing objects between each other, and, crucially, communicating via symbolic exchanges. Human cognition is the outcome of such relations.

The attempt to develop a unified model of embodied cognition is an attempt to construct a conceptual framework which can specify a 'research program' (Lakatos, 1978). This obviously is not, in itself, a detailed explanation for all the phenomena falling within that framework; rather, it identifies what those phenomena are, and in doing so determines what sort of questions are relevant and what techniques need to be applied. It directs discovery, and good frameworks are productive in expanding understanding. The argument is that the symbolic framework's productive power is waning. It constrains us to look in the wrong or peripheral places armed with unhelpful questions. The challenger embodied framework moves our focus to previously peripheral areas, employing new techniques to address surprisingly different (under the old framework) questions. For example, a repeated issue throughout this text concerns the sensorimotor neural structures that have become adapted to facilitate skilled hand actions, and one technique for exploring this issue (described in Chapter 3) is experimental archaeology; an example of which is analysing activity and adaptation in the brains of human participants while they fabricate Palaeolithic stone tools. Such topics do not find a place in many current textbooks on cognitive science. Before we turn to such empirical concerns however we must examine some of the, often implicit, philosophical bases of the contending frameworks.

A trope of much of cognitive science is to treat humans as detached from the world in which they dwell and to regard their brains as devices for discovering truths about the world by inferring the world's states on the basis of evidence of its effects on sensors. Perhaps it is not surprising that scientists are comfortable with such a frame, after all it does mirror what they do as scientists. As a group they commit to seeking truth by gathering evidence from which they can infer the validity or otherwise of theoretical conjectures. They are detached from the phenomena which they seek to understand and must necessarily view them with specialist tools of enquiry. But it is a destructive confusion to adopt this method of knowing as a model for cognition. Daniel Dennett (1993) used the term 'Cartesian theatre' to characterise this way of thinking about the mind *in general*, believing it to signify a residual influence of Descartes's dualist solution to the mind–body problem, in what are intended to be strictly materialist accounts. It is as if the world of objects, events and actors is 'projected', in the form of neuronal activations, to higher regions within the brain and understood when processed by what amounts to an internal homunculus.

This is not a fruitful metaphor for the larger part of our behaviours which, as we will see shortly, some refer to as 'everyday coping'. These are better thought of as being the outcome of a synergetic coupling between an agent and their world leading to a profound immersion of the one within the other. In an attempt to clarify and elaborate what these statements mean we will first discuss some trends in modern philosophy that start by explicitly rejecting the Cartesian model and focus on what it is to 'cope in the world'. We will consider three versions of this phenomenological philosophy in turn, before discussing its relevance to embodied cognitive science.

Phenomenology Sketched

There are three phenomenological philosophers most commonly associated with embodied cognition: Husserl, Heidegger and Merleau-Ponty. Their influence in the development of embodied approaches to understanding cognition will be made explicit as we proceed. We will focus on the claims of phenomenology for which, in later chapters, we are able to provide favourable empirical evidence; effectively we will pilfer from phenomenology without subscribing to it. First though there is an admission or qualification to do with the general limits of the relevance of their thinking to our concerns here.

The qualification is as follows. Phenomenology is often said to be about lived experience. This philosophical school starts with a premise that it is possible to systematically analyse the contents of our mental life from a first-person perspective. This is not meant to be mere introspection, but a methodology, as rigorous as any in science, to describe the content of the investigator's phenomenal experience. As such, it appears to have nothing in common with the natural sciences, which are necessarily third-person descriptions. But, a phenomenologist might argue, when the subject of the scientific enquiry is a sentient being the third-person perspective misses something vital. It seems to have nothing to say about what it is like to be that being. So, to consider a classic example, we have a good understanding of the neurological basis of colour perception but almost nothing to say about how it is that red is experienced as red. This is truly the hard problem (Chalmers, 1995), which, wisely, we will not attempt to solve here (except to suggest, in the final chapter, roughly where it might be fruitful to look for a resolution). So, fortunately, this aspect of phenomenology is not the most pertinent to our concerns here.

The starting point for the varieties of phenomenology of interest to embodied cognitive science, as understood here, is the work of Husserl in the early 1900s (see Zahavi, 2003, for a contemporary discussion of his philosophy). This may seem an unpromising beginning given that its author was concerned to reject rationalist and reductionist accounts of the natural world, especially when applied in psychology. In its later formulations Husserlian phenomenology adapted a transcendental approach to knowledge, as opposed to an empirical stance. Consciousness cannot be understood by a reduction to, for example, neurological processes. It cannot be treated as just another object. It is not like an atom, a rock or a galaxy. Rather it must be understood independently of any assumptions about the physical world. It is how we come to know the world of real and imagined objects, and therefore precedes our understanding of them. It is the job of the phenomenologist to describe the structure of consciousness by a systematic, first-person investigation of its contents: sensations, perceptions, memories, thoughts and their kin. The understanding of our mental processes in this sense is a precondition for the validity of understanding anything. How can we claim to understand something if we fail to grasp the fundamental basis of our sensing and knowing what evidence is pertinent and how our decisions or beliefs based on it are arrived at? The transcendental reduction consists in this recognition that consciousness is not an object in the world and can only be appreciated by detaching oneself from practical engagement with the world. As we will discuss in the next section this gulf in perspective has not prevented some cognitive scientists from attempting to integrate Husserl's philosophy with their empirical work; in particular his insistence that the 'lived body' is at the centre of his investigations has obvious resonance for embodied accounts.

Subsequent strands of phenomenology provide further scope for a partnership with cognitive science. The work of Heidegger obviously connects with some aspects of the embodied approach, particularly his notion of being-in-the-world (1962) and the nature of a person's relationship with their material environment. The hyphens of being-in-the-world mark it as referring to a unified, and novel, concept, revealed by phenomenological analysis. It does not refer to something (a being) contained within a receptacle (the world). Rather it is meant to capture the inescapable connectivity of a sentient being (Dasein in the human case) with its world. Again, an understanding of being-in-the-world necessarily precedes an understanding of the things in the world.

According to Heidegger, humans are embedded in a world with which they are largely familiar and for which they have acquired the skills necessary to achieve the satisfaction of their needs in relationship to their interests. The skills are essentially mundane and practical, and our actions are mostly ways of coping. Moreover, the world is not merely a collection of physical objects that we passively sense. The objects solicit behaviour and, again mostly, a distinction between them and us is lost in their use. These artefacts present themselves to us as *equipment* with which we pursue our aims. Such things as hammers, combs, keyboards, smartphones and pianos are typically not scrutinised to discover their identity. Typically, they are manipulated skilfully to achieve a purpose, without any explicit consideration of their appearance or physical properties. Heidegger termed this relationship between a sentient being and a tool as readiness-to-hand. When engaged in skilled acts the entities involved disappear into the background. The carpenter or pianist is not aware of the hammer or the keyboard, or *themselves*. The subject–object distinction is dissolved, and the unfolding skilled action is the foreground of awareness. Obviously, there are other states of awareness that involve scrutiny of objects. I can gaze in appreciation at the shiny new smartphone I hold in my hand. I can see its elegant and flawless construction. Now the subject–object distinction is foreground: I am regarding another entity. For Heidegger this is a distinct category of awareness, which he termed presence-at-hand.

The aims of skilled activity are revealed only as a part of a systematic network of an agent's engagement with the world. As I use my smartphone to find the location of the meeting I must get to, it becomes ready-to-hand, part of the equipment I use to get to the meeting. Like the handle of the door of the taxi I called to get me to the building whose lift I operate to get me to the room where the meeting is to be held. Now another set of involvements may be evoked. Perhaps I am attending the meeting so as to report on it for my employers, eliciting a set of activities using another set of equipment of ready-to-hand objects. The seat I occupy as I type notes on the laptop of the discussions I listen to, and so on. This flow of (highly skilled) activity is the result of an effectively unbounded set of other involvements in the world. I attend the meeting because it contributes to achieving things that matter to me: a livelihood, a social good, pursuing my curiosity about the topic under discussion, meeting other people, and so on. Our activity in the world is governed by the things that concern or matter to us which we pursue by a set of projects. This activity, moreover, takes place with others within a material and social culture having established sets of practices. And here 'others' does not:

mean everyone else but me – those over against whom the 'I' stands out. They are rather those from whom for the most part, one does not distinguish oneself . . .

By reason of this with-like being-in-the-world, the world is always the one that I share with others. (Heidegger, 1962: 118)

The ideas of Merleau-Ponty are seemingly the most amenable of our three strands of phenomenology for cognitive science, particularly as described in his *Phenomenology of Perception* (2002). His view was that its relationship with the natural sciences should be one of mutual enrichment, consequently he used results from psychology and biology to clarify his investigation of subjective experience. He was particularly concerned to analyse perception, both as a phenomenologist and as a natural scientist. The analysis leads to, again, a rejection of the relationship between the perceiving agent and the world as that between subject and object. Perception is not properly described by accounts that treat the human body as the receiver of elementary sensations that are processed in the sensory pathways and brain to form representations of the world for the perceiver.[3] The body is at the core of our perceptual involvement with the world, but it is not the body as revealed by the natural sciences. Rather it is the body as experienced as a result of having one: 'The body is the vehicle of being in the world' (ibid.: 160). From this perspective, the world is not a set of seen objects but a set of potential actions.

The set of potential actions are of course constrained by the constitution of the observer's body.[4] Distances and slopes and accesses are scaled by the capacity of the body for movement and exertion and manipulation. But, very importantly, these capacities are not fixed. They may be extended as a consequence of skill acquisition, increasing our capacity for 'coping' in the world and thus adjusting the set of potential actions made available by the world. They may be further extended by creating artefacts that effectively extend our bodies. Cultural changes and skill transmission thereby open up new aspects of the world to the members of that culture. When coping in our world, available to us given our skills and our inherited material culture, we are absorbed in the flow of skilful activity, requiring no reflection on what we are doing. A dynamic balance is achieved between the potential actions available in the world and movements within it. Merleau-Ponty likens this to a soap bubble in which the final configuration, a sphere, is produced by a balancing of local forces acting within the soap film. When behaviour is so determined we have achieved a 'maximum grip' on our world, so that:

---

[3] Such accounts continue to be the dominant view in the science of perception, as we will describe shortly.

[4] The use of the term 'observe' is now a little dangerous given it implies the very subject–object distinction that is being rejected by the phenomenological tradition. It is difficult to avoid and that this is so indicates the hegemony of Cartesian ideas.

My body is geared into the world ... when my motor intentions, as they unfold, receive the responses they expect from the world. (ibid.: 225)

On this way of thinking the relationship between action and perception is entirely synergetic. Our acting body provides access to the world, thus a strict duality between the observer and the observed cannot be maintained. Moreover, the action–perceptual *system* is strictly instrumental in that objects are always perceived as pertinent to the actor's intentions. They are not, in our normal skilled coping in the world, objects for scrutiny, rather we apprehend them in terms of what can be done with them. The enmeshing of a body within its world together form, to use Merleau-Ponty's term, an intentional arc that provides the means of knowing how to move in the world, to 'allow oneself to respond to their call' (ibid.).

Most importantly, as noted previously, the world in which the actor is so enmeshed is enlarged by skill acquisition. Cristiano Ronaldo's prodigious goal scoring is not the result of a more careful than normal scrutiny of balls and goals, rather it is their incorporation into his action–perceptual system, so that:

The field itself is not given to him, but present as the immanent term of his practical intentions; the player becomes one with it and feels the direction of the goal, for example just as immediately as the vertical and horizontal planes of his own body. (Merleau-Ponty, 1967: 168)

The world is also enlarged by skilful tool use; so, when we drive a car, in another example employed by Merleau-Ponty, our 'body' is extended to the boundaries of the vehicle so that we become implicitly aware of its proximity to other solid objects. Importantly a human's place in the world is that which is open to them as a consequence of their skilled bodily capacities, that is:

not my body as it in fact is, as a thing in objective space, but as a system of possible actions, a virtual body with its phenomenal 'place' defined by its task and situation. (Merleau-Ponty, 2002: 291)

Language use is also tied to the body and language is an extension of the body, under some interpretations of Merleau-Ponty's enigmatic comments on language use. He focused on speech itself, rather than the formal structure of human languages, and claimed speech was a form of gesture in which the meaning was visible or manifest. Gestures do not require interpretation. To use one of his examples: angry gestures do not *lead me* to think of the anger underlying the expression it *is* anger. The meanings in speech are not latent so do not require decoding. On the face of it this seems an absurdity given the general consensus that language is conventional, that is a system of commonly agreed, arbitrary signs for events, states and objects organised by rules of combination. To evade such a challenge he discusses the origins of language in non-arbitrary expressions, beginning with emotional expressions, shaped by their cultural contexts which account for the diversity of forms of gestures, and thereby, languages. All behaviours, including speech, carry meaning as a consequence of their immersion in the world. To again use one of his illustrations: just as one cannot separate musical meaning from the sounds that express it, behaviours, including speech, and their meaning are inseparable. They are similarly the vehicles of meaning, rather than codes from which meaning has to be extracted.

Importantly 'speech, in the speaker, does not translate ready-made thought, but accomplishes it' (ibid.: 207). Language does not, therefore, reflect universal patterns of human thought processes, with different 'dialects' simply reflecting alternative symbol systems for representing those same thoughts. Speech is the means by which we accomplish thought and, of course, the means for shaping the thoughts of others. Taking the meaning offered in the speech of others is to have one's body inhabited by the intentions of others. But also, my own speech, silent or spoken, may surprise me and teach me new things. Speech thus opens up the world. We return to language in Chapter 6 and consider how it might have arisen among groups of highly dextrous and social primates and conclude that Merleau-Ponty is largely correct.

The final aspect of Merleau-Ponty's thinking that has the potential to cast light on what follows is his insistence on rejecting the subject–object distinction. This is of course, as we have shown, a common thread in phenomenology, but he had a particularly vivid and distinct argument which may contribute to discussions of the relations between agents and objects and collaborative action in later chapters. In *The Visible and the Invisible* (Merleau-Ponty, 1968)[5] he attempts to elaborate and generalise his earlier, well-known discussion of the paradoxical notion of 'touch' that occurs when we grasp our right hand with our left hand:

In this bundle of bones and muscles which my right hand presents to my left, I can anticipate for an instant the incarnation of that other right hand . . . [that] initiates a kind of reversible reflection. (Merleau-Ponty, 2002: 106)

It is not clear in this case that there is a sharp distinction between an object being grasped and the subject doing the grasping. Rather, the relation is akin to a 'chiasm' in which the two entities may cross over their identity:

[5] An incomplete text published after his death.

the touched becoming the toucher and the toucher the touched. Though distinct the two things are entwined: we cannot touch ourselves, or, so Merleau-Ponty claims, another without having the phenomenal experience of being the touched. This model of a chiasmic relationship is generalised, in his later work, to the relationship between a human and their world. Being-in-the world as a subject is to be entwined with an object or another agent so that the one invades the other. Again, subsequent discussions, in Chapters 2, 3 and 4, will provide such notions with some empirical support.

These ideas have been mostly ignored by mainstream cognitive science. There have been occasional noisy skirmishes between the orthodoxy and rare adherents of versions of phenomenology,[6] but things are changing as a consequence of the growth of embodied approaches and the next section considers attempts to align the two traditions.

Phenomenology Tamed

To naturalise a branch of philosophy is to make it continuous with natural science. This is a particularly tough task in the case of phenomenology. Even though we have decided to largely ignore the 'hard problem' of accounting for qualia, such as how we explain the phenomenal experience of colour, we are left with the, probably, equally hard problem of reconciling an insistence that an understanding of our being-in-the-world as a subject must precede the understanding of ourselves as an object for scientific enquiry, with the presumption that natural science is necessarily detached from subjectivity. We will duck this problem too (but see Zahavi, 2004 for an example of an attempt to confront it). Rather we will pilfer different elements of a phenomenological perspective to clarify the new, embodied framework for cognitive science. It will be claimed that a phenomenological perspective contributes to making better sense of several reoccurring controversies in cognitive science. Examples of the latter include the degree to which perception is 'direct' or 'computational', the representational status of brain states, how to solve the 'frame problem', the dichotomy between rational and reflexive mental processes, the basis for, and validity of, a theory of mind. This piecemeal strategy, it will be argued, is the means by which embodied cognition may become a naturalised phenomenology.[7] Perhaps a better way of putting it is to say that we aim to tame phenomenology rather than naturalise it.

[6] Dreyfus (2007) provides an interesting description of early examples of this in MIT during the early flourishing of work in artificial intelligence during the 1960s.

[7] Stealing the good or useful bits of phenomenology is akin to accepting the mutually beneficial friction between phenomenology and cognitive science as recommended by Wheeler (2013), rather than attempting to resolve it.

What *is* clear is that in the last two decades or so the interest in continental European philosophy has grown enormously among those working in the cognitive sciences (see as examples Varela, Rosch and Thompson, 1992; Gallagher and Zahavi, 2013). A seed for this development may well have been the famous, and prescient, critique by Dreyfus of the work in artificial intelligence which dominated during the 1960s and 1970s (Dreyfus, 1972, 1992). His primary targets were the notion that the everyday knowledge evinced by every human could be encapsulated within a rule-based computing system and the wildly optimistic claims that the early success of such systems in their 'understanding' of linguistic materials within highly restricted micro-worlds were demonstrations that a physical symbol system could be elaborated to create and explain intelligence in general (Newell, 1980). Dreyfus focused on the frame problem to illustrate what he took to be a fatal weakness of the rule-based approach. That is how does a rule system select the appropriate subset of rules appropriate for a given context and how does it update itself in the light of changes in the world? No algorithm could be devised that could conjure up just the set of appropriate rules that governed a given situation in anything like the fluid manner and had anything like the scope to deal with an almost boundless set of situations as it appears that humans can. Common sense is just as programme resistant as qualia, and presents us with yet another hard problem.

There is no such frame problem on the phenomenological account. In a sense, its solution is built-in. Being-in-the-world is being connected to it in just the right way, so as to allow its states and its changes to modulate an agent's behaviour in relevant ways. The world is open to the agent, and it does not require computation to work out its states and relevant behaviours. The world presents itself as, to borrow Merleau-Ponty's term, 'solicitations' and for Heidegger being-in-the-world is to operate skilfully in it with understanding. But stating this is the case is very different from *explaining how* it is so!

To say being-in-the-world solves the frame problem is unsatisfactory, given we have no explanation of the basis of this sort of immersion or embeddedness. In fact, the notion gives rise to more questions than answers. And this is its great virtue. When faced by a degenerating research programme (Lakatos, 1978) it is wise to reconsider the problematic phenomena using different ideas which demand answers to different questions. One of the aims of this text is to explore the issues and questions in cognitive science that are suggested as foundational by a, broadly, phenomenological approach. In doing so it will become apparent that a consequence of making empirical sense of being-in-the-world has consequences for problems in cognitive science that extend beyond qualia and the frame problem. Some of the questions that become foreground are as follows. What is our perceptual access to the world? If we reject, what seems like a reasonable claim using the old frame, that we must infer its states from sensory simulation and accept the claim that it is 'direct' in some sense, how is this achieved? How do aspects of the world 'solicit' responses appropriate to their identity and the aims of a human agent? How is 'equipment' ready-to-hand and in what sense does it become incorporated into the body? How are 'others', that is other human agents, part of our presence in the world? What is the role of skill acquisition in determining our place in the world and what are the impacts of such changes on human capacities? How do we adapt to changes in the 'equipment' of the world, that is its material culture, and, again, how do these changes modify human capacities? What distinguishes ready-to-hand from presence-at-hand as forms of access to the world? How do symbolic exchanges, especially human language use, relate to these two modes of being? And, of course, the body: to what extent do the specific character-istics of our body determine our place in the world and therefore sculpt our cognitive capacities?

There is now a large, and growing, body of work which draws on some aspects of phenomenology so as to answer questions like these. It is referred to by a variety of terms, with the most general being embodied cognitive science. The embodied approach regards mental processes to be strongly conditioned by the whole body, not just the brain (for reviews see Wilson, 2002 and Anderson, 2003). Within this general framework there are nuances with slightly divergent perspectives on what to regard as the definitive properties of mental processes: the extended, enactive, embedded and affective approaches to the mind. The extended approach removes the body–world boundary and argues that mental processes may include essential elements that are objects in and states of the world (Clark and Chalmers, 1998). The enactive approach stresses the role of the body as an autonomous living system (for example see Di Paolo and Thompson, 2014). The embedded approach focuses upon the mutual and dynamic interaction between a body and its environment (for exam-ple see Beer, 2014). The affective approach stresses the degree to which the human body is instrumental in the expression and perception of emotion (for example see de Gelder, 2016). This family of ideas has been dubbed 4EA cognitive science by some (Kiverstein and Wheeler, 2012).

In summary, this developing framework causes us to shift our gaze from the lone thinker whose brain acts as a computational interface between them and the world, to an agent whose body moves skilfully so as to provide direct access to those aspects of their social and material world which are pertinent to their concerns. The purpose of this text is to put a little flesh on these bare bones, particularly empirical flesh, in an attempt to provide a coherent and unified account of how human cognition is built on foundations of a body's sensorimotor interactions with the world and other bodies. The next section provides an overview of the main steps in the argument.

Assembling the Argument

As the title of this book hints at, the end point of its arguments is a claim about how human agents relate to the other things in their material environment. These things include other bodies and other objects, in particular the artefacts that constitute our material culture. We will conclude that the boundaries between these entities, between artefacts and bodies, and between bodies and bodies, are less absolute than is commonly supposed. We enjoy a form of direct access to other bodies and our artefacts are *literally* a part of us. The key to understanding human cognition is to found in this network of bodies and other objects. Critically language, and symbol systems in general, are artefacts in the sense being used here. What binds these elements together is joint activity within a material culture.

There now follows an outline of the twelve major steps towards these conclusions, and, hopefully, a consequent loosening of our addiction to the orthodoxy of the last several decades. It is an attempt to provide a drone's eye view of the terrain before we descend and risk losing our way in the thickets and swamps on the ground. Accordingly, there is simply a list of claims and conjectures, with no evidence for their validity or many clues as to their origins.

Step one. The first step is a large one. In reframing our investigations, it is necessary to specify our place in the world so framed. Place here is used in a special sense and refers to those aspects of the material and social universe in which we, as individual agents, are immersed or embedded in such a way that we have unmediated access to it. The connection between an animal and its environment in such a case is one of reciprocal influences. An illustration is a fish holding its position in a swiftly flowing stream, constantly adjusting its body posture and the power in the sweep of its tail to adjust to the varying force of the currents acting upon it and thereby affecting the current flow around it, the global effect of which is to maintain the forces in equilibrium over time. Notice that nothing in the animal is calculating the opposing forces so as to 'work out' how to produce a countervailing force with its body. The body's *skilful* responses are adaptations to its niche which constitute a large part of the animal's place in the world: fish swim in water.

Similarly, a human's place is delimited by the set of skilled responses to their environment. Humans are adapted for a (mostly) terrestrial niche, unlike fish, therefore their movements are not largely a question of fluid dynamics, but metaphorically they do swim in light. That is the moment-by-moment relationship between their body and the world depends on (among other things) a similar strong coupling of events in the visible world and their muscular-skeletal system. Sensorimotor coordination of this sort provides an important part of the foundation upon which our broader cognitive abilities are built. Viewed in this way our perception of our world is rarely a detached 'observation', it is almost always an active exploration. This perspective is explored in detail in Chapter 2.

Step two. A consequence of step one is that we have to shift our scientific gaze in the search for some of the structure that supports cognition. If an organism is conceived of as adapted to respond to significant structures in its niche, an account of its behaviour must include a description and understanding of what those structures are. In some cases, this shift of gaze can be a massively simplifying move, as will be suggested when we discuss Gibson's notion of direct perception in the next chapter. To paraphrase a famous dictum: we should have regard for the richness of the perceptual world in which the head is inside of, before speculating about what structures might be inside the head.

Step three. The human brain should be regarded as fundamentally a biological mechanism for the control of bodily responses in space and time. It cannot be usefully likened, at this fundamental level, to a general-purpose computer. So, for example, sensory information is not processed to 'infer' facts about the world which then form the basis of a motor 'programme' in response. A corollary of treating the brain as a mechanism for controlling the body is that it should not be seen as the 'location' or 'container' for the mind. Such spatial metaphors are seriously misleading. The notion of mind makes sense only in the context of a community of agents, with brains, acting together within a niche. Arguments and evidence for this assertion occur throughout the text, and it is returned to in the final chapter.

Step four. Humans have a sensorimotor system that includes specific adaptations to exploit their exceptionally dexterous upper limbs, which are inherited from our brachiating (branch-swinging) ancestors. This yields hugely more than the simple mechanical advantage of having an opposable thumb. The need to control skilful hand actions on objects within reaching space required the adaptation or construction, during evolution or individual learning, of brain networks dedicated to events and actions within this peripersonal space, and independently of networks dealing with far space. In this text we will, for reasons that will become clearer as we proceed, refer to peripersonal space, together with the neural adaptations that underpin skilful action within it, as the 'toolspace'. These issues are discussed in the first part of Chapter 3.

One of the most significant of such adaptations is the coupling of visual and motor responses in such a manner that the sight of graspable objects within reach evoke, in a human observer, the actions required to handle them. If I were to attend to a largish, graspable object within my reaching space, for example, my motor system would be provoked into state in which a power grip is facilitated (but not necessarily executed). The object affords the grasp and in this way the agent is immersed in their material culture in a manner akin to the fish in the stream; their access to it is unmediated. We discuss visual object affordance of this sort in some detail in Chapter 2.

Step five. Hominins were toolmakers above all else. Their manual dexterity both enabled and was boosted by the development of toolmaking and use, first evident in the ancestors of *Homo sapiens* about 2.6 million years ago. Such early material *cultures* had a twofold impact. First, they were an engine for further adaptations in sensorimotor networks as these coevolved with increasing refinements in tool technology. Second, the material culture itself constituted an evolutionary niche, with new opportunities and challenges, thereby further sculpting evolutionary change. The impact of material culture on human development continues to the present, of course. These issues are discussed in Chapters 3 and 5.

Step six. Cognitive science has until recently tended to neglect the effects of human material culture, which we now know can be profound. So, for example, the tools we make, and use extend our toolspace and are, in a sense, incorporated into our bodies. These effects occur over several time scales. A skilled violinist will have differences, compared to the nonmusician, in cortical networks involved in, for instance, the control of the fingers of the left hand as a consequence of their tens of thousands of hours of practice. In contrast, there are instant effects of your grasping of an object, say, a small pointing device, that extends your reach. Your toolspace would be literally extended; you would judge objects and locations to be nearer than when not holding the pointing tool. Notice that the boundary between the body and the tool is not clear in these cases.

The effective human body is not fixed or defined by its fleshy boundaries. These effects are considered in Chapters 3 and 5.

Step seven. As illustrated by the case of tool incorporation in the example of the violinist, neural plasticity is a key feature of human development. That is the ability of the human brain to develop new patterns of connectivity over a lifespan, by the pruning of existing connections or the development of new ones. This plasticity is of course uneven: it is far greater in the early years of life than later.

The impact of the greater plasticity of the human brain in its early years is amplified by the fact that human infancy and childhood is exceptionally long. The period during which young humans are dependent on the help and guidance of others, adults and other juveniles, is greater than any other primate. The opportunity for cultural transmission is thereby enhanced and this would include the material culture in which the infant and juvenile developed. In much of our prehistory, for most individuals, the transmission would have taken the form of an extended apprenticeship in the manual skills that supported their material culture. Just like a contemporary violinist, the brains of our ancestors would have been rewired by the tens of thousands of hours of practice at their craft, which probably would have begun the moment they were physically capable of grasping the tools and artefacts in their culture. Discussions in Chapters 3, 4 and 5 are related to neural plasticity and human development.

Step eight. Individual humans adapt to their material and social cultures as a result of associative learning. Far from being a dead end, as once thought within mainstream cognitive science, modern statistical and computing insights or discoveries reveal the startling power of associative learning procedures. Importantly these new ideas appear to be entirely complementary with new unified theories of brain function. These ideas and models will be introduced in Chapter 4.

The skill acquisition that associative learning allows is the key to creating a place in the world for an individual human. Sensorimotor development during childhood and beyond is shaped by the need to move fluently in physical space, handle objects and artefacts, collaborate with others in work practices, sing, dance, chant, communicate, and so on. The total set of such *skilled* practical activities constitute the unmediated access to a material and social niche. Variations in the set of skills is the source of cultural variation. Cultural transmission is largely the outcome of an extended apprenticeship during a period when the body is growing, and the brain is at its most plastic.

Step nine. Adaptations to a material culture may be 'locked in' and transmitted across generations by a number of routes. Inheritance is not solely the genetic transmission of a programme of development for an organism so as to fit a given niche. Some organisms, but particularly *Homo sapiens* and their ancestors, have coevolved with their niches. That is, there is a dynamic relationship, during development, in which the individual organism is shaped by its environment while simultaneously adapting that environment. Both these changes may be transmitted to future generations. The plastic adaptations during development may themselves become sources of variation for natural selection. The changes in the environment form, a non-genetic, cultural heritage affecting the development of subsequent generations. As do the behaviours and skills that are transmitted across generations. This extended theory of evolution is discussed and used in Chapters 5 and 6.

Step ten. Humans are not just immersed in a material culture; they enjoy a similar relationship with their social world. Our place, in the specific sense introduced here, in that social world is also delimited by unmediated access. Other human agents evoke responses in a human observer akin to the manner in which a seen graspable object evokes a grasping response in a human, or the current in the stream evokes the movements of a fish's body. A better metaphor, which has been often suggested, is to liken human to human interactions to dancing together. That is a collaborative set of highly skilled behaviours which depend on synchrony of complementary actions. Importantly it requires, in the case of a couple, that each can predict what the other is going do next, and it seems that we are especially good at this, as will be pointed out, and illustrated, in Chapter 4.

Step eleven. One relatively recent part of the legacy of the ancestors of *Homo sapiens* is symbolic communication and ultimately language. Language is a hugely significant case of niche construction. Or rather the end point of a progressive elaboration of the niches of, probably, early hominins. Our dexterous ancestors enriched their environment by increasingly sophisticated toolmaking and use. The brain adaptations which coevolved with this technological progress also supported increasingly sophisticated communication systems which, in themselves, extended the niche in which subsequent generations developed. The toolspace became an arena for a gestural system of communication, elaborated with sounds and then extended by combining the elements into sequences of utterances, spoken and gestured, in a manner which reflected the organisational necessities of combining actions in their technological practices, including the dynamics of agents engaged in joint action. Language, therefore, is a relatively recent artefact. It is a *tool*. It is made from, initially, skilful movements of hands, and the vocal apparatus. It reflects its origins in the coordination of practical activity, so coevolving with elaborations in such practical concerns. It was not the result of purely genetic transmission. Chapter 6 is devoted to the evolution of language

Step twelve. The final step, like the first, is a big one. The evolution of spoken language, followed by symbol systems in general, such as written languages and mathematical formalisms, provides an access to a far, far wider world than that of our ancestors who lacked any form of language. Language provides a second *mediated* access to the world. The two forms of engagement with the world, skilful bodily interactions and symbolic interactions, often based on language, are reflected in the very common dual process categorisation of mental phenomena. It is also related to the similar distinction between ready-to-hand and presence-to-hand. We will attempt to make sense of this distinction in the final chapter.

The next chapter starts the work of attempting to justify these various claims with an attempt to clarify the notion of place as it has been introduced here. To do so it describes some long-established currents in cognitive science which until recently have been considered a little contrary to mainstream thinking. These are those theories of perception which treat it as direct in some sense. The ideas will be discussed in relation to visual processes, but it will be assumed that similar principles can be applied to the other senses.

2   Vision and Action

One aspect of the conceptual changes currently underway in the cognitive sciences is the renewed regard for action-oriented accounts of perception. In this chapter we trace the journey of the counter-culture in the perceptual sciences, exemplified in the work of Gibson (2014) and others, towards the mainstream.

Representing the World: a Cartesian Approach

Perhaps influenced or troubled by the Cartesian image of an observer connected to the world only through their senses, the primary task of perception was taken, by the mainstream, to be the derivation of *veridical* internal models or representations of the world from sense data. Perception then is a form of remote sensing similar in principle to how we may observe, say, distant galaxies by constructing devices that provide information about them, from which we can infer their properties. It is tempting to apply this frame when we think of our ordinary seeing: that we ordinarily observe the world laid out before us through our visual system, a device constructed by evolution, rather than engineers, to gather evidence about pertinent features about the environments so that we infer its properties. In the case of human vision, the sense data was constituted by the retinal image. The derivation of information about the world from a two-dimensional image is a very deep problem indeed. A brief reflection will reveal the gulf between the properties of the (proximal) retinal image and the (distal) properties in the world that give rise to it. The world is three-dimensional, whereas an image only has two. An image of an object varies with viewpoint so that, for example, a profile view of a face differs massively from a frontal view. Equally profound changes in an image are produced by changes in the light sources that illuminate a scene.

Reflection also seems to suggest that what we see when we open our eyes is the distal properties of the world. How is this seeming miracle accomplished? How does the visual system derive a stable description of objects, their three-dimensional properties, their arrangement in space and their identity under huge variations in their retinal projections? David Marr (1982) provided, arguably, the most complete answer to this question. In an impressive attempt to integrate conceptual, computational and physiological accounts of vision he proposed that the brain constructs a hierarchical set of descriptions. The first of these, the Primal Sketch, is derived from processes taking as their input the intensity values (shades of light and dark) of the image cast on the retina and recorded by the firing rates of the photoreceptive cells within the retina. These processes discover and record the location of, potentially, significant changes in intensity, such as those that might coincide with the boundary of an object against its background. This raw description is then the subject of various Gestalt-like grouping processes to deliver a full Primal Sketch that might be thought of as analogous to a pencil sketch or drawing of a natural scene.

It is easy to underestimate the difficulty of constructing such a representation. Perhaps, it might be thought, all one needs to do is to record intensity across the retinal image and locate changes bigger than some threshold. This does not work. The solution required the simultaneous measurement of rates of changes in intensity in all directions in the image over several bands of spatial resolution, so as to be sensitive to different types of feature. Marr's demonstration of the effectiveness of the procedures by their actual implementation as algorithms that could construct a full Primal Sketch from a real-world image is the more impressive because they appeared to be entirely consistent with the neurophysiology of the early stages of the human visual system. That is a plausible brain mechanism for implementing the measurements needed for the raw Primal Sketch are the centre-on and centre-off neurons found in the retina itself and the lateral geniculate nucleus neurons which they signal to over the optic tract. Moreover that these measures need to occur over a range of spatial resolutions seemed to make sense of the previously discovered existence of independent channels in the early visual pathway, each tuned to a different range of spatial frequency (Campbell and Robson, 1968).

The derivation of the Primal Sketch, accomplished by the prodigious computational processes occurring in the retina and the early part of the ascending visual pathway, is a solution to the problems of early vision. Marr's theory proposes a further two levels of description. A set of parallel processes takes the Primal Sketch as input and collectively derives the 2.5D Sketch. As its name suggests this is a partial description of visual space, encoding the orientation and distance of visible surfaces in a scene relative to a viewer. The final level of description, in the theory, is the 3D Model, which is meant to be a view-independent encoding of the three-dimensional shape of an object sufficient for its recognition. Neither of these stages has been implemented in subsequent work. Only partial insights into how something like a 2.5D Sketch might be derived have been offered and we have no clue how to construct a view-independent three-dimensional representation of shape in a brain. Viewed from the distance of more than thirty years the project to build on the startling success of the work in early vision appears to have run into the sand.

Why has this work not progressed? Because, some would answer, it had a flawed conception of what vision *is*. For Marr:

Vision is a process that produces from images of the external world a description that is useful to the viewer. (1982: 31)

The remainder of the work described in this chapter will challenge both these claims. It rejects the assumption that the input to the human visual system is anything like an image projected onto the retinal surface and it rejects the further assumption that the primary, or sole, outcome of visual processing is a description or set of descriptions of the seen world in the brain of the perceiver.

The Ecological Context of Vision

J. J. Gibson was an early member of the counter-culture, remaining defiantly outside of the mainstream, as this transformed from behaviourism in the first half of the twentieth century to cognitive psychology in the second half. He would probably have not described himself as a phenomenologist, but several aspects of his approach to understanding perception in general and vision in particular echo the ideas we sketched in the previous chapter.

Central to Gibson's (2014) reformulation of the problem of perception is a demand to examine the world in which the perceiver is immersed. Experimental investigations of perception had abstracted from this world by testing lone participants in highly controlled laboratory conditions. Typically, their movements were restrained, using chin rests for instance, and highly simplified stimuli were briefly presented at a fixation location. These conditions are very distant from those of a perceiver in the world. Outside the laboratory our visual experience is characterised by richness and complexity, not simplicity, and our movement affects it profoundly. The starting point for any theory of vision must start with recognition of these ecological conditions, for which the human visual system is adapted, not an abstraction from them.

An ecological account of vision must develop a new language to capture the visual complexity of a human perceiver's world. For Gibson, the starting point for this endeavour was the discarding of the centuries-old metaphor of vision-as-optics, illustrated in countless textbooks by schematic illustrations in which a very simple external object is shown seemingly superimposed on a featureless background. Rays of light are shown reflected from the object, passing through a lens and thereby projecting an (inverted) image of the object onto a two-dimensional surface behind the lens. This particular form of illustration is also an explicit avowal of the camera metaphor of visual perception, showing the seductive parallels between the two systems. These are highly misleading analogies.

There are two fundamental flaws with these ways of conceiving of the problem of vision. First, simplifying the stimulus has actually prevented the discovery of solutions to some of the deepest problems. Rather than discover a limiting case that applies to these simple instances and then generalised to the more complex, real world, we have missed solutions that are only possible *because of* the complexity and richness in the real world. Take, for example, the knotty problem of size constancy. Given that the size of an object's projection onto your retina depends on both its actual size and its distance from you, how, despite this confounding of variables, do you normally have no problem in distinguishing big distant objects from close little ones? Gibson provides an answer that is jaw-droppingly simple, once we reintroduce complexity *to the world*. Objects, outside of the psychophysics laboratory, do not present themselves to us floating against a blank background. They almost always appear in front of some background or other and this background is not featureless. The features produce a texture that varies in density with distance (think of a gravel path receding into the distance). There is no ambiguity about foreground object size in this world: a given object for a given viewer covers up the same proportion of textured background when near or far. In Gibson's theory there is no need for complex computations in the brain of the viewer in order to disentangle the confounding, in the retinal projection, of object size with its distance. Object size is perceived *directly* in an *invariant* feature, in this case the constant ratio of object size and background texture.

This simple case illustrates the general assumption of Gibson's ecological theory of perception that we perceive the world directly, unmediated by internal processes, by picking up the invariants in the sensory stimulation. The brain is adapted to be sensitive to precisely those aspects of the world that have been significant for survival during its evolution. What happens in a perceiver's brain is best described as a set of physiological processes that allow the picking up of those invariants, not a set of computations that construct a model of the world. We do not need a model in our brain because of the direct access we enjoy to the world.

But wait a minute, the mainstream, represented here by Marr, might object. The ratio of object size to background texture presupposes a method of distinguishing background from foreground, and it has just been shown in the discussion of the description of the Primal Sketch that even detecting features that might include the boundaries between an object and its background requires very intensive computations which cannot be understood in purely physiological terms. Information processing models are also needed in accounting for them. The Gibsonian response is to point out that very often objects are simply revealed by movement. An object that moves relative to a viewer, for instance, traces a characteristic path against its background: progressively covering texture in the direction of movement and uncovering texture in its wake. This objection and response reveals the second flaw in the vision-as-optics metaphor. That is, sensory stimulation, in the case of vision, is not a single glimpse of the world projected onto the retina.

Movement is intrinsic. Our sensory stimulation is affected by, almost, constant motion of various types. The viewer constantly transforms their sensory experience by moving their eyes within their orbits, by moving their head relative to the rest of their body, and by moving their entire body. Each of these produces different and characteristic global changes in sensory stimulation, easily distinguished by the viewer from the localised changes that result from something else in the world moving relative to the viewer, as in our previous example. The vision-as-optics metaphor, and its associated vocabulary is simply too impoverished to capture this constant change in a complex world.

Gibson developed what he called a 'ground theory' of vision so as to describe a world of textured surfaces, to replace the previous 'air theory' and its world of points and planes (the vocabulary of vision-as-optics). Subsequent elaborations arrived at what is a central idea of the ecological approach: the optic array that replaces the retinal image as the starting point for vision. The optic array is the solid sphere of structured light that a viewer is centred within. In all directions light converges on the central point of observation as a result of it being scattered and reflected by the (textured) surfaces and objects present within the array. The structure in the light contains information, in the form of invariant properties, about what gave rise to it. So, for example, the statistical properties of textures indicate the distance and orientation of surfaces, since texture density varies with distance.

Critically the centre of observation is not static. It is moved purposely. Observer movement produces global changes within the optic array referred to as optic flow. Were the viewer to move forward a characteristic (and information-bearing) set of changes would result. Elements in the array would appear to flow outwards, expanding from a central node. Two vital sorts of information are carried in such a transformation. First, the direction of flow of elements entails forward motion. It would be reversed and become an inward flow if the viewer were to retreat backwards. Second, the central node of no change informs the viewer of the direction of their movement. The claim is that within the flux in the structured light produced by the movement of objects and observers there are invariants that provide the observer with further significant distal properties of the world directly.

This reformulation of the problem of perception entails radical changes in how the relationship between the perceiver and the world is conceived. The use of the expression 'sensory stimulation' above is, from the ecological perspective, questionable. The division between a sensory receptor (the retina in the case of a human) and a source of stimulation does not capture the dynamic relation that actually exists between a perceiver and their world. The actual relationship is better captured by the phenomenological sense of being-in-the-world. The perceiver is an active explorer of the world. These explorations reveal both the world and their self to the perceiver. Their self-movement elicits changes in the optic flow, which allow the detection of invariants that reveal other objects as distinct from themselves as well as their own trajectory. The means of revealing the world in this way depends on not just the possession of sensory receptors but also on the body that they form a part of and that allows exploratory activity. The retina, located in eyes, which can be moved at will to sample different portions of the optic array, that are located on a body, which can move the perceiver to another point of observation within the optic array together constitute a perceptual system. We see the world with our body.[1]

The final element of Gibson's reformulation of the problem of vision is the reappraisal of what it is we achieve when we see. It may seem self-evident that the purpose of seeing is to discover what our local, physical environment 'looks like'. We look so as to discover the colours, shapes, distances and identities of things around us. Having discovered these various properties, we may then use them in actions in pursuit of our goals. You see the cylindrical, shiny and translucent object on the table, recognise it to be a glass, and reach to grasp it so as to quench your thirst. For Gibson, however, this common-sense account of the purpose of

---

[1] The same principles also apply to the other senses.

vision conceals a central aspect of our engagement with the visual environment. The phenomenological notions of 'readiness-to-hand' or 'solicitations' are close to capturing this missing aspect.[2]

Affordance is the term introduced by Gibson to refer to invariants in the optic array that carry information about behavioural possibilities. The physical environment of all animals contains opportunities for behaviour, which depends on their physical capacities. Humans are bipedal animals of a certain size and physical prowess. Our movement must be attuned to the physical structure of our cluttered environment in the light of these capacities. Given the critical importance of successful, purposeful movement our perceptual systems are adapted to pick up the information needed, for successful locomotion for example. Directly. Invariants in the optic array specify whether it is possible to move in a given direction, that is whether it affords walking in that direction.

> A path affords pedestrian locomotion from one place to another, between the terrain features that prevent locomotion. The preventers of locomotion consist of obstacles, barriers, water margins and brinks (the edges of cliffs). A path must afford footing; it must be relatively free of rigid foot-sized obstacles. (Gibson, 2014: 36)

Similarly, objects afford the actions that are possible on them. An apple can be grasped, a chair can be sat on and a ladder can be climbed. The claim is that these behaviour possibilities are also detected directly as a consequence of the affects the objects that afford them produce in the optic array.

Tools are a particularly interesting class of physical object. These are objects, probably modified to attune with some aspect of the users' physical capacity (such as being easily held in the hand), and used for a specific purpose. When used, are they part of the body or part of the environment? Gibson's answer to this question is profound:[3]

> When in use, a tool is a sort of extension of the hand, almost an attachment to it or a part of the user's own body, and thus is no longer part of the environment of the user . . . This capacity to attach something to the body suggests that the boundary between the animal and the environment is not fixed at the surface of the skin but can shift. More generally it suggests that the absolute duality of 'objective' and

---

[2] Given the strong affinities with phenomenology highlighted in this account of Gibson's ideas, it is surprising that there is not a single reference to Husserl, Heidegger or Merleau-Ponty in Gibson's 'The ecological approach to visual perception'. This is despite the claims that he, Gibson, spoke of being influenced by Merleau-Ponty (Baldwin, 2007). This perhaps illustrates the gulf at that time between anglophone and European continental intellectual cultures; perhaps making references to the continental tradition was regarded as a little suspect among members of the former.

[3] And for this text a focus of attention, as will become clear in subsequent chapters.

'subjective' is false. When we consider the affordances of things, we escape this philosophical dichotomy. (ibid.: 41)

So how valid is the ecological approach to perception and what evidence is there to support it? Naturally its theoretical foundations were, and continue to be, challenged by the mainstream (vision as the computational derivation of representations of the world in the brain of the perceiver). One important debate concerned the concept of 'direct perception' in ecological theory (see Fodor and Pylyshyn, 1981; Ullman, 1980 for critiques of the idea, and see Turvey et al., 1981, for the ecological school's defence). One part of the opposition to the idea of perception being, somehow, direct, is that it is unclear how to conceive of the process by which the 'invariants' in the optic array are 'picked up'. Gibson tended to rather brush these issues aside, referring to the brain as 'resonating' to the invariant structures, rather than performing computations on sensory data, at some level or other, to extract them. It has only recently become possible to glimpse a resolution to this issue as a result of developments in computing architectures which attempt to be 'brain-like'. Artificial neural networks or connectionist systems consist of simple interconnected units, each of which signals their varying activity level via their connections with the other units. The network adapts to external objects, states and events by changing their connection strengths. When so adapted to properties of the world they can be shown to respond to 'known' or 'learned' states of the world by 'relaxing' to a stable configuration of activity levels across the units. These configurations may include units executing motor responses which change the states of the world. Though a form of computation it is not a set of formal operations on symbols, rather perturbations in both domains affect the other. They are locked together in a synchronous dance of phase changes. Hopefully this sketch of the relationship between a brain in a body and the world will be made less mysterious in Chapter 4. There we will discuss such connectionist systems in greater detail and argue that this sort of process best captures the Gibsonian notion of 'direct' and our notion, deployed in Chapter 1, of 'unmediated' and so makes sense of our being-in-the-world.[4]

The other term which arises in this debate is of course 'representation'. On the mainstream account, it is a central concept: brain states model and intrinsically reference world states. That is how we gain access to the world. But what of the brain states that, in the direct or unmediated accounts of perception, are coupled synchronously with aspects of the

---

[4] See Dreyfus (2002) for a similar argument.

world? Do they represent? Our broad answer to this question is no. As John Searle has argued extensively, representation is not intrinsic to a formal system (see Searle, 1989 and 1980 for examples). Meaning can only be attached by someone external to the system. By extension, but probably contra to Searle's arguments, brain states have no intrinsic meaning. Meanings only arise, it will be argued as this text proceeds, when such brain states occur in brains in bodies in exchanges with other human bodies and objects. To look for meanings inside heads is to look in the wrong place.

Another, often cited, problem with Gibson's theory is how, precisely, to make sense of the notion of affordance. It seems plausible that information about some global behavioural possibilities can be carried by invariants in the array of light. The distance and orientation of surfaces from the statistics of texture is one such example. The extension to higher-order vision–action relations, requiring ever higher-level invariants, is less compelling. What invariant in the light reflected from a smartphone specifies *all* the actions that it potentially elicits: finding a location, listening to music, emailing a friend and, even, making a phone call? The attempt to answer this question, and therefore establish the utility and limits of the notion of affordance, will occupy a major part of the rest of this text. The answer, summarised in the final chapter, depends on insights from a wide range of disciplines introduced in the chapters that precede it, and will reveal affordance as a building block of cognition. And, of course, in making sense of affordance we will provide an elaboration of the phenomenological notion of objects being ready-to-hand.

An evaluation of one other aspect of Gibson's thinking will also occupy us further as this text progresses. This is the startling claim that the use of tools somehow collapses the subject–object distinction. This has been mostly ignored in discussions of ecological theories (at least within mainstream cognitive science) but in Chapter 3 there is a discussion of tool use and recent evidence for tool incorporation in human and non-human animals. These insights will be deemed significant for subsequent discussions of the development of human material culture, in Chapter 4, which in turn will be said, in Chapter 5, to provide the foundations of social forms of exchange, which can be described as representational.

First, in the rest of this chapter, the relationship between vision and action is discussed in greater depth, partly as an attempt to clarify the notion of affordance, but also so as to continue to weigh the claims and counterclaims about the role of representation in the perception of the world.

Multiple Visual Systems: a Possible Resolution

One readily available resolution of the conflict between direct action-oriented and representational theories of visions is to recognise that visual systems serve a number of functions. The requirements of escaping predators and harvesting food sources are very different. In the former a rapid detection of a looming object, followed by a rapid flight that avoids obstacles, without being concerned with the precise colour and number of the feline's whiskers is required. In the latter, what is needed is the ability to scrutinise the precise three-dimensional shape and shade of colour that might be critical in distinguishing the edible berry from the toxic variety that is very similar in appearance. Yes, this is 'eco-babble' but it does illustrate a basic distinction between two sorts of visual processing: the one rapid and closely tied to action, the other richer in detail and linked to the perceiver's knowledge of the world. Moreover, some fundamental aspects of the anatomy of the human visual system seem to map neatly onto functional distinctions of this sort.

Early discussions of a 'two visual system' conjecture can be found in Trevarthen (1968: 301)[5] that, from the outset, regards as a given what is to be one of our primary conclusions in this chapter. That is in the primate:

Visual perception and the plans for voluntary action are so intimately bound together that they may be considered products of one cerebral function.

Action here means bodily action: turning, walking, climbing, reaching, grasping and so forth. These may be divided into two broad categories, for which there exists two distinct types of visual processing implemented by different neural circuits. One category of action is concerned with moving the body relative to its environment, such as turning the head or walking. These actions are controlled by, or implemented within, the ambient visual system,[6] which detects relevant spatial properties of the animal's world, such as the location and movement of objects. The second category of action involves actions on a particular place or object. Such actions arise within the focal vision system, which allows the detailed visual analysis needed for the identification of objects and their manipulation by the hands[7] of the observer.

---

[5] This paper is a superb, and rare, example of a combination of physiological, behavioural, ecological and phenomenological analyses. It is highly recommended.

[6] Remember the assumption: action and perception are the product of a single cerebral function, so it is not the case that the ambient visual information is derived and then passed to a separate motor control system.

[7] It will become clear as this text proceeds that the human visual system, and indeed the cognitive system in general, cannot be thoroughly understood without taking account of the perceptual-motor system that allows the skilful use of hands.

Primates' forward-facing eyes ensure that the lateral portions of any observed scene stimulate the nasal portion of the retina, a region of relatively low acuity. As the animal moves forward in space or rotates their head this region will be transformed at the greatest rate and is, according to Trevarthen, the basis for detecting surfaces and obstacles which determine possibilities for gross movements of its body. In contrast the central region of the retina, the fovea, has higher acuity which may be directed at a small region of space, while the animal stands on two legs or sits or squats. This region may, importantly, include nearby objects and the two hands with which they may manipulate those objects. The two systems were also said to contribute differentially to visual awareness, with the primary contribution coming from focal vision, compared to only a dim awareness of the contents of the ambient system.

The further anatomical separation between the two modes of vision is evident within the projections from the retina to the brain, in their dependence on two of the several distinct visual pathways in the primate brain, it was claimed. The primary visual pathway proceeds from the retina, via the optic tract, to the mid-brain body of neurons in the thalamus, in each of the hemispheres, known as the lateral geniculate nucleus (LGN hereafter). These LGN neurons in turn project to the area of cortex on the surface of the brain known as, variously, primary visual cortex, striate cortex, Brodmann area 17 or V1 (V1 hereafter) located near the back of the head on the left and right.[8] This pathway was postulated to be the basis of focal visual processing. Another set of projections from the retina bypasses the LGN and V1, terminating first in mid-brain regions, before projecting to the cortical surface adjacent to V1. This pathway was said to serve ambient visual processing.

Evidence cited in support of the ambient and focal visual system distinction included the preserved visual ability in animals with experimental lesions within the postulated pathways. The most striking case is a female rhesus monkey, whose V1 was removed[9] (Humphrey and Weiskrantz, 1967; Humphrey, 1974). Initial observations of the animal, while she was

---

[8] There will be frequent references to brain areas in this text, but there will be no figures illustrating them because knowing their precise locations will add nothing to the arguments. The following very simple description of the human brain will suffice for our purposes here. It is broadly divided into two, roughly symmetrical, hemispheres each of which is divided into four lobes. The occipital at the back of the head, the temporal at the side, the frontal above the temporal and at the front, and the parietal above the temporal and between the occipital and the frontal lobes. Most of the references in this text will refer to cortical areas, that is the outmost surface of the brain made up of layers of densely organised neurones.

[9] Actually, a very small portion was spared. Subsequent testing determined that this was not likely to be the reason for her preserved visual ability.

housed within a laboratory cage, indicated little preserved visual function, beyond a gross sensitivity to light. Over a period of months however it was noticed that she was orienting towards moving objects, turning her head or eyes towards them. Subsequent shaping of orienting behaviours, using food rewards, revealed residual visual function that allowed the detection of, *and reach towards*, stationary high contrast objects such as a black object against a light background. When, five years after the visual cortex was removed, she was rehoused from her cage and allowed to explore large-scale environments, including woodland, further developments in visual abilities were observed: in time she could move around an arena littered with obstacles in a search for food rewards. Particularly pertinent to our concerns at this point is the manner in which she found and grasped the small food items. As described by Humphrey (1974):

Somewhat surprisingly, her preferred method for picking up the currents was to take them directly with her mouth rather than her hand ... When she did reach with her hand she would ... bring her hand down on top of the object ... she never used fine finger movements in the way characteristic of a normal monkey. (245)

And:

Most of the observations of her ability to avoid obstacles were made while she was searching out currents. She would wander around until she spotted one and then run over to it. While she ran she would usually keep her eyes fixed on the current and it seemed clear that she used peripheral vision to guide her way around any intervening obstacle. (248)

But exhaustive testing showed that she:

could classify stimuli in terms of visual salience but of visual salience only ... With the important exception of her spatial vision she appeared in fact to be totally agnosic. After years of experience she never showed any signs of recognising even those objects most familiar to her, whether the object was a carrot, another monkey, or myself. (252)

It should be obvious that the dramatic contrast between this animal's fluent whole-body movements within a cluttered, three-dimensional space, and her impaired abilities to recognise and *handle* discrete objects within that landscape supports the sort of distinction in visual function suggested at the outset of this section. It is also clear that it supports aspects of Gibson's ecological perspective. First, in general terms, it demonstrates that vision also needs to be investigated outside of tight constraints within the laboratory. It was when released from the cage, and able to engage in large-scale, exploratory movement that the monkey's preserved 'ambient' visual capacity was uncovered. Surely, it follows, there may be much to discover about human vision by releasing human participants from their chin rests and fixation crosses. The second, more specific, aspect of the ecological approach that accords with the animal's behaviour is that movement by the observer provides vital information about the behavioural possibilities or affordances in its environment. But notice that it also motivates a reappraisal of the notion of affordance. That she was able to detect the affordances for walking, running and climbing, but not those required for the precision grasp of an object suggests the need for the refinement of the notion that makes sense of this contrast. Much more will be said about this as we proceed.

The primary impact of animal V1 ablation studies was not to do with affordance however. It was quite simply that such animals would be expected to be blind, in the conventional sense of the total loss of a visual sense and therefore the behaviours that depend on it. Damage to V1 in humans was long known to produce blindness in the region corresponding to the site of the lesion.[10] So how does a blind animal continue to engage with its visual environment? Subsequent work with human participants revealing similar, seemingly, paradoxical behaviour confirmed the existence of 'blindsight'. Again, a single-case study was particularly influential.

Patient DB had a large portion of V1 in his right hemisphere removed to extract a tumour, and the consequences for his visual capacity within the resulting blind region in his left visual field were investigated over a period of decades (Weiskrantz et al., 1974). As with the rhesus monkey, significant residual visual function was observed in his blind field. In summary, DB could, some few months after surgery, point with an extended forearm to the location of a spot of light; distinguish vertical lines from horizontal and diagonal; and distinguish an 'X' from an 'O'. That DB could comment on his own performance added to the drama of these observations. When shown a video of his accurate pointing and discrimination of line orientation, for instance, he was astonished, insisting that he been guessing. Blindsight is now an established phenomenon.[11]

---

[10] V1 is organised in such a manner that it preserves the spatial relations of the visual scenes to which it responds, so adjacent locations in the world produce activation in adjacent locations in V1. Therefore, damage to regions of V1 will produce visual field loss in corresponding regions, referred to as a scotoma. In addition, the visual field is lateralised: the left projects to V1 in the right hemisphere and the right to the left hemisphere.

[11] The interpretation of these data in terms of their being truly 'blindsight', that is recognition without awareness, naturally produced refutations. Some argued that the preserved recognition performance was a consequence of light scattered from the object into the intact field providing cues to recognition, others that it was the result of islands of intact visual cortex within the apparently ablated regions and, yet, others that performance reflected a shift in DB's response criterion. A response to these challenges can be found in Weiskrantz (2009).

Discussion of the ambient–focal distinction, and the underlying sub-cortical and cortical brain structures it is associated with, has faded, becoming overshadowed by another formulation of a two-visual systems hypothesis. The possibility of there being two, relatively independent, visual pathways within the cortex itself was based on further ablation studies of monkeys, in which the different effects of lesions in temporal and parietal regions of cortex motivated the distinction between a ventral and dorsal visual pathway (Ungerleider and Mishkin, 1982; Mishkin, Ungerleider, and Macko, 1983). Broadly, lesions in inferior temporal cortex were seen to produce impairments in an animal's ability to discriminate between objects, while its visuospatial skills, such as locating objects, were preserved. In contrast lesions in parietal regions impair visuospatial performance but did not disrupt discrimination. Accordingly, the two pathways were dubbed the 'what' and 'where' systems respectively. Subsequent investigations have elaborated this two visual system hypothesis, confirmed its validity in the case of the human visual system and collected impressive evidence in its support, to the degree that it is now close to orthodoxy (see Milner and Goodale, 2006, for the most complete account). It will be described in greater detail next, before examining its claims in relation to our intentions of making sense of affordance.

Both the ventral and dorsal visual systems originate in V1. The ventral pathway projects to lower or inferior temporal cortex (IT hereafter) and the dorsal pathway projects to the rear or posterior parietal cortex (PP hereafter). That these two pathways constitute different visual systems, serving distinct functions, is supported by work in electrophysiology, brain imaging, monkey ablation studies, human single-case studies and psychophysical investigations. This converging evidence, a portion of which we review below, is said to reveal the ventral pathway to be the basis of a primate's perception of the world, while the dorsal pathway serves the visual guidance of their actions in general (and thus is not simply a 'where' system as in the original formulation of the ventral–dorsal distinction).

The most compelling evidence for the vision–action distinction, and its mediation by the ventral and dorsal pathways, is, naturally, the dissociation of the two functions that is observed in humans with localised brain damage. The putative independence of, and distinct functions served by, the two pathways predict the results of damage within them. Ventral pathway damage would be expected to produce deficits in recognition processes but spare the ability to execute actions on the basis of visual information. In contrast, damage in the dorsal pathway should impair actions and spare recognition. And this is broadly what is found.

Damage to the region of parietal cortex in which the dorsal pathway terminates produces so-called optic ataxia, a condition in which a patient can report the visual properties of an object but not use that information in, for example, grasping it.[12] In order to grasp an object within reaching space a hand must be transported towards the object, rotated around the wrist so as to align it with suitable grasp points on the object and a grip formed so as to close on the chosen grasp points. The precise details of these actions depend of course on the particular characteristics of the object: its location, its three-dimensional shape, its function (which will determine which part of it should be grasped), its orientation relative to the agent, its weight and so forth. Optic ataxia patients have been observed who can report the relevant properties of an object but are unable to perform the contingent actions. So they misdirect a reach towards an object they can locate or cannot align their hand to an object whose orientation they can report or fail to form a size-appropriate grip on an object whose size they can report (Perenin and Vighetto, 1988; Jakobsonet et al., 1991).

The converse of optic ataxia, in which a patient with ventral pathway damage is seemingly unaware of visual properties that they can act on, is relatively rare but has been observed, notably in the case of patient DF (Goodale et al., 1991). She suffered devastating brain injury after carbon monoxide poisoning. The damage included areas in ascending ventral cortex beyond V1, the latter being largely spared. The consequence was a form of visual agnosia that impaired her recognition of objects and their properties, despite her not being blind in the conventional sense (such as the blindsight patient DB). For instance, she could not distinguish between (graspable) square and elongated rectangular plaques. Nor could she indicate their width by adjusting the aperture of her thumb and index finger when looking at them. Yet when asked to reach and pick up a plaque her performance was entirely normal. The adjustment of her thumb and index finger aperture as her hand approached each plaque was accurately tuned to its size, despite the failure to make precisely the same adjustment when passively viewing the plaque. A similar dissociation between reporting and acting on object orientation was observed. When confronted by a letter-posting like slot oriented at a particular orientation within a vertical plane she was unable to report its orientation either by saying, selecting a similarly oriented line on paper or turning a card, held in her hand, to match the slot. If, however, she was asked to post the (same) card through the slot, then performance was normal.

---

[12] Such patients do not have a general problem of motor control. It is specific to vision, so they are able to use tactile information to perform a grasp that they cannot form from vision alone.

DF participated in many subsequent investigations of her condition of which Carey, Harvey and Milner (1996) is particularly relevant to our discussion here. She was required to reach for and grasp common objects and pantomime their use. When objects were oriented so that their graspable part was oriented towards her (so the handle of a spoon was pointing towards her for example) her reach to grasp was not distinguishable from a normal control group. However, when the object was oriented with the handle pointing away her performance was far from normal, with grasps of the non-handle end as likely as a grasp of the handle. Clearly her grasping of objects was not influenced by their functional use, which, of course, depends on their identity. She was able to grasp an object, as an object, but not as a tool ready for use. Her pantomimes of an object's use were also far from normal in that, although largely accurate, it depended on a tactile exploration of each object following the grasp. These observations should give us reason to pause for thought on the concept of affordance: that is, there appears to be a distinction between an object affording a mere grasp, so as to possess it, and its affording a grasp for use. We will return to this distinction later.

It should now be clear why some have been tempted to reconcile direct and representational theories of vision by reference to the ventral–dorsal distinction (examples are Neisser, 1994; Goodale and Humphrey, 1998; and Norman, 2002). The ventral pathway can be regarded as implementing a computational visual system that derives, from retinal stimulation, increasing abstract descriptions of the visual world. The higher-level internal representations form the basis of a viewers' conscious visual experience of the world. They may also engage with the viewers' memory and knowledge systems serving recognition. The dorsal pathway in contrast works to control bodily responses to the visual environment. These include whole-body responses, as in obstacle avoidance, but also eye movements and reaching towards objects with the hands. This system is encapsulated in that high-level cognitive processes do not modulate it and its operations are largely (or even entirely) unconscious. While the systems are independent there has to be some coordination between the two. Goodale and Humphrey (1998) liken this to tele-assistance, analogous to a human operator of a remote robotic device. The human operator, in this scenario, observes the robot's environment using a remote camera link so as to identify objects of interest, which the operator than directs the robot, via a second communication channel, to act on. In a similar manner the ventral system constructs a detailed model of the visual world, revealing the identity of objects. Based on the current goals of the agent it may direct attention to a relevant object, which the dorsal pathway also processes in order to execute the intended actions. How should we evaluate this highly plausible model, which is supported by such an impressive range of evidence? At this point we will consider two aspects, which on closer inspection provoke doubt, certainly from an embodied perspective.

First, is the division of primate vision into two systems too much of a simplification? A brief examination of any contemporary text on the neuroscience of visual perception will remind the reader of the multiplicity of routes from the retina to the cortex. Has our fondness for binary distinctions forced the categorisation all these possible projections from the retina involving subcortical and cortical regions and their numerous recurrent links into just two sorts of process? It seems odd that the earlier focal–ambient distinction has been displaced by the ventral–dorsal. Putting together the data on primate vision that motivated both suggests *at least* a tripartite division; broadly: vision for whole-body movements (subcortical perhaps), vision for object manipulation (dorsal) and vision for recognition (ventral). As we proceed in this text we will introduce another vital task for human vision: recognising and *interacting* with other humans: social vision perhaps? By the end of this chapter it is hoped that a model of vision will emerge in which multiple, distinguishable visual brain networks with highly dynamic links coordinate actions in the world. Think of the parent running to the bus stop to give his child her pencil case, which she has forgotten, before she hops on the bus for school. His visual system must enable him to guide his body through the cluttered ambient environment, locate his daughter at the crowded bus stop, coordinate his body posture and reach towards her in a way that takes account of her location and orientation. Her visual system must allow her to locate her father, recognise that the object in his hand is the forgotten pencil case and is being moved towards her so she can take it, control a reach to the pencil case and grasp it with a hand orientation and posture that takes account of the location of her father's grip on it. A remarkable achievement that is comparable to the performance of Olympic relay-team members. Also, as with the athletes, this is the outcome of extended and intensive training (from birth) leading to the highly *skilled* visuomotor behaviour, which is concealed by it being mundane and allows each of us to cope in-the-world. This behaviour is not captured by the tele-assistance metaphor.

The second concern about the ventral–dorsal account is its assumption that the results of ventral processing are (largely) conscious and those of dorsal processing are (largely) unconscious. This seems obviously wrong. While some aspects of visuomotor coordination, assumed to be undertaken, by the dorsal system rarely reach awareness, such as the precise details of my grip on an object, others seem ever present. Moving my body within my visual environment provides me with the vivid sense of self that arguably must accompany any conscious experience at all. Eye, head and whole-body movements produce transformations in my field of view that both locate me and distinguish me within it. Perhaps this is not the sense of being conscious that is meant to be associated with the ventral system. Rather it is being aware of, and consequently being able to report, the appearance of things and events within my visual field. How to make sense of this is of course one of the deepest puzzles that exist, it is the hard problem again. For now, it should be noted that the fact that activity occurs within a particular brain area rather than another does not seem to solve the puzzle (see Bach-y-Rita, 1972 and Noë, 2010 for discussions pertinent to this issue). It is hoped that towards the end of this text we will have a mere glimpse of a solution. This is to locate this sort of ability not within a single brain but within a community of agents.

What of affordance? It has already been noted that the ambient–focal distinction introduced the possibility of there being multiple classes of affordance. So, in ecological language, the agent's ambient visual system picks-up invariants in the optic array that specify the spatial properties of their environment. These afford actions such as 'walk forwards', 'pass between' and 'reach towards'. But not it seems 'grasp the object between thumb and forefinger'. Or at least not in the case of Humphrey's (1974) monkey with induced blindsight. The subsequent work with visual agnosia patients such as DF suggests a further refinement. The discovery described in Carey et al. (1996), that DF could successfully grasp an object in the sense of reaching to it and picking it up with an appropriately adjusted grip, but not necessarily in a way that allowed it to be used, suggests a further refinement of the notion of affordance. They indicate a further class of affordance: a 'reach-to-grasp-to use for x' affordance, where x is a function of the affording object. A hammer affords a grasp with your dominant hand around its shaft. It is not immediately clear how to regard such cases in either the ecological or ventral–dorsal framework. Are they examples of indirect affordance, or ventral stream affordance? The next section will address these and related issues in a general evaluation of the notion of affordance.

Affordance Revisited

Until recently most of the empirical investigations of vision and action that explicitly test, in humans, the validity of the affordance concept has been of the sort of action that we discussed above in relation to the putative ambient visual system. For examples studies of activities like stair climbing, walking through gaps in obstacles and sitting on seats (Warren, 1984; Mark, 1987; Warren and Whang, 1987). The results of these suggest that at least some aspects of what we see are scaled to our body. To judge, as an example, that one can walk between two obstacles the gap between them must be estimated as at least wide enough to allow the viewer's body to pass. Warren and Whang (1987) showed that this estimate was a constant ratio of shoulder width to gap size for a range of different walkers, big and small.

Work of this sort, which might be said to address the issues of affordance in body-centred space, has been supplemented more recently by investigations of affordance in hand-centred space, in particular object grasping. To reach to pick up a hand-sized object within reach requires the coordination of a number of muscular and skeletal systems (Jeannerod, 1981). One must choose the hand to use for the grasp, reach with the hand towards the location of the object, while adjusting body posture to accommodate the reach. As the hand approaches the object, the hand shape must be adjusted, along with its orientation, so as to arrive at a location of the object which fits the three-dimensional shape and orientation of the hand and allows the application of sufficient force to grip and lift it. Rather like the earlier example of the parent running to the school bus this is a mundane activity that conceals much of its massive complexity. Yet the ability of patients with visual agnosia, such as DF, to successfully complete such actions, despite not being able to report the relevant properties of the object to be grasped, suggest their dorsal visual system origins. Can objects therefore be said to afford the precise parameters of a reach to grasp?

Evidence for this being the case is provided by studies of how a seen object affects a viewer's motor responses. In one such study participants viewed an image of a familiar object (a teacup for example) in order to judge whether it was upside down or not, indicating their decision with a left- or right-hand key press (Tucker and Ellis, 1998). Their response was faster and more accurate whenever the object was oriented such that it would be optimal to reach and grasp it with the responding hand, compared to the incompatible case. It was easier, for example, to press a key with the left hand, than their right hand, whenever the teacup's handle was oriented towards the left side of their body, and vice versa. Other elements of a reach to grasp action are similarly afforded by the sight of an object. Ellis and Tucker (2000) had participants categorise the pitch of a tone as high or low while viewing a *real*, single, graspable object, which they were told to remember for a subsequent recognition test. In one study participants had to rotate their wrists either clockwise or anticlockwise to indicate the pitch of the tone. Each viewed object was oriented relative to the participant so that, were they to pick it up, a wrist rotation would be required. An upright bottle for instance would require a clockwise rotation; while a pencil aligned left to right relative to the participant would need an anticlockwise rotation (from a neutral starting position with the thumb at an 11 o'clock position). Performance was facilitated when a response matched the orientation of the viewed object. It was easier to classify the pitch with a clockwise rotation of the wrist than anticlockwise when looking at an upright bottle. The reverse was true when looking at the pencil. A second study demonstrated entirely analogous effects in the case of hand shape or grip type. The viewed objects were now either small and needing a precision grip between the thumb and forefinger to pick up (a coin for example), or large, and needing a power grip between the four digits and palm of the hand (a hammer for instance). Participants signalled the pitch of the tone by squeezing a small switch with a precision grip or large switch with a power grip. Again, ease of performance depended on the relation between the response grip and the grip needed to act on the seen object. It was easier to perform a precision grip, than a power grip, when looking at a small object such as a coin. The reverse was observed when participants looked at a large object such as a hammer.

This facilitation of components of a reach to grasp by the mere sight of an object, in the absence of an intention of actually reaching to grasp it, was said to be evidence for micro-affordance. This term was meant to distinguish it from Gibson's (2014) notion in that it refers to a different level of action specification. Rather than an object affording a generalised 'can-be-grasped', it also affords the specific elements of grasp including the values or parameters for the elements, such as hand shape and orientation.

Perhaps it is not surprising that seeing an object elicits the actions commonly applied to them; maybe it is just yet another demonstration of associative memory, not unlike the smell of a rose evoking a memory of its appearance. Clearly any account of vision, embodied or not, would be consistent with this possibility. The visual system might, for example, extract or compute from the retinal image of a hammer a description of its three-dimensional shape (as in Marr, 1982) and this representation allows access to the object's identity, which thereby elicit the associations. This would work for actions such as grip type, since this is, in many cases, intrinsic to the identity and function of familiar objects. A hammer is associated with a power grip, a nail with a precision grip.[13] Such an account is less plausible for the micro-affordances of hand (left or right) and hand orientation. Both these parameters of a reach to grasp depend on contingent or extrinsic facts about the (spatial) relationship between

---

[13] Many issues are glossed over in this contrast, such as the contrast between grasping for use and grasping for possession or manipulation, the fact that some common objects are tools, which are fashioned so as to fit human bodily capacities and so forth. We will return to these concerns.

the object and the observer. They are candidates for dorsal visual system processing perhaps. Some more recent studies shed light on the nature of micro-affordance: one investigates, using electroencephalography (EEG), the temporal properties of motor activation elicited by seen objects, another examines motor activation to unnoticed graspable objects and a third investigates a case of 'alien hand'.

EEG involves recording electrical potentials at multiple locations on the scalp that results from the brain activity beneath it. In order to chart brain responses to seen objects averaged EEG measurements over repeated presentations of an object can be calculated to produce event-related potential (ERP) data. Goslin et al. (2012) measured ERPs while their participants responded to images of common, handled objects, whose handles were oriented towards the left or right side of the participant. The participants classified the objects as either tools or kitchen implements and pressed a button with their right or left hand accordingly. Electrodes over the primary motor cortex measured ERPs indicating the preparation of a left- or right-hand response (by comparing the differences in potentials in the two hemispheres over time). This revealed the preparation of a hand of response[14] that would have been optimal for grasping the depicted object that began just 100 milliseconds after the onset of the image and continued up to 400 milliseconds before the actual response was made (which of course may have been with the afforded hand or its contrary). The claim is that the action activation precedes the identification of the potentiating object.

Two other ERP components were also modulated by action properties: P1 and N1. These labels refer to what are generally regarded as early signatures of purely visual processing, with P1 being the first observed positive deflection in the EEG waveform and N1 being the first negative going deflection following the onset of a visual stimulus. The amplitude of N1 is usually said to be affected by various visual properties of a stimulus and levels of attention to it, P1 amplitude is modulated by attention (Mangun and Hillyard, 1995; Handy and Mangun, 2000). Goslin et al. (2012) observed, in data pooled across posterior and occipital electrodes, maximum deflections marking P1 at around 100 milliseconds, and N1 at about 150 milliseconds following presentation of an object. In both cases the amplitude was greater, across both hemispheres, whenever the hand afforded by the object was the same as that used in the subsequent response. Clearly this difference did not reflect a difference in visual properties among stimuli. Exactly the same image of the same hammer produced different P1 and N1 values when its handle was congruent with

---

[14] Or more accurately: activation of motor cortex contralateral to the afforded hand.

a later response than when it was not. Rather, a plausible account suggests an early attentional effect that is the consequence of an action intention combined with the grasp afforded by an object. The authors suggest that they represent a neural signal of object-based attention (Egly, Driver and Rafal, 1994). We will return to the interplay of visual attention and affordance in general later in this chapter.

Taken together these lateralised readiness potential[15] data demonstrate a very early involvement of a seen object's action properties within *visual* pathways. In this case reflecting a relationship between its micro-affordances and the viewer's action intentions. An account in which seen objects are represented within the visual system, leading to its identification and this identity subsequently activate actions associated with it is not tenable in the light of these data. This conclusion is provided with additional support by the finding that unseen, or unreportable, objects afford actions. McNair, Behrens and Harris (2017) had their participants view and identify two briefly images of graspable and non-graspable objects. The pairs were presented with very brief intervals between each of the pair, which tended to make the second unreportable (an example of the so-called attentional blink phenomenon as reviewed in Shapiro, Raymond and Arnell, 1997), or a longer duration, allowing the second object to be reported. Motor-evoked potentials were measured in the right hand after the application of transcranial magnetic stimulation (TMS)[16] over the left hemisphere 250 milliseconds after the second image was presented. The evoke potentials were significantly higher for the graspable objects, compared to those that were not graspable, and this effect did not depend on whether the object had been identified or not. Notice that in this case, unlike the last, the participants were not intending to use the afforded hand.

Another, very different, source of evidence for the role and nature of micro-affordance is alien hand syndrome (AHS). As the term suggests, this rare, neurological condition consists of a disruption of the normal sense of ownership of the action of one or both hands. AHS patients report that apparently deliberate actions, such as reaching to an object close to

---

[15] A term used to refer to electrical activity that reflects the preparation of motor activity on one side of the body.

[16] TMS involves placing a magnetic field generator close to the head so as to induce electrical activity in discrete brain regions. In the case of motor areas such stimulation will evoke muscular electrical activity in connected effector systems, referred to as motor-evoked potentials (MEPs). In effect then it is a non-evasive version of the electrical stimulation used by Penfield to map sensory and motor cortex. It may be used to detect covert motor preparation, as in the case described in the main text. That is, differences in MEPs under a constant TMS reveal differences in motor system excitability (see Schütz-Bosbach et al., 2008, for a review.)

them, are not the result of their volition, and they may be unable to release a grip in the affected hand. One such patient, with AHS in both hands, was unable to entirely suppress an afforded action in order to carry out a contrary, specified action (Riddoch et al., 1998). When asked to reach to a cup placed either to her left or right side and use the hand on the same side of her body to reach with, interference errors were observed. That is if a left-side cup had its handle oriented to the right she might reach to it with her right hand contrary to the instruction. McBride et al. (2013) pursued this apparent inability to ignore or suppress micro-affordance in a study of a second patient, with AHS confined to her right hand. Her susceptibility to micro-affordance was tested using a standard procedure. That is, images of graspable objects were presented with handles oriented towards her right or left hand, and she was required to classify them as tools or kitchen implements, responding by squeezing a response device in her left or right hand. The micro-affordance effect (faster responses with a hand optimal for actually grasping the depicted object) was confined to the alien (right) hand. Moreover, the speed advantage for the alien hand was of the order of five times greater than in age-matched healthy individuals tested with the same materials. The authors conclude that AHS results from a failure in the inhibitory processes, that are present in healthy individuals, needed to suppress actions afforded by seen objects but not relevant to an agent's current goals.

Earlier in this text micro-affordance was said to be different from the Gibsonian notion on account of the scale of the actions afforded. The examples just described are all to do with affordances of hand actions, whereas the prominent studies of affordance within the ecological tradition have focused on affordances of whole-body actions. Are there other differences? Yes, and more significant, perhaps, than contrasts of scale. The authors of the micro-affordance idea intended it to serve as the basis of visual object representation, which is of course at odds with the ecological claim that perception is direct. There are a variety of reasons for supporting a representational account of micro-affordance. One is the observation that its effects do not differ between responses to real objects and their depictions. The earliest demonstrations of the facilitation of reaching and grasping by the sight of object, and almost all of those since, have participants viewing an image on a screen. Their environment did not literally afford a reach to a graspable object.[17] This surely entails the viewer of the scene regarding it as being something other

---

[17] Ellis and Tucker (2000) did use real objects, but they were presented within a light box, with a sheet of glass between object and viewer, so again an actual reach to grasp the object was not possible.

than it actually is. How can that count as the direct detection of a behaviour possibility? The viewer must be treating the scene 'as if' it included a graspable object. This is seen even more clearly in a study that investigated the effects of obstacles on responses to affording objects (Costantini et al., 2010). Participants, in experiment two, had to respond to computer-generated images of handled objects, depicted within reaching space, but in some cases behind a (depicted) transparent screen. The usual micro-affordance effect was obtained but only in the absence of the obstacle. The authors interpret their finding as demonstrating that affordance only arises when an object is really ready-to-hand, that is falls within the viewer's reaching space. But in neither condition was this the case; rather, the participants viewed depictions of two scenes. One depicted a reachable object, the other depicted a non-reachable object. Both objects were not actually ready-to-hand.

There are a number of paradoxes here which we need to attend to. The paradox of a response being afforded by an object actually consisting of coloured pixels painted onto a two-dimensional screen, and this effect being eliminated by superimposing a similarly *depicted* barrier implies a representational account of micro-affordance. The behavioural possibilities affecting the viewer's responses are not literally in their environment, but part of their current representation of it, what they take it to be. In the language of phenomenology most of the procedures which report micro-affordance effects are concerned with objects that are present-at-hand rather than ready-to-hand. How is this to be squared with an ecological account of direct perception? A possible resolution is to acknowledge that the relationship between the participants in these experiments and the experimental stimuli is not that of an actor within-the-world. The visual scenes that constitute the stimuli are actually symbols of things and events in the world. They are scrutinised by the participants in order to make a judgement on some property. In a sense, the participants are *commenting* on their perceptual experiences when they act on the responses devices. In later parts of this text (especially in Chapters 5 and 6) we will develop arguments that the capacity for representing the world is a consequence of communicative exchanges between human agents which have evolved into symbolic systems. The ability to describe objects and events to others brings with it the ability to describe them to oneself. The mental representation of a visual scene is a form of self-commentary. Yet in representing the objects as being graspable or not, that is, in taking them to be such or in describing them to be such, it seems that the motor system responds as if the represented objects were actually present and ready-to-hand. This is entirely in accord with the account of language to be developed in Chapter 6. Language will be shown to have been built from, and grounded in, sensorimotor elements. A straightforward demonstration of this grounding of language in sensorimotor activity is the finding that the words naming graspable objects also potentiate actions: Tucker and Ellis (2004) show that both an image of a hammer and the word 'hammer' facilitate a power grasp. Rather than a paradox the findings may be a key to understanding human symbol systems (see Borghi and Riggio, 2009, 2015 for a closely related discussion).

In order to serve as a sensorimotor grounding of a representational state such as 'that image depicts a hammer',[18] it is obviously necessary that the afforded actions have arisen in the context of real grasping of real hammers, and that the same sensorimotor brain activity occurs as that occurring during its actual use. It seems reasonable to suppose, therefore, that somehow visual and motor system responses have become closely integrated, in order that the motor circuits for grasping an object are active whenever an object, or a symbol for it, are seen.

Learning must surely account for the very close integration of the visual and motor systems evinced by micro-affordance. Reaching to grasp an object is a hard-won skill, acquired as a consequence of extensive training during the period when the human brain is most plastic and therefore adaptable. The integration of sensory and motor processes that is critical to success during learning has been likened to natural selection (Edelman, 1993). This theory of neural Darwinism proposes there is a gradual adaptation of neuronal networks as a result of the selection of those involved in a successful outcome, such as bringing the hand into contact with an object (Sporns and Edelman, 1993). This process of adaptation to both a physical environment and a material culture[19] results in the formation of so-called 'global neural mappings' that couple together motor and sensory systems. These mappings not only serve as the neural basis of the skilled behaviour, but also the basis of the categorisation of objects and events. Motor activation provides the grounding for mental representation. The motor activation observed when an observer categorises a visual event or object is not merely associated with a semantic representation that the observer may be deemed to have, by virtue of their commentary on it, that is their correct categorisation, it provides content to that conjecture about the world. As we develop our thinking on these tough problems through this text it should become clearer that brains alone do not represent states of the world; rather, they control the bodies

---

[18] Importantly it should be noted that it is not being claimed that this representational state is available for report by the bearer of it, as McNair, Behrens and Harris's (2017) demonstration of the affordance effects of unreportable objects shows.

[19] Of which much more will be said in the next three chapters.

of agents engaged with the world, which includes symbolic exchanges with others.

We are now in a better position to confront a common criticism of the affordance idea, which was alluded to earlier in the description of the ecological approach. That is, it does not seem credible that culturally specific artefacts such as postboxes, hammers and smartphones can be perceived directly, unless in some vacuous sense (Fodor and Pylyshyn, 1981). What invariant in the optic array is picked up whenever one sees a hammer? What invariant can possibly be shared by all cases of hammer-in-view other than their being hammers? The invariance is located not in the optic array but in the relationship between the viewer and the tool which has developed during learning. This is a further revision of the notion of affordance, at least as it is used within the ecological tradition where most insist it is a property of the environment (Turvey, 1992; Reed, 1996; Michaels, 2003). Yet some within the community have questioned this assumption. Heft (2003), for example, has argued that for some cases of affordance:

the relevant information is embedded within a temporally extended flow of events that includes the perceiver's history of engagements with the environment. Said in other words, we might begin to look at this question in the context of perceptual learning and development. (158)

Some micro-affordances of reach to grasp may well be such cases, particularly when they involve an artefact or tool.

In summary, this section has, in revisiting affordance, described evidence and reasons for significant modifications of the idea originally proposed (but actually not clarified) in Gibson (2014). First, there appear to be different classes of visual affordance, which may be served by different visual systems. Whole-body affordances that provide an agent with the gross characteristics of their environment in terms of being able to walk, climb, sit, stand, pass through, and so forth. The observer generated fluxes in their optic array might be thought of as directing such actions rather like the current in a fast-flowing stream modulates the movements of a fish swimming within it. We primates swim in light. This form of seeing appears to be closely related to the functions postulated for the ambient visual system. In contrast, there appears to be a set of affordances to do with the manipulation of hand-sized objects and there appears to be distinct classes of them. One way of talking about these distinctions is in terms of their specificity. Tucker and Ellis (2004) suggested that the motor activations associated with object categories can only be broadly specified: the hand of grasping and whether it is a power or precision grasp say. Whereas there must be another class of visual to motor effects which are far more finely tuned so as to allow successful prehensile actions: the precise posture of the digits as they close on a grasp point for example. Another way of expressing the same distinction is that between stable and variable affordance as suggested and discussed by Borghi and Riggio (2009, 2015). Stable affordance are invariant features of an object, whereas variable affordances are to do with contingent aspects, in particular the spatial relations between an object and an agent. Stable affordances may, according to the authors, be further categorised as canonical or not. Canonical affordances are those associated with the characteristic contexts in which an object is used. A cup, for instance, affords a precision grasp to its handle, rather than a whole hand around its body, because of this being highly associated with its use as a drinking vessel.[20]

These hand–object affordances do not seem to map neatly onto the dorsal–ventral distinction. At least some appear to be dependent on representational states, which of course would suggest either a ventral origin if one were to accept this as being a representational brain system,[21] or their being an outcome of an interaction between the two systems. But there may also be purely dorsal sources for some of the actions performed on objects. Alien hands (as in AHS) and patient DF's errors in grasping tools might indicate that some affordances of the hands are those that specify the optimal grasp for an object in view given its three-dimensional shape and orientation, irrespective of its identity or function or intentions of the viewer. Some have argued (Creem and Proffitt, 2001, for example) that affordances of the latter type are dorsal in origin, whereas those that allow effective tool use are ventral. Others (Borghi and Riggio, 2015) have suggested a finessing of the notion of dorsal visual function by drawing on the claim that the dorsal pathway is made up of two parts: the dorsal–dorsal and ventral–dorsal subsystems (Rizzolatti and Matelli, 2003), with the former having the role prescribed in the original formulation of the dorsal stream, and the latter being involved in mappings between objects and actions, including those that make up the class of stable affordances.

This is clearly now a crowded and noisy arena with many competing claims. What does seem established is that the human visual system is not

---

[20] Of course, this distinction between types of hand-centred affordance is not absolute. Tools are crafted to exploit human bodily capacities, their handles, for example, being essentially visually salient protuberances that accommodate a secure and comfortable grip, appropriate for its use. We return to this important interplay between the human body and tools in the next chapter and Chapter 5.

[21] Which we have just suggested is not the case. Further clarification of this issue may be provided in our subsequent discussions of how symbolic exchanges between human agents have evolved.

modular and is closely integrated with the motor system in particular, with, probably, multiple networks specialised in different aspects of sensorimotor coordination. Some things are missing obviously however. The first is other people. The descriptions and theories have been concerned with a lone agent acting on a world of seen objects. Yet many of our activities in the world depend critically on coordinating our actions with others, as when we, in a simple case, pass them an object. Might there not be special purpose visiomotor networks for person to person actions like this? There are. In fact, Rizzolatti and Matelli (2003) claimed that their postulated ventral–dorsal subsystem also played a role in understanding the actions of others. We return to this in detail in Chapter 4. A second absence from our accounts of vision so far is any mention of how it reveals the *visual* appearance of the world to us. The next section attends to this.

Visual Phenomenology and Visual Attention

There probably is a gathering sense in the reader that our concern with the relations between the body and seeing has obscured the primary characteristic of vision. Ironically, given the claimed phenomenological influences on embodied cognition, we seem to have ignored the phenomenal properties of vision. Seeing is not just the revealing of behavioural possibility. It is obvious that to see, at least in the human case, and in the sense of see as normally used, is also to enjoy a particular phenomenal experience, which may be reported by the individual having that experience. Accounting for this aspect of seeing is surely one of the deepest of the many mysteries of perception, and one that is not obviously solved by a conventional representational account or the ecological approach.

Except that some have argued that the phenomenal aspects of seeing are themselves the result of skilled bodily activity (O'Regan and Noë, 2001; Noë, 2004, 2010). More specifically seeing depends on the possession and use of sensorimotor knowledge by the viewer. It is therefore continuous with, and complementary to, the ideas, sketched above, that perceptual systems adapt themselves to a material culture and physical environment. But it also goes beyond the claim that a primary purpose of vision is the detection of action possibilities. It asserts that seeing *is constituted* by action and so is termed an 'enactive' theory of perception, which we will now consider in a little more detail.

The discovery of 'sensorimotor contingencies' during development is the basis of seeing. Agents actively explore their visual world with whatever bodily capacity they possess at their particular stage of development.

An outcome of this extensive and intensive training is the discovery of the underlying regularities that govern the changes in the retinal flux that are caused by bodily activity. Moving the eyes, head and body produces changes in the retinal flux that have a lawful relationship with the objects and events that the eyes pass over.[22] As an illustration consider the effects of moving your eyes left to right in an otherwise stationary visual scene. Elements in the scene will be cast onto incrementally different portions of your retina and because of structural changes in the retina across its surface an individual element will elicit very different responses in the brain's ascending visual pathways. The density of photoreceptor cells varies across the retina with the highest at the centre and gradual reductions towards the peripheral regions. Accordingly, responses to an element in the scene[23] in, say, V1 will vary in extent in a regular fashion. The distribution of colour-sensitive photoreceptors (cones) and achromatic photoreceptors (rods) also varies across the retina, with the former concentrated in the fovea. Accordingly, there will be a change in colour responses as the eye moves across an element. One region of each retina contains no photoreceptor cells (it being the point at which axons from the retina are bundled together to form the optic tract that connects to the ascending visual pathways). The resultant blind spot, about 8 degrees by 5 degrees centred at about 15 degrees temporal, therefore may well move across an element in the visual field, resulting in an effective blink for the duration of the conjunction. These, and other, simultaneous changes in the responses of the visual systems as a consequence of moving your eyes are systematic and, as a result of co-occurrence during learning, predictive of aspects of the external world. Similarly moving your head and body introduces further sensorimotor contingencies whose rules can be discovered. For example, moving around a solid, discrete object will yield characteristic transformations in its appearance that depend on three-dimensional geometry and the transmission of reflected light. Different parts will come into view during the movement and other parts will disappear. The shapes of surfaces will mutate as the viewpoint changes: rectangles become trapezoids as orthogonal views of them become oblique.

In a highly skilled visual animal (that is almost all of us) these relationships have become embedded so that they form a body of implicit knowledge that provides the basis of *expectations* of the consequences of various types of visual exploration. Sensorimotor contingencies do not lead to the

---

[22] In Chapter 5 we will discuss learning in artificial neural networks that appear to be capable of discovering such regularities.

[23] The problem of what constitutes an element is passed over here.

recovery of information, which is then or thereby represented in the brain. Rather they provide the means of accessing the external world that may be explored, more or less at will, according to the current goals of the viewer.

That seeing is the skilful exploration of the outside world, guided by implicit knowledge of the rules governing the changes in sensory data that result from the exploration, is consistent with two phenomena that are puzzling under more traditional accounts: visual adaptation and sensory substitution. Generations of psychology undergraduates have been introduced to visual adaptation via the work of Kohler on the effects of wearing inverting goggles (Kohler, 1963). In one example the goggles inverted the image on the retina in the sense of rotating it through 180 degrees. Up became down, and down became up. In other examples the inversion was left to right. In both cases when first worn the initial effect is not a simple, corresponding inversion of the world. Rather the wearer's visual world becomes chaotic and highly unstable. Head movements produce bizarre transformations of objects, which dissolve and combine in impossible ways. Walking causes surfaces to tilt, wave and loom in alarming ways. Yet after some days of constantly wearing the goggles normality returns.[24] The point, for the enactive account, is that the wearer, by moving and acting in the world, has acquired the new sensorimotor contingencies created by the optical inversions. If the wearer now removes the goggles, their visual world is again chaotic and a further several days of adaptation is required for them to see as normal.

The second phenomenon consistent with an enactive model of vision is sensory substitution, which is probably even more startling to our (Cartesian) intuitions about vision than the effects of inverted images. An example of sensory substitution is tactile stimulation replacing visual stimulation, which was extensively explored by Paul Bach-y-Rita in a decades-long search for effective devices to replace the loss of vision after brain trauma (for examples see Bach-y-Rita et al., 1969; Bach-y-Rita, 1972; Sampaio, Maris and Bach-y-Rita, 2001). One early such device consisted of an array of stimulators (electrical or mechanical) attached to, often, the back so that tactile stimulation could be applied to the skin. The array was connected to a head-mounted camera, the input of which activated the tactile array. When equipped in this way, a blind person would be encouraged to move and explore their environment. With practice the user reported an experience of exploring a three-dimensional space and could make accurate judgements about the presence of objects within that space. They report this world as being laid out

---

[24] Or more likely a resemblance to normality. See the discussion of inversion in O'Regan and Noë (2001) for a more careful description of the phenomenological effects.

in front of them, not across the tactile array. A quasi-visual experience can it seems be derived from tactile sensory data. The point is that the tactile array preserved some of the sensorimotor contingencies transmitted by the camera stream, and from these some sort of visual experience was derived.

These observations of adaptation and sensory substitution are difficult to evaluate because, in part, they depend on reports of a person's phenomenal experience. While in both cases there is clear evidence that visually derived behaviours may be adapted or restored,[25] the concurrent changes in phenomenal experience may be disputed and for a variety of reasons. These include an aversion to phenomenological reports in the mainstream and a recognition that we are dealing here with something close to the 'hard problem' of consciousness (Chalmers, 1995). But, perhaps ironically, there are also good empirical reasons for doubting the reliability of our reports of our own experiences of seeing, which we will focus on next.

We open our eyes and there the world is. Its rich detail is revealed to us, seemingly without effort. That is how it seems. Our surprise at demonstrations that in fact we can be utterly impervious to huge changes that occur in front of our open eyes is a measure of the strength of the illusion of completeness. One such demonstration is the phenomena of change blindness. McConkie and Currie (1996) showed that large-scale changes in a visual scene were missed if they occurred during a saccadic movement of the eye. More startling, perhaps, were subsequent demonstrations of similar blindness to change during eye fixation. Participants viewed alternating pictures of a real-world scene that were identical except for some, one might have supposed, obvious difference (Rensink, O'Regan and Clark, 1997; O'Regan, Rensink and Clark, 1999). For instance, a large section of tree-covered, coastal background appears and disappears in the otherwise identical image pair of a sea kayaker. A change like this is indeed obvious. Were the two images to be viewed simultaneously or in succession it would simply 'leap out' to any viewer. However, if between the alternating images a third frame appears (a blank field or a pattern of random 'mud-splashes') the change becomes very difficult to detect. It is presumed that without the intervening visual event the change between the two images captures the viewer's attention because of the visual transient it causes. The additional visual changes introduced by the intervening field mask those caused by the image change, so attention is

---

[25] Therefore, both clearly illustrate neural plasticity, the possession of which has profound consequences for human development and cognition as we will see in the discussions that follow.

not drawn to it and it is not seen. The conclusion is that attention is required to notice the change. One can look without seeing, to see one must attend. A claim which is supported by the observation that once the change has been detected or pointed out it is not possible to not see it again, even with the intervening frame. With moving images and real-world scenarios, where visual transients cannot draw attention to any particular change, the failures become even more spectacular. Levin and Simons (1997) presented video clips of human actors engaged in everyday activities. During a change in camera angle some object in the scene was changed. In the majority of cases these changes were missed by participants viewing them. In the most striking case a person was seen moving to answer a telephone, with the action, during the first and second halves of the clip, performed by a different actor wearing different clothes. Only 33 per cent of forty participants noticed the change, despite being told to scrutinise the scene so they could write detailed descriptions of what they saw. Simons and Levin (1997) extended this astonishing finding to real-world interactions. Stooge actors engaged participants in conversations and during a staged interruption a second actor replaced the stooge. Again, a minority of participants reported seeing the change in actor.

Some have argued that change blindness implies that the visual system is representationally sparse. Given we seem to miss so much, despite our illusions to the contrary, our visual representations are far from a complete description of what is currently in view. An additional tenet of sensorimotor contingency theory (O'Regan and Noë, 2001; Noë, 2004) is that the world serves as an external memory. Detailed internal representations are not required because as skilled visual animals we can consult the world according to our current interests. Our skilful visual exploration provides access to the external world, that is:

seeing is casting one's awareness onto aspects of the outside world made available by the visual apparatus. (O'Regan and Noë, 2001: 946)

The degree to which this direct theory of visual awareness is in fact entailed by the empirical demonstrations of change blindness is disputed. Simons and Rensink (2005) have pointed out that they are also compatible with representational theories in which visual transients or interruptions disrupt the *internal* comparisons required to detect change.

What does not seem in doubt is that change blindness reveals our misconception about what is available to awareness, and can be reported on, at any point in time. This appears to be limited to attended aspects of a visual scene. Attention may be drawn by external signals, such as those associated with visual transients, or directed at will by the viewer according to their current goals. Broadly you see what you need to see as determined by your current goals. This is certainly suggested when change blindness is investigated while participants are engaged in acting on the world rather than just scrutinising it. In studies in which participants sorted virtual reality stimuli, the probability of their detecting a change, such as the size of an object was more likely to be detected if size was relevant to their task (Triesch et al., 2003; Droll et al., 2005). For instance, if an object changed in height after it had been grasped this was more likely to be detected if its height was relevant to where the grasped object should be subsequently placed. Analysis of hand and eye movements during the actions suggested their tight coordination, tuned to the particular task demands. It is tempting to describe this behaviour as following a just-in-time principle; like efficient manufacturing rather than store large quantities of materials needed to construct a complex object it is better to have what is needed delivered at the point and location it is needed in the unfolding sequence of actions.

This tight coupling of acting and seeing appears to go very deep. Symes et al. (2008) show that hand posture may modulate what is noticed. Their participants had to detect a change within a standard change-blindness procedure. Stimuli were arrays containing twelve objects, one of which changed identity in otherwise identical alternating images, separated by a blank grey screen. All the objects in the displays were of such a size that they would normally be grasped with either a precision grip, such as a grape, or a power grip, such as an apple. The change was such that the grip association did not vary between the two objects, so a grape became a strawberry for example. If participants viewed a sequence of alternations and pressed a response key when they detected the change, an effect of change blindness was observed, in that the average time to respond was nearly five seconds (compared to a small fraction of this had the intervening visual transient not been present). If instead of preparing a simple key press to signal detection of the change, participants had to form a precision or power grasp, then whenever the prepared grip was compatible with the change object, the time to detect the change was reduced by an average of 372 milliseconds. For instance, preparing to respond by pressing a key between one's thumb and forefinger makes it easier to see a grape and strawberry swapping with each other in the alternating scene. Literally the shape adopted by the hand formed with the intention of acting modulates what is seen. In a related study Ellis et al. (2007) showed that selecting one object from another required the inhibition of the actions associated with the ignored object. Their participants had to respond to one of two abstract, three-dimensional objects, with the target identified by its colour, with a precision or power grip. Whenever the ignored object was compatible with the grasp made to the target there was a decrement in performance. This effect was not seen when the target appeared at a fixed location, leading the authors to conclude that affordance is the outcome of object-based selection processes. Directing our attention to an object 'as an object' necessarily potentiates the actions associated with it.

Other studies have shown the importance of the location and posture of our hands in modulating visual attention Abrams et al. (2008) showed that visual attention close to one's hands is enhanced. The simple act of having participants position their hands close to a screen on which three classic visual attention tasks were presented changed their performance. For example, in a visual search task (identifying a target letter among an array of distractor letters) participants search time was longer whenever they grasped the side of the display device compared to when their hands were resting in their laps. It seems that visual analysis of the close-to-hand stimuli was more extensive or careful or thorough. Thomas (2013) also showed that grasp posture alters visual processing in the region around the hands in a manner that seems related to the sort of ongoing actions that such postures are typically associated with. For instance, a precision grip may be associated with actions that require high spatial precision, such as threading a needle, while a power grip may be associated with fast and, relatively, spatially coarse actions, such as catching a ball. Accordingly, participants were required to complete motion detection or form detection tasks, while their hands were close to the target display and forming either a power or precision grip. The power grip facilitated the motion detection task, consistent with a specialism for temporal precision, whereas the precision grip facilitated form detection, consistent with a role in fine-grained spatial tasks.

In sharp contrast to these low-level action effects, visual attention may also be affected by conceptual action information. Humphreys and Riddoch (2001) demonstrated that unilateral visual neglect, that is the failure to notice visual objects in the visual field opposite to the site of brain damage, could be reduced by action cues. Patient MP, for instance, would miss target objects on the left of an array of objects when asked to search by name (find the cup) or colour (find the red object); however, when asked to search using an action term (find the object you would drink from), his neglect was reduced. An interaction of high- and low-level action systems in seeing is indicated by the fact that this reduction in MP's neglect was observed only whenever the target object was oriented with its handle towards MP. The handle orientation in the absence of the action cue did not reduce neglect, suggesting that a combination of goal and affordance is necessary for the capture of attention in this manner.

This chapter has discussed work in vision to illustrate the role of embodiment in human cognition. Several tentative conclusions can be made at this point.

Drawing the Threads Together

An ecological and enactive approach to vision (and perhaps to perception in general) has the potential to liberate our understanding from the very restricted glimpses offered by evidence drawing on passive viewing experiments. Active exploration, using a perceptual system, allows the use of changes in visual properties as access to the world, that are not, by definition, available in a single glance and a resultant retina image. Changes that result from the nature of the world and the perceptual apparatus used to engage it effectively embed the perceiver in the world. When engaged in active exploration they do not view the world they become part of it. The agent's actions modulate their perceptual experience in concert with the changes in the world that those actions produce. More surprisingly the agent's action intentions also mediate their perceptual experience, with action goals directing what is attended to. Passive viewing may play a relatively small part in our perception of the world.

However, empirical support for the ecological and enactive approaches is relatively sparse. Part of the reason for this is simply that it is difficult to study 'perception in the wild'.[26] Yet the potential rewards seem obvious, as illustrated by the transformation in the understanding of preserved visual capacity in a monkey with no striate cortex when released from her cage. Understanding what happens in the visual brains of agents as they move through and act on their world is perhaps increasingly obtainable given advances in virtual reality and brain imaging technology.

Gibson's assertion that the neurological mechanisms by which information is 'picked up' are of no concern for the psychological understanding of vision was unhelpful. Not only, as has often been pointed out, did this neglect obscure the complexity of the neural structure which allows the pickup, it also concealed important distinctions in the ecology of vision that had been missed by a purely ecological analysis. Distinctions in brain function and structure suggest the need for important revisions to the notion of affordance. The broad categories of ambient and focal vision suggest a division between whole-body and hand affordance that was

---

[26] Hutchins (1995) illustrates the benefits of such an approach in the case of non-perceptual cognitive processes.

absent, or at least rare, in the literature until recently. This relationship between brain organisation and types of action is probably reciprocal of course. A more detailed classification of actions and the bodily systems they depend on may well provide clues to a higher-resolution understanding of the architecture of the visual system. Although the evidence for there being multiple visual systems is very solid, the preceding argument that a closer examination of categories of action systems may have implications for understanding divisions within visual processing in the brain suggests that the currently dominant binary distinction may be too broad to capture distinctions among important categories of visually guided behaviour. For example, what of bilateral actions, involving the two hands in cooperation in a single task such as stabilising an object with the left hand while striking it with the right, such as hammering a nail or knapping a flint? What of actions which involve cooperation with other agents? Each of these cases is far more representative of our mundane actions as we cope in the world, than passively scrutinising a visual scene so as to make a judgement or arbitrary response. It might be suspected therefore that dedicated visiomotor systems will exist for such classes of action, yet we actually know very little about the neural basis of such activities. Later chapters will consider some recent work relevant to these issues.

Visual attention is tuned to action. The traditional view of attention being a consequence of information processing limitations (Broadbent, 2013) has largely been replaced by it being a requirement to select among potential objects for action, and is necessarily limited because of the limitations in our effectors (Allport, 1987; Humphreys et al., 2010). Just as the various kinds of action systems may depend on functionally distinct visual brain circuits, distinct attention mechanisms may be associated with the different action systems. Evidence for there being specific attentional mechanisms for the space around the hands was mentioned in this chapter. In the next chapter we will discuss the dissociation of attentional phenomena in far and reaching space. There can be little doubt that there are other action-specific attentional effects and systems to discover. Whether or to what degree seeing involves representational states has not been clarified by our discussion thus far. The purely representational theory of vision, typified here by the discussion of Marr (1982) has been rejected given its theoretical flaws, and the growing evidence for an ecological and enactive approach. The Gibsonian tradition is clear in its rejection of representation in favour of perception being direct, as are some advocates of sensorimotor contingency theory (Noë, 2010). But it is not the case that an enactive theory of vision *must* reject *any* role for representation states, despite this being strongly associated with it.

Some of the evidence for the affordance of grasping by the sight of artefacts, described above, suggested the notion of seeing something *as* a tool with particular functional potential, thus affording a particular grasp for use, as against a grasp simply to pick up. Is this 'seeing as' a representational state? Some of the change-blindness effects could actually be accounted for by the influence of representations in the form of expectations. Understanding what is happening in a video clip of a person leaving a desk at the sound of a telephone and then reappearing at another location to answer that call (Levin and Simons 1997), depends on understanding narrative structure, among many other things. Might not the failure to detect the change in identity across the two perspectives indicate the presence of a representation of the unfolding scenario? We will defer attempts to answer these questions to later, since they will also be seen to depend on understanding how an agent is affected by their culture, both material and social. We will eventually conclude that commenting, to others or oneself, on a flow of visual experience is also a skill that is subject to culture adaptation. It follows therefore that naive phenomenology is misleading, if taken to offer a genuine first-person account of the contents of experience, which is somehow prior to other forms of knowing. Our surprise at change-blindness phenomena reveals how false is our common-sense understanding of perceptual experience. The key to understanding this gulf is to examine the source of this 'common sense'. Before we get to that discussion however we need to extend our understanding of the impact of human dexterity and tool use on cognition.

3   Tool Use and Tool Incorporation

We have shown that the relationship between a human and the objects that share their world is not simply one of an active agent acting on a passive thing. The varieties of affordance that were described suggest that objects may summon behaviour and agency is thereby shared with the person. In this chapter, we deepen our enquiry by considering a special case of this relationship: tool use. Tools will be taken to be objects that are fabricated or modified in order to fulfil a function, and restricted, here, to those that are for hand use. We will re-evaluate old ideas about tool use being a key to understanding (in particular) human cognition, alongside recent empirical work demonstrating the adaptation of body and brain during tool use over a range of timescales. First though we examine our hands, which cognitive science has tended to treat as the end point of cognitive processing, rather than, as will be argued, one of its foundations.

Hands

Standing up brings dramatic changes! This is true in the development of the species and an individual human. In the former case the freeing of the upper limb allowed the further development of the hand, including its most sophisticated form in humans. The human upper limb with the hand at its end is an adaptation of the brachiating arm of a tree-dwelling ancestor species. There are good reasons for regarding it as a very valuable gift, for the arm we brought to the ground (Wilson, 2010) is the basis of huge advantages for our bipedal ancestors.

Brachiating is a method of moving along a branch of a tree by swinging beneath the branch using successive hand holds on the branch. Compared to the smaller, lighter animals that skilfully moved along the top surface of the branches, it requires some specific new features of the upper limb and the supporting muscle and skeletal systems. One feature is an increase in the mobility of the upper arm allowing the hand to be moved to most of the reaching space surrounding the shoulder joint. In addition, the twisting of the arm required for the swinging motion and the power grip required to support an animal's weight entailed flexibility of the lower arm from the elbow to wrist, along with adaptations of the hand.[1] Modifications such as these provided important capacities for the bipedal inheritors of this arm. These were not just modifications of muscle and bone but also the neural sensorimotor networks controlling the musculoskeletal system. The refined ability to reach into more extensive regions of space would have had entailed increases in the brains capacity for sensing the regions, sensing where the body, and the limb in particular, is within the extended space and moving the limb towards locations. The increased ability to twist the lower arm and form power grips, provided the first stage in the development of the critical ability to wield the weapons needed for predation of, and protection against, those with sharp teeth and claws. Subsequent refinements of the hand in the long trail, of some 3 or 4 million years, from the ground dwelling australopithecines to *Homo sapiens* included another critical development: the ability to bring the thumb into opposition with the other four fingers and therefore an increase in the range of types of hand holds possible, including precision grips in which an object is held between the thumb and one or more of the other fingers (Napier and Tuttle, 1993). Again, these developments were not simply adjustments in joints, tendons and muscle, but also in the complementary sensorimotor networks in the brain.

The evolution of a system allowing powerful, but also dexterous, deployment of the hands in space around an agent would require the development of sensory systems in support of such actions. To reach and grasp an object with a hand is a huge achievement. An appropriate body posture must be adopted and constantly adjusted during the reach. An arm must be 'selected' and extended by 'choosing' a sequence of configurations of joint adjustments, at the shoulder, elbow and wrist, so as to bring the hand to a position adjacent to the object, which allows for an optimal grasp given the three-dimensional shape and orientation of the object, and, often, the intended use. As the hand approaches the object that is to be grasped, the fingers progressively adopt a posture that will allow it to enclose the object and bring them into contact with it such that their positions form a balance in their opposition of forces as they squeeze

---

[1] The reader will gain a more vivid insight into these actions from a visit to their local play park where they may well find 'monkey bars' with children illustrating the movements and demonstrating the perseveration of this behaviour in humans. They might even get a go.

together in the grip, taking into account the weight and fragility of the object simultaneously. This sequence of actions demands the continuous satisfaction of mutual constraints between the body and the object, that depend on a moment-by-moment coordination of body movements and sensory systems (detailed commentaries can be found in Jeannerod, 1981, 1988 and Grafton, 2010).

When the object is grasped its use will necessitate similar coordination in space and time. A typical action, such as hammering a nail into wood, may now involve collaboration between the two hands. The left hand will position the nail to receive the hammer blow towards the end of the swing action of the right hand, so that it falls with sufficient force squarely on the head of the nail, without injury to the fingers which grasp it with a precision grip. The effects of the actions must enter into the control of the unfolding action sequence. So, for example, were the nail to be sensed as deflected from the vertical by a hammer blow, the next would be adjusted so as to strike a glancing blow offset to the side of the nail's head and with an adjustment in force so as to realign it. A skilled carpenter can repeat this task, practically flawlessly, at great speed. Japanese carpenters will clad roofs with shingles of the bark of cypress trees and work so fast that they stuff their mouths with nails, spitting one out as needed, as they proceed in their work, rather than slowing themselves by having to reach into a container of nails.

Humans are the undisputed world champions in manual dexterity. No other animal hand or, yet, robot hand can match the dexterity of a skilled human hand. It will be argued here that the refinement in sensorimotor control within reaching space that such dexterity requires is central to understanding human cognition in general. This development was of course progressive in that it built on the achievements of our ancestor species and was driven, in large part, by the benefits accruing to those who could make and use tools, an ability which we will now focus on.

Making and Using Tools

With the hand, eventually, came tools. Tool manufacture and use pre-dates the modern human hand, and the detail of the conjoined development of hand and tool is not easy to discern. There are relatively rich archaeological data on tools and their development, but relatively little on the parallel development of the hands that made and used them. Some key aspects of the latter, as expressed in the modern human hand, are worth noting however (Marzke, 2013). One is the increasing refinement of the thumb, in both power and flexibility. A characteristic of the modern human hand is the long thumb relative to the fingers, combined with a skeletal and muscular system that allows a particularly powerful compression force on objects held in a precision grip. A second characteristic is the orientation of the surfaces of joints around the thumb and index finger, which allow cupping of the hand around an object. A third is the structure of wrist bones allowing a flick of the wrist such as occurs towards the end of a hammer blow.

Each of these adaptations makes for a particularly skilful maker of early tools, such as a simple stone blade that might be used for cutting or scraping, as is revealed by experimental archaeology. Detailed observations of people (usually other archaeologists) making and using stone tools provides some clues as to the abilities of those who made and used the originals (Marzke and Shackley, 1986). A stone blade, for example, is made by modifying a suitably sized and shaped stone fragment, the core, using a larger, round hammer stone. Clearly two hands are needed for this task.[2] In modern, right-handed humans the preference is to hold the hammer stone in their right hand and stabilise the core in their left hand. Flakes are removed from the core by carefully aimed strikes with the hammer stone. Another obvious requirement is to form grips on both stones that avoid striking flesh rather than stone, so the ability to perform powerful precision grips is highly advantageous. Such a grip is the cupping of the entire hand so that the pads of finger and thumb ends can be aligned to squeeze against the edge of a stone, so exposing a large surface area to work on. Another is the 'three-jaw chuck' grip of a stone using the thumb in opposition to the index and middle finger. The force of a strike of the hammer stone on the core is increased significantly by a flick of the wrist. Use of the blade made in this way, to scrape residual fat and flesh from animal hide, say, requires yet another grip, clamping it between the pad at the end of the thumb and the side of the index finger.

The earliest stone tools found in the archaeological remains, and replicated in these studies, were certainly not made by *Homo sapiens*. Conventionally they are associated with the earlier hominid *Homo habilis* (or handy man) at sites in South and East Africa from about 2.4 million years ago.[3] It should be clear however that the development of the hand, towards its modern human form, and the development in the sophistication of the tools which became possible based on the resultant increases in the dexterity and power of object manipulation were intertwined. But

---

[2] This observation is deceptively mundane. We will discuss the profound consequences of bimanual actions for the development of lateralised functions, in species and individuals, later.

[3] More recent work has toolmaking earlier and therefore associated with earlier species (e.g. see Kivell et al., 2011).

what was the engine of this progress? A tempting answer is that skilled tool manufacture and use provided such significant survival advantages that it was selected for. But another possibility is that the dexterous hand was the by-product of other evolutionary pressures and tools were consequential to this more fundamental factor or factors. Given our state of ignorance, the claim that the advantages to survival of tool use were themselves the engine of evolutionary adaptations in the hand can only be conjecture (for a discussion of this issue, see Biro, Haslam and Rutz, 2013).

There is far less uncertainty about the actual tools that were made by early and modern hands, with rich material evidence that records their development (Ambrose, 2001). The Oldowan Industrial Complex refers to some of the earliest sites of toolmaking (Leakey, 1971), dated as early as 2.5 million years ago, and containing the blades and hammer stones we discussed above. Their manufacture appears to be the work of very skilled individuals[4] able to direct very precise blows to the edge of a stone, detaching flakes to yield well-shaped blades with only rare marks of mishits. Only after a further one million years do new tools appear, which give rise to the Acheulean Industrial Complex, from 1.5 million to 0.3 million years. The new tools include large cutting blades, which could function as axes or cleavers. Importantly these new blades appeared to be fashioned to a common design using a range of materials in a range of sizes, rather than a simple opportunistic modification of exiting forms evident in Oldowan tools. By the end of the Acheulean period the pace of development increases, leading to composite tools (such as stone tips mounted on wooden shafts) and some evidence of cultural variation in their precise form. The remains from a few tens of thousands years ago contain harpoons, buttons, needles and much more, made from stone, bone, shell and ivory. It seems clear that:

With the appearance of near-modern brain size, anatomy, and perhaps of grammatical language ~0.3 Ma, the pace quickens exponentially ... A mere 12,000 years separate the first bow and arrow from the International Space Station. (Ambrose, 2001: 1752)

Brain and Cognitive Architecture for Tool Use and Toolmaking

As we have noted the adaptations in the hand that provided these increasing skills in toolmaking and use were not simply adaptions of muscles and

---

[4] A skill that is beyond that of any other modern primate apart from humans, as illustrated by failed attempts to train, over three years, a bonobo (pygmy chimpanzee) to make blades (Schick et al., 1999).

bone. They would have entailed concurrent adaptions in the brain. It is a central contention of this text that some of the architectural features of the human cognitive system are the result of these adaptations. We will begin here with a discussion of some such possibilities and provide further elaborations as we proceed.

Precision manipulation of objects in near space clearly benefits from specific, and probably, independent sensorimotor networks in the human case. Some of the assumed characteristics of both the dorsal and focal vision system may seem to be adaptions for efficient and dexterous handling of objects. The increased demands a hand places on sensing the location and three-dimension shape of objects in near space may, however, justify a refinement of such fairly gross classifications of sensorimotor networks. There is evidence for several such refinements that are plausibly linked to, what might be deemed, our 'toolspace'.[5]

As was indicated in Chapter 2, contemporary theories of visual attention tend to treat it as a set of special purpose mechanisms serving particular action systems, rather than a homogeneous searchlight on the world (Rizzolatti et al., 1985; Humphreys et al., 2010). There are good reasons to suppose that the reaching space of an observer is served by a specific, and relatively independent, attentional mechanisms of this sort. Some forms of visual neglect suggest this for example. Visual neglect is a relatively common consequence of brain injury, mostly in the form of inattention to the left visual field (following right hemisphere damage). Such a patient, when asked to bisect a horizontal line on paper with a pencil, will make their mark, erroneously, displaced towards the right of the line, reflecting, it is said, their neglect of their left visual *field*. Actually, such gross clinical assessments probably mask a range of attentional deficits (Halligan et al., 2003), one of which involves either near or far space, rather than simply left or right fields. In such a case (Halligan and Marshall, 1991) a patient who, after a right hemisphere stroke, exhibited left-side neglect as evinced by his poor performance on the line-bisection task when completed using pen on paper, was shown to be significantly more accurate if he used a light pen to bisect a line located about 2.4 m in front of him. The converse case has also been observed (Vuilleumier et al., 1998). That is a patient who had pronounced left neglect in far space but not near. This double dissociation of function is particularly good support for the notion of independent sensorimotor neural systems for reaching space and far space, and this is complemented

---

[5] Which is clearly related to the commonly used term 'peripersonal space'. However, as we show shortly, what counts as near or far for a human depends on what they hold in their hands. Toolspace is intended to capture this characteristic.

by brain imaging data. Weiss et al. (2000) measured, by positron emission tomography (PET), cerebral blood flow in healthy humans, while they performed the line-bisection task and pointed to targets in near and far space. These data indicated largely dorsal system involvement in near-space actions and largely ventral system involvement in far space. Note also that the near–far distinction maps onto an upper–lower visual field distinction. That is, when looking directly ahead, objects within reaching space will be located in the viewer's lower visual field, whereas distant objects will lie in their upper visual field. Previc (1990) has argued, in a comprehensive review of a variety of literatures, that the increased specialisation of lower visual field processing in primates is actually the origin of the dorsal and ventral separation. Asymmetries in several psychophysical functions between the two regions (such as reaction times, motion perception, eye movements, attention and visual thresholds) suggest an upper field advantage for visual search and recognition, along with a lower field advantage in motion tracking and stereomotion detection of three-dimensional shape. It is easy to see how a facility in tracking moving objects and recognising three-dimensional shape would support the skilful control of hand actions on objects.

This separation of reaching and non-reaching space is not confined to skilled makers and users of tools of course. The efficient grasping of food items with a hand[6] and bringing them to the mouth may well depend on the distinction, as is suggested by studies of non-human primates. Rizzolatti, Matelli and Pavesi (1983) revealed similar far and near distinctions in ablation studies of the macaque monkey for instance. But some specifically human adaptations have been associated with the requirements of toolmaking. Orban et al. (2006) suggest that some differences in parietal cortex between humans and other primates is a consequence of adaptations for skilled tool use in humans. They review an extensive series of comparisons of neural activity, measured by functional magnetic resonance imaging (fMRI), in humans and macaque monkeys while engaged in a variety of visual discriminations and conclude that the human brain includes an evolutionary recent adaptation of posterior parietal cortex to the sensorimotor demands of skilful object manipulation. In the human brain this portion of cortex contains a greater number of subregions, each having a functional specialism. For instance, there are four separate regions responding to moving stimuli, probably also involving the derivation of three-dimensional shape from motion. Four areas respond to two-dimensional shape, that is respond more to intact than scrambled figures, and three deal with central vision.

---

[6] Or indeed a beak (Goodale and Graves, 1982).

The authors speculate that this complex of brain regions is the basis of what was termed toolspace earlier in this text. It allows a maker or user of tools to coordinate the movement of their hands with objects within a central region of their visual field.

Of course, tool use requires more than an ability to grasp objects and move them. A grasp made in order to use an object for a specific purpose may be very different to one in which the intention is simply to pick it up. Often the initial grasp is rather awkward to ensure that the final state of hand and object are appropriate for the intended use (Rosenbaum et al., 1992), such as when one grasps an upside-down drinking glass with the hand rotated so that the thumb and index finger are below the other fingers, allowing for a wrist rotation after grasping and lifting the glass to bring it to an orientation that allows a drink to be poured into it. It can get far more complicated than this of course. Consider hammering nails again. This requires 'knowing' where to grasp the hammer in order to use it with the right degree of force and how to place the nail on the surface so it can be driven into the wood, and this is just a tiny part of what a skilled carpenter needs to know.

Frey (2007) suggests that the 'how' of complex tool use of this latter sort has required the development of additional brain networks, in humans, to supplement those postulated to account for the simple grasping and handling of objects. He points to the aforementioned dissociations between the ability to grasp an object and the ability to grasp it appropriately for its use in brain-damaged patients: the agnosia patient DF's inappropriate grasps of objects given their function (Carey et al., 1996). But also, some apraxic patients show preserved abilities to grasp artefacts at the same time as failing to be able to use them for their designated function (Buxbaum et al., 2003). These data indicate that in the intact brain, there must be some means by which sensorimotor systems for grasping are coordinated with those determining the functional properties of a seen object. On the basis of fMRI studies of healthy participants, Frey postulates that a network of brain areas in the temporal, frontal and parietal regions of the left hemisphere, which include portions of both ventral and dorsal systems, is specialised for behaviours reflecting the functional properties of tools. Participants who planned but did not execute actions, *with both left and right hands*, on tools showed activation in these four left-hemisphere regions. We will return to these left-hemisphere networks in subsequent discussions of language evolution to discuss the intriguing link between the apparent lateralisation of language and skilled, complex tool use.

A more obvious human adaptation for tool use involves another class of lateralisation: handedness. About 85 per cent of our population would use their right hand by choice for a wide range of tasks. This so-called hand dominance[7] is found in earlier toolmakers too. Toth (1985) noted that stone cores from up to 1.9 million years ago bore fracture marks which suggested that they were rotated clockwise in the hands of their maker as they struck it with a hammer stone more often than anticlockwise. This bias suggests a preference for holding the hammer stone in the right hand, and the core in the left hand. To see this the reader should try rotating each of their hands clockwise and anticlockwise in their frontal plane. The left hand allows far more movement in a clockwise direction compared to the right. This mere hint of very early lateralisation in hand function is reinforced by a variety of sources which together tend to confirm that handedness was a, *perhaps unique*, feature of toolmaking hominids and their descendants. Steele and Uomini (2005) summarise the evidence. First, the finding of further traces in archaeological data of handedness in tool use, but also in skeletal remains and even artwork, as the following examples illustrate. The wear pattern of axes and cleavers dating from about one million years ago reveal a preponderance for right-hand use. The skeletal remains of Neanderthals reveal a robust right arm compared to the left and dental marks from cutting food held between their teeth point to a strong right-hand preference. The wonderful hand stencils found in Upper Palaeolithic art of about 40,000 years ago, and illustrated on the cover of this text, have a greater frequency of left-hand stencils, which is compatible with their being made by an individual holding a blowing tube in their right hand and spraying ochre pigment over their left hand pressed against the cave wall.

A second set of observations of modern, non-human primates (also summarised in Steele and Uomini, 2005) suggest that handedness, at the level of species, may be unique to those species adapted for complex toolmaking and tool use. Chimpanzees, in the wild, use tools: they crack open nuts with stones and fish for termites using sticks or straw, some of which they modify. They do not, clearly, have the ability to shape a stone axe head and bind it to a shaft of wood. Nor do they demonstrate a species level handedness. Observations of spontaneous hand actions within particular groups reveal them as ambidextrous for behaviours such as reaching for an object or grooming another individual. More complex actions often elicit a hand preference at an individual level, in that a given animal will demonstrate a preferred hand for termite fishing, for example. There is no consistent bias at the population level among these animals,

---

[7] Actually, limb dominance, since any action with a hand is also necessarily the action of the complex muscular and jointed skeletal system to which it is attached. Hand will be used in this section as referring to a limb system.

however, with groups showing a left preference, others a right preference, some divided equally and yet others demonstrating ambidextrous behaviours. This is very different from modern humans of course, who exhibit a clear right-hand bias across all populations, with no population observed to have a left-hand preference.

Why is there an association between species level hand laterality and complex tools? One approach to this question is to focus on the role of both hands in a given action sequence. That is rather than hand dominance, the lateralisation is the result of hand specialisation during bimanual object manipulation. Guiard (1987) asks us to consider the performance of a violinist in which the two hands and limbs play complementary roles, neither of which could be considered dominant. This bimanual collaboration is the typical manner in which tools are used, and, the author asserts, its development was an important factor in hominisation. The collaboration has entailed that each hand is responsible for specific elements of a task. In a right-handed individual their left hand stabilises and adjusts an object, while their right hand performs precision actions on the object proffered by the left hand. Think once more of the core stone in the left hand gradually being rotated clockwise so as to allow blows with the hammerstone held in the right hand. Or writing a letter, adjusting the sheet of paper on the table with the left hand, while writing with the right. In these cases, the left hand is providing a spatial frame for the right and therefore, in a sense, leads the right hand. Also, the two hands are moving within different spatial scales: the left tends to be used for high-amplitude movements, the right for high-resolution or precision movements. It is fairly obvious that early toolmaking would have benefited from just this sort of lateralisation of function. The fact that it is preserved in the structure of the modern human brain, that is inherited not acquired during postnatal development, is remarkable, suggesting that the benefits derived from skilled, bimanual actions drove brain adaptations.

The making of even a simple stone tool is not just the result of random hitting or a fixed pattern of hitting of a core held in one hand with a hammerstone held in the other. Each blow is a stage in a progression from the raw core to the finished blade, with 'decisions' required as to which path to take, of the several possible paths, to the end state. Certainly, this seems true of tools being made about 1.4 million years ago, which are referred to as bifaces. These have characteristic two-dimensional shapes forming what are probably intended to be hand-axes and cleavers. One approach to understanding the implications of such activities for the individuals and societies in which they occur is to analyse the sequence of operations that are required to fabricate their artefacts. In reviewing the changes in Palaeolithic material culture Stout (2011) frames toolmaking as a hierarchy of actions, which evolved to enable the increases in technical complexity. Such activity may be represented within a tree structure with several levels branching from the superordinate goal of achieving the tool's final form. Lower level goal nodes would include gathering the raw materials, examining the core, selecting a target on the core for striking, positioning the core and so forth. Within this structure some activities will consist of behavioural loops, such as the repeated flaking until some high lever goal, such as edge construction, is achieved. The complexity of such tree structures increases to reflect increasing sophistication, and at some point an important new element seems to have been added. By the early Acheulean period (1.6–0.9 million years ago) cores were modified, rather than simply selected, so as to be suitable shapes for further flaking into a desired final form. That is one or more subordinate flakes are removed to provide a suitable core for the iterative, primary flaking to achieve a cutting or scrapping edge. As Stout (2011) notes this nesting of flaking within flaking actions is recursive, haveing the potential power of all recursive operations. Clearly these developments depend on not just sensorimotor adaptations, but also seem to require abilities that would be usually described as cognitive.[8] To keep track of where one is in a complex network of activities requires, surely, means of mentally representing and retaining such structures. Combinatorial structures with recursion are, of course, characteristics of natural languages.

Again, there may be a link between the needs of complex toolmaking and use, and language. Later in this text we will assemble an argument that the benefits of these adaptations for skilled toolmaking and use did indeed provide the basis for the evolution of human language. It will be claimed that complex toolmaking and use, combined with social learning (discussed in Chapter 4) within a material culture (discussed in Chapter 5) was the driver of language evolution (discussed in Chapter 6) and therefore the creation of *symbolic* cultures. Meanwhile, in the next section, we consider the effects of tool use over shorter timescales.

The Effective Body: Remapping Sensorimotor Systems and Neural Plasticity

Some phenomenologists have claimed that tools, when used skilfully, become effectively part of our body. Heidegger's notion of ready-to-

---

[8] But this assumption will be questioned later in this text.

hand suggests that a tool is largely unnoticed by its wielder, akin to our ignorance of the what our hands are doing as they reach and grasp an object. Merleau-Ponty claimed that a body is extended to the boundaries of a skilfully employed artefact. Gibson too claimed that tool use abolishes the subject–object distinction in some manner. Anthropologists have referred to the stone axes of our ancestors as 'secretions' of the wielder's skeleton (Leroi-Gourhan, 1993). There is now good, and accumulating, evidence that such notions of tools becoming incorporated into the body when used skilfully is not merely an 'as if' relationship but is literally the case. That is, tools have been shown, largely by neuroscientific investigations, to be incorporated into the body's sensorimotor system over a range of timescales, with some such effects being immediate and others being long-term adaptations during individual development.

A celebrated study is that of Iriki, Tanaka and Iwamura (1996) who trained macaques to use rakes to retrieve food rewards that were beyond their unaided reach. Brain activity in intraparietal regions, which combine visual and somatosensory information in bimodal neurones, was recorded during this skill acquisition. Some neurones were identified which responded to somatosensory and visual stimulation at or near the hand, and whose visual receptive fields tracked hand movements. After only five minutes' use of the rake to retrieve food some of these 'hand' neurones had expanded visual receptive fields that now covered the length of the tool. Similarly, bimodal neurones with somatosensory receptive fields around the shoulder and neck, and visual receptive fields around the space reached by the arm, adapted to rake use, with some showing expanded visual receptive fields covering the space reachable with the arm and rake combined. These adaptations followed only after active use of the rake, mere grasping was not sufficient. The visual receptive field expansion was only observed for neurones having somatosensory receptive fields on the arm or hand, but not the fingers. It seems that the rake was incorporated as an extension of the arm's reach.

Related effects of tool use have been observed repeatedly in humans. We discussed above the cases of visual neglect in which a disassociation was demonstrated between reaching and far space. Berti and Frassinetti (2000) describe a patient with left-side neglect following right hemisphere brain damage confined to near space. Thus, when required to bisect a horizontal line using a projection light pen her responses were biased to the right side of lines within reaching space, but significantly less so for lines positioned beyond her reach. Remarkably if instead of pointing with the light pen she reached with a stick towards the more distant lines her performance declined so that the right bias was equivalent to that for near lines. It seems that merely holding a stick had, immediately expanded peripersonal space, or, as is preferred here, toolspace.[9] Even more remarkably a similar remapping of toolspace occurs when observing the actions of others reaching with tools. Costantini et al. (2014) tested a hemisphere neglect patient, with the neglect confined to near space, on bisection of far and near lines using a laser pointer and a stick. The patient performed the laser pointer task both before and after observing the experimenter perform the same task with a stick. The neglect patient's performance, prior to the observation phase, replicated that of Berti and Frassinetti's (2000) patient: the neglect was confined to near space when using a laser pointer but became equally bad for both far and near when using a stick. After observing the experimenter perform the task with a stick the patient's performance was transformed so that his own bisection performance using a laser became identical to that when he used a stick, that is neglect was evident for both near and far lines. Intriguingly this transformation occurred if he had held a stick during the action observation but not if he was empty-handed.[10]

A similar remapping of toolspace when another person is observed using a tool can be inferred by its impact on affordance. Costantini et al. (2011) had participants respond with a pantomime of a reach-and-grasp action while viewing depictions of graspable mugs with handles oriented to the left or right. The typical micro-affordance effect was elicited: responses with a hand congruent with the handle of the depicted object were faster than incongruent cases whenever the object was depicted within a hand's reach, but not when beyond. There then was a training phase in which participants used, or viewed an experimenter using tools to reach towards real objects. They then repeated the stimulus–response compatibility experiment. If, in the training phase, participants themselves had reached towards objects with a 1-metre-long garbage picker, the objects which were beyond the unaided reach of a hand now afforded a compatible response, but only in the hand that had used the tool. Passive holding of the same tool in the training phase did not modulate affordance. If instead during the training phase

[9] In fact, this is a rather neat demonstration of the benefit of the proposed renaming, given that the special purpose sensorimotor systems underlying hand actions, in the phenomena under consideration here seem to be attuned to the effective space of hand–tool combinations. The term peripersonal itself has become more nuanced since its early use in Rizzolatti et al. (1981). An overview of recent thinking on this topic can be found in Brozzoli et al. (2011) and a specific argument for there being a variety of such peripersonal spaces can be found in De Vignemont and Iannetti (2015).

[10] A lot more will be said about the impact of the observation of the actions of others on the sensorimotor systems of the observer in the next chapter. Interactions of this type will be seen to be critical to the central themes of this text.

participants viewed another person reaching with the garbage picker, a similar modulation of the affordance to that caused by actually using the tool themselves was observed, but only if the participant also passively held a similar tool while observing the other's actions. If empty handed or passively holding a tool which would be ineffectual in the task of grasping the distant object, no modulation of affordance was observed. Viewing others acting on the world with tools produces the same adaptation of toolspace as the actual use of the tool, that it is remapped to include the space within the effective reach of a hand holding the tool, but only if the observer has a similar extended capacity by virtue of holding a similar tool. The authors suggest that this dynamic reconfiguring of toolspace reflects the requirements of coordination between agents. On this perspective toolspace is a shared space which is configured to take account of the effective capacities for *joint* action. We will reconsider this important conclusion in the next chapter when we look in more detail at the coordination of joint action on objects.

Dynamic reconfiguration of the toolspace has also been demonstrated in participants without brain impairment. Brozzoli et al. (2009) had participants discriminate between touches on either their thumb or index finger of their hand as they merely viewed a graspable object, a small metal cylinder, or reached and grasped it with a precision grip. They used, as a measure, the magnitude of the so-called cross-modal congruency effect (CCE) on their reaction times. This refers to the finding that judgements of the position of tactile stimulation on the body are affected by the position of simultaneous, but irrelevant, visual stimulation (Spence et al., 2004). Spatially congruent visual stimulation enhances performance compared to incongruent ones (the CCE). In the case of the present study the cylinder to be viewed or grasped had two LEDs attached, one above the other, which were therefore congruent with either the thumb or index finger of the participant. The CCE varied as a reach to grasp was executed: at the initiation of the reach it increased markedly from that observed with a static hand and then increased further when the precision grip on the cylinder was executed. The authors attribute this modulation of the CCE to the real-time reweighting of the visual and tactile information relative to the acting hand.

The implication of these data is that the toolspace inherited from our handy forebears is not just specialised in the sense of having dedicated sensorimotor brain networks, which integrate sensory information around our hands and track objects within their reach, it also adapts in real time. It responds dynamically to events within that space, remapping space and sensory events, as hands move towards objects, and as hands grasp tools. It is in fact the effective space of hands and tools.

This dynamic response of sensorimotor systems to the *effective* capacities of a body is reflected in human perceptual judgements also. One finding was mentioned in the introduction to this text: objects appear nearer when the viewer holds a tool with which they intend to reach towards it (Witt et al., 2005). There are a host of similar observations which involve sensorimotor systems other than toolspace and so suggest that a body's effective capacity in general is dynamically linked to our perceptual systems (for a review, see Witt, 2011). Softball players see the ball as larger when they are playing well. Successful tennis players see the net as lower compared to the less successful. Physically fit individuals judge hills to be less steep than the not so fit. People with narrow shoulders perceive doorways to be wider than do those with wide shoulders. Observers carrying a heavy load see distances as greater and hills as steeper. That these affects are affects on perception literally and not merely a judgement bias of some kind is suggested by their occurrence with covert manipulations of bodily capacity. Schnall, Zadra and Proffitt (2010), for example, demonstrated that participants who drank juice sweetened with sugar saw hills as less steep than others who drank juice with non-sugar sweeteners.[11]

Sensorimotor adaptations occur then over a range of timescales: those that are thought to have occurred during the evolution of our species and those that occur moment by moment as we act and move within our world. There are also changes that occur within the lifetime of an individual human as they learn the specific skills demanded of them in their particular culture. These are particularly important for key arguments that are to follow. Such adaptations are possible because of neural plasticity which allow changes in brain networks as a consequence of experience. While these processes have long been recognised as a feature of young brains during critical developmental phases, more recently it has become clear that the human brain should be regarded as permanently plastic (Pascual-Leone et al., 2005). Changes in environmental contexts and learning new skills have been shown to produce enduring changes in brain networks throughout the lifespan. We will discuss such adaptations in greater detail in Chapter 5's discussion of material culture and the significance of skill acquisition, but an illustrative example, for our purposes at this point, is the modification in brain structure associated with learning to juggle (Draganski et al., 2004). After three months of daily training, the brains of newly competent, adult jugglers showed increases in grey matter, revealed by MRI, in cortical regions associated with

---

[11] The experimenters ensured that there was no detectable difference in taste between the drinks.

motion analysis. Three months later, without any further juggling practice, this grey matter had reduced to only just more than that measured before any training. It seems that the human brain, although the product of natural selection, is moulded millisecond by millisecond, day by day, month by month, year by year by what we habitually do in our world. What we do habitually is of course determined by the specific social and material culture which we inhabit. We will get back to this insight repeatedly, as we proceed, in this text.

Natural-born Toolmakers: Genetic Inheritance and Cultural Transmission

This chapter has discussed the coevolution of toolmaking and use, and the brain of *Homo sapiens*. The conclusion is that significant architectural features of our brains are the consequence of progressive adaptations in sensorimotor networks that formed the neural basis of a toolspace. That is special purpose sensory, motor and attentional systems to deal with events and objects within reach, of the effective body, have become hardwired. Importantly this system is modulated as a result of both instantaneous adaptation, as when a tool is gripped and therefore the effective reaching space is expanded, and longer-term adaptation as the result of skill acquisition. The consequence is that the genetic endowment becomes overlaid or sculpted by a lifetime of practical activity within a human culture. Clearly toolmaking and use did not, and does not, occur in a social vacuum. Toolspace, in the sense used in this text, is a product therefore of both genetic and social transmission. The transmission across generations of increasingly complex technical skills is itself dependent on a number of aspects of social interactions that are, debatably, most fully developed in humans. Language is the most obvious of these, but there are other conduits, probably uniquely human, that appear particularly important for skilled actions. Imitation of observed actions may be one such source. A surprising finding, for most, is that non-human primates appear to favour novel solutions when required to solve a problem that they have observed another agent solving, whereas humans often appear to prefer to simply imitate what they see. Nagell, Olguin and Tomasello (1993) showed that 2-year-old human children who had observed a demonstrator retrieve an out-of-reach object by using a rake, in either an efficient or inefficient manner, subsequently copied what they had observed: those who had observed the inefficient rake technique reproduced it. In contrast chimpanzees who observed similar demonstrations were not entrained by what they had seen, but emulated the performance of using the rake to successfully retrieve the object. For some this tendency to imitate rather than emulate[12] is a key to understanding the massive expansion in human material culture compared to non-human primates. Tennie, Call and Tomasello (2009) have described the rachet effect which characterises the uniquely human accumulation of culture. Modifications in skilled actions, such as those in tool manufacture and use as previously described, tend to pass down through generations, with imitation ensuring the fidelity of transmission.

Tomasello et al. (2005) concluded, in a survey comparing humans with other primates, that non-human primates, both apes and monkeys, learn from the observation of the actions of other members of their group about the causal powers of *objects* within their environment, which allows them to invent means of attaining goals. Whereas, they speculate, the imitation learning seen in humans depends on an understanding of the intentions of others, and such understanding arises from early social interactions which are unique to human societies. We will examine these possibilities in far greater detail in reviewing evidence, in the next chapter, that humans are bound to each other by obligatory responses to the observed behaviour of others.

---

[12] But as Whiten et al. (2009) point out, the distinction between imitation and emulation is neither sharp nor straightforward. Their more nuanced approach nevertheless reveals a surprising tendency to simply copy observed actions in young, human adults, particularly in more cognitively advanced individuals.

4   Agency, Objects and Others

Earlier in this text we claimed that Penfold's homunculus better represented the essence of human mental processes than Rodin's statue of *Le Penseur*. Yet they share an obvious deficit: both depicted lone agents. A better caricature would be a community of the troll-like creatures busy in their world acting together to achieve their common purposes. The focus on this chapter is on the ways in which individuals become connected with others within a material culture and what should become clear is a sense that humans share a world, effectively integrating other agents when working together, and thereby share agency, and that the mechanisms by which we form relationships with the animate and the inanimate have a common basis. First though we will consider claims that humans are uniquely social primates in the sense of the strength and synchrony of the relations within human groups.

The Emergence of the Social Brain

There is broad consent for the idea that an important engine of hominin evolution was the change in social relations that supported, and were supported by, the increase in technical skills. Increases in toolmaking sophistication would have demanded additional means of coordination among individuals, in gathering the required materials and transmitting the technical skills. The use of the tools would have allowed more effective exploitation of natural resources which would have created the conditions for larger social groups. These entailed changes in social relations would themselves have elicited adaptive responses in the individuals, some of which would have been selected by virtue of their contribution to fitness. Those adaptations would have in turn expanded the possibility of innovations in technology. A particular variant of this sort of account is termed the 'social brain' hypothesis (Barton and Dunbar, 1997). This emphasises the close relationship between an increase in the size of the communities[1] of our ancestors and the observed increases in brain size deduced from archaeological data. The claim is that, broadly, the *prime* driver of hominin brain evolution was social complexity itself.

More specifically the increasing social complexity of primate societies is said to account for the marked increase in their brain to body ratio compared to other animals. In modern primates, particularly the anthropoids, this is reflected in a strong positive correlation between the social group size and their relative brain size, the relationship being particularly strong in the case of regions in the frontal lobes and the neocortex (Dunbar and Shultz, 2007). Extrapolating this correlational data to modern humans leads to an estimate of about 150 individuals for their social groups, a figure which tends to be supported in surveys of personal social networks (Gonçalves, Perra and Vespignani, 2011).

A very important moment in the evolution of the social brain is the dispersal of a group so that all are not always present to each other. This was already the case for some of the earliest toolmakers of the Oldowan period whose stone artefacts were transported over distances greater than 10 kilometres, which suggests a range greater than modern apes. Cooperative behaviour among these early hominins would have required the taking account of the actions of both those immediately present and those elsewhere. This seemingly requires a form of disengagement from the flow of sensorimotor interactions so as to represent the invisible others, to imagine them in other words. Similar disengagement in the fashioning of a stone object so as reduce it to a final form which, it might be assumed, must also be imagined. There is a debate, to which we shall return, as to whether the additional social demands provided the basis for the brain adaptations which formed part of the basis of the capacity for making tools or the converse or whether the social brain and the toolmaking brain co-evolved.

Interestingly, the correlation between group size does not apply to other mammals or birds. What is strongly associated with brain size in these taxa is the form of bonding between individuals: those that pair-bond, that is form male and female relationships lasting for a breeding season or longer, have bigger brains than those that do not. In pair-bonding birds, those that pair-bond for life have bigger brains than those that do not. It is presumed that the bigger brains are a consequence of the increased cognitive demands of defending territory, coordinating behaviours with a partner, and so forth. Dunbar (2009) conjectures that at some point early in the evolution of the primate brain the form of affective pair-bonding found in

---

[1] The sense of community used here is of set individuals who may be divided into subgroups dispersed over an extended area rather than a single group that is always together.

mating pairs was generalised to all group members. Dunbar is tempted to call this new form of bonding 'friendship'. The shift to generalised pair-bonding is claimed to bring with it brain and cognitive adaptations that form the precursors of later developments that include the ability to predict and understand the actions of others.

The social brain hypothesis concentrates on the requirement to develop the social skills needed to cope with ever larger communities entailing increasingly complex relationships with others to account for the evolution of the hominin brain. This text, thus far, has focused on the sensorimotor skills required of members of communities possessing increasing sophisticated material cultures to explain similar brain adaptations. Which account is correct? Almost certainly, both. It seems very plausible that the two sets of skills coevolved. The sort of collaboration needed for all but the simplest of stone technologies required exchanges with others and the transmission of the associated skills, in particular, required both complementarity between the actions of individuals and also, probably, an affective bond between the collaborating individuals. The enhancements in technical prowess would have provided the basis for societies capable of supporting greater numbers in any given natural environment and so required further adaptations of social skills. The relative contributions of social and technical competence to adaptation would have fluctuated over the eons but any attempt to disentangle them is misguided. In fact, this view is shared by the advocates of the social brain hypothesis:

Instead of either competence leading the way towards an explanation, they work in tandem as co-evolutionary partners in a system of mutual influence. (Gamble, Gowlett and Dunbar, 2011: 119)

An illustration of this mutuality will be provided in Chapter 6 when it will be claimed that the development of language depended on the prior development of toolspace, and of course the development of language massively expanded the social space of those with that competence. Using language is a social *and* technical skill.

We will now consider the evidence for there being the sort of bonding and synergy between individuals in modern primates suggested by the social brain idea, beginning with the startling evidence that our understanding of the action intentions of another is as direct as our understanding of our own actions.

Mirror Neurones in Monkeys and Humans: Action Understanding and Imitation

In one sense, other humans are simply other objects in our material culture with which we interact. We will see, in the foregoing discussions that, just like artefacts, observing other humans elicits obligatory responses in the motor system of the observer. So-called mirror neurones, which underlie these influences, have been used to answer many questions in cognition, from the origins of empathy to language use. Here, in contrast, a case will be made for treating the mirror neurone system (MNS) as part of a larger system that supports joint action on objects.

In another very important sense, other humans are very different from the artefacts we face in that they are animate, and their behaviour is driven by intentions, which may not be directly observed.[2] In order to accomplish the simplest of cooperative actions, say, receiving a proffered glass of wine, we must 'read' the intention of the giver, and predict the location, orientation and time of arrival of the offered glass within our reaching space. We must also form a grip that complements the grip used by the other. In this chapter we will describe behavioural investigations that reveal the meshing of agents and objects within a dynamic network of mutual, sensorimotor influences. It will be further claimed that these networks provide the building blocks of higher cognition, in particular language. First though we will examine the evidence for mirror neurones.

The discovery of mirror neurones, first in the macaque monkey, was happenchance. Investigators at the University of Parma were using single cell recording techniques in an attempt to understand the role of premotor cortex in the control of grasping actions. Measuring in an area generally referred to as F5 they wanted to separate the responses of neurones to movements of the monkey's hand and to the object that it was grasping. Accordingly, they trained the monkeys to reach and grasp objects of various shapes and sizes while recording the activity of neurones in F5. While conducting the studies they noticed that a large proportion of these neurones also responded to the actions of the experimenters, as they grasped and placed food items during the training procedure. Pellegrino et al. (1992) described some of this class of visuomotor neurone as being mirror-like, in that they were responsive both to the execution of a particular action by the animal, such as when making a precision grip on a peanut, and when they observed the same grip being executed by an experimenter. Gallese et al. (1996) extended these findings. Of the 532 neurones they investigated, 92 had mirroring properties, responding to both actions of the monkey and similar actions observed in others, mostly involving actions with the hands or mouth on objects. A large proportion of these discharged when the animal observed a hand approaching and grasping an object, some of which were specific with regard to the type of grip, such as a precision grip or a whole-hand grip. Others were selective

---

[2] But, of course, this may be changing as developments in robotics accelerate.

for actions placing objects, manipulating objects, holding objects and bimanual actions on objects. It is important to note that the mirror responses were dependent on the observation of the combination of the action and the object acted upon. Either in isolation did not elicit a mirror neurone response. Also, and this is significant for our subsequent discussions in this chapter, some exhibited a hand preference, with some of these neurones responding preferably to the observation of ipsilateral and others to contralateral hand actions in the experimenter.

Subsequent work has revealed the existence of an MNS extending beyond F5 in monkeys and an analogous system in humans. In the case of the human, brain imaging suggests an extensive network. Molenberghs, Cunnington and Mattingley (2012) performed a meta-analysis of 125 human fMRI studies which had identified brain regions which appeared to mirror action execution and observation. Among these studies fourteen distinct neuronal groups across nine different Brodmann areas were consistently identified as having mirror properties. These included two predominately motor areas: one frontal, around the inferior frontal gyrus;[3] and the other parietal, around the rostral portion of the inferior parietal lobule. These latter two sites have sometimes been referred to as the core or classical MNS in humans, and are said to include the analogue of F5 in the macaque. But other areas revealed as having mirror properties included areas within the primary visual cortex, the cerebellum and the limbic system.

Additional support for the existence of a human MNS is provided by observations of the affects on hand muscles of observing actions in others. Fadiga et al. (1995) measured motor-evoked potentials (MEPs) in muscles in the hands of participants while they viewed the experimenter grasping an object. MEPs were significantly raised in a muscle group also shown to be active when actually executing the same grasping action. Mirror properties in neurones have also been revealed by direct, single cell recordings in humans. Mukamel et al. (2010) describe data from a group of patients with severe epilepsy who were undergoing exploratory surgery using micro electrodes in attempts to identify the loci of their seizures. Recording in frontal and temporal cortex while patients observed or executed grasping actions, they found a significant proportion of neurones which responded to both observation and execution, some showed an excitatory response, others were inhibited.

---

[3] A gyrus is a ridge on the cortex. The inferior frontal gyrus is one of the four gyri of the frontal lobe and includes Broca's area, a circumstance clearly of significance for our discussions here.

It is easy to understand why the properties of the MNS have provoked great excitement. Surely, it can be argued, brain regions which are active both when performing and observing actions are conduits between agents. If my brain reflects your actions by reproducing the activation patterns that are the neural basis of my performance of the same action, it seems that brains can be synchronised, to a degree. Accordingly the MNS may be the basis of non-linguistic understandings between agents. Also of course the MNS appears to be a plausible neural candidate for a mechanism of imitation learning which, as previously noted, appears to be particularly important in the human case.[4] We will consider each of these two possibilities in turn.

One form of understanding that the MNS is said to provide is the understanding of the actions of others. The argument for this claim is simple enough:

Each time an individual sees an action done by another individual, neurons that represent that action are activated in the observer's premotor cortex. This auto-matically induced, motor representation of the observed action corresponds to that which is spontaneously generated during active action and whose outcome is known to the acting individual. Thus, the mirror system transforms visual infor-mation into knowledge. (Rizzolatti and Craighero, 2004: 172)

Two studies with monkeys have tested the idea that the MNS is the basis of action understanding. Kohler et al. (2002) described neurones in the F5 region of macaques which discharged when they either performed an action or heard a sound associated with it, such as the sound associated with breaking the shell of a peanut. The majority of these neurones also responded to the observation of the associated action. Umilta et al. (2001) measured the responses of F5 mirror neurones in macaques, while they observed an experimenter reaching towards and grasping an object. The final phase of the grasping action was either in full view of the animal or concealed behind a screen so that the interaction of the hand with the object could not be seen. But it could be inferred of course, and the fact that the majority of the mirroring neurones that were tested were found to respond whether or not the final phase of the action was visible implied that an internal representation of the completed action was formed in the animal's brain. Importantly the action represented was that of a reach-to-grasp an object, since the same neurones failed to respond to the same actions pantomimed in the absence of an object. The authors concluded that the monkey MNS is the neural basis of action recognition.

[4] And, yes, that is contradictory given that monkeys also have an MNS. This distinction between humans and other primates is clearly not absolute, but one of degree.

The immediacy of the inference that MNS activation represents actions, thereby constituting the understanding of them, masks a number of difficulties in interpretation. First, how does a resonant brain state constitute understanding? To assume that it does, is to adopt a highly contentious solution to the mind–body problem, that is to assume their identity as an empirical fact. There are very long-standing philosophical objections to such a brutish mind–brain identity theory and the idea that activity in a part of the brain can be said to constitute a mental state (Kripke, 1980 is one such objection).[5] Another difficulty with evaluating the claim that MNS activity constitutes understanding is the various senses of 'understanding'. Importantly, is it meant to entail an explicit or consciously held insight into an activity? This is certainly hinted at in the notion of the MNS transforming visual information into knowledge. Or might the understanding evoked be implicit or procedural? Closer to the understanding I have of riding a bicycle, say.

As we proceed, a case will be made for, at least, some forms of understanding to reside not in individual brains, but in a community of skilled agents acting cooperatively and competitively within their material culture. Their skilful interactions are made possible by the possession of sensorimotor systems, including the MNS, which allow an individual agent to *incorporate*, as well as use, tools and other agents in their unfolding activity. Some aspects of these sensorimotor systems have been shaped by natural selection as brain development was driven by ever more dextrous hands and increasing technical powers within social groups. Others are shaped within an individual lifespan by, it will be argued, powerful associative mechanisms, as the individual adapts to their material culture.

The tendency for humans to imitate the bodily actions of other humans is so great that it has been likened to the response of chameleons in changing their skin colour to match their surroundings (Chartrand and Bargh, 1999). This analogy is meant to capture the obligatory nature of the imitative response. Most of us come to know, perhaps uncomfortably, that the crossing of arms and legs, yawning, verbal tics, even accents are copied without intention or awareness. Chartrand and Bargh (1999) confirmed these anecdotal insights in a study in which participants worked in pairs, with one of the pair being a confederate of the experimenters. During a task in which the two took turns in describing a set of photographs, the confederate adopted a behavioural mannerism: either

---

[5] In at least some of the studies associating action understanding and MNS activation there is also the analogous problem of the validity of reverse inference whereby a cognitive process, like understanding, is inferred from the brain activation (Poldrack, 2006).

rubbing their face or tapping their foot. The frequency of foot tapping, and face rubbing were all reliably increased in those participants exposed to them. Moreover, they were not aware of these mannerisms in the confederates with whom they worked. When asked, after the task had been completed, whether any of their partners had distinctive behavioural traits, no participant mentioned face rubbing or foot tapping.

The human tendency to imitate extends far beyond behavioural tics and includes detailed aspects of the body movements of those we observe. Fine-grained aspects of hand posture, for example, seem to be influenced by merely observing other human hands. The participants in Brass et al.'s (2000) study were required to make a series of binary judgements of visual stimuli by lifting either their index or middle finger while their hand rested on a table. The stimuli consisted of five frames of a video of a human hand also resting on a table, mirroring the participant's hand and also performing either an index or middle finger lift. One set of trials entailed the participants responding to the number '1' or '2' which was superimposed on the hand image. Despite the action of the actor being irrelevant to their task, it influenced their performance: the time to initiate finger lifts was 56 milliseconds faster whenever the finger was the same as that seen moving in the video sequence, compared to when it differed.

The obvious candidate for the neural basis of imitation effects of this kind is the MNS and there is evidence that this is so. Iacoboni et al. (1999) measured brain activity with fMRI while participants performed a task similar to the finger-lifting procedure just described. Now, though, in one condition, they passively observed the animated sequence of the hand lifting one finger from a table and this was compared to conditions in which they explicitly imitated the finger lifting and conditions in which they responded with finger lifts to either symbolic or spatial cues. Two brain regions were identified which were active both when passively viewing finger lifting and when executing the same movements, with a relative increase in activity in those cases when the execution was a response to observing the movement. These mirror-like responses were found in regions of the left-side, frontal cortex and right-side parietal cortex. The former area corresponded to Broca's area, which is regarded by some to be the human analogue of F5 in monkey (Binkofski and Buccino, 2004).

Why is this human compulsion to imitate important? Because it provides the basis of social learning of various kinds is one answer, which as we alluded to above is particularly important in human cultures. One intriguing possibility links language learning with the MNS, given a core component of the latter is Broca's area and Broca's is the motor area for speech production, damage to which results in expressive aphasia.

Obviously learning to speak a language involves imitating the sounds made by fluent users of that language. Also, so-called motor theories of speech perception, which claim that the basis of speech perception is the perception of the 'gestures' of tongue, mouth and so forth which produce the speech sounds (Liberman and Mattingly, 1985) would appear to be supported by the mirroring properties of Broca's area (but see Lotto, Hickok and Holt, 2009 for an objection to this notion). We will return to these possibilities in Chapter 6 where a far more extensive discussion of language evolution and acquisition will be attempted.

Observational motor learning is another class of social learning that is plausibly related to the MNS. Rather than the incremental learning of a new motor skill via the conversion of a set of symbolic instructions, verbal or other, into motor acts that are gradually automated during skill acquisition, simply watching what another does can achieve the same ends. The learning of motor skills by imitating what others are seen to do does seem an obvious candidate for a function of the MNS. Buccino et al. (2004) used fMRI to measure the brain activity of novice guitarists as they learned chords. Notice that the learning of the hand actions involved in playing a musical chord go beyond the observer merely reflecting actions in their existing repertoire. Imitative *learning* entails the enactment of novel sequences of behaviours, with elements of the sequence being resonant responses within the MNS. Measurements were taken while the participants observed a skilled guitarist play a guitar chord, during a pause following the observation, while they then attempted to repeat the chord and during rest. The key finding was that the brain areas implicated in this particular example of imitative learning included the inferior frontal gyrus, and the inferior parietal lobule, which, as noted above, is regarded as the core MNS in human. In addition they suggest the involvement of the middle frontal lobe (Brodmann area 46) in modulating the MNS so as to construct the required sequence of resonant activity.

Many have argued that imitative learning of this sort is very, very important in that it may account for the unique power of human cultural transmission and forms the basis of important elements of social cognition in general (see Hurley and Chater, 2005, for a representative set of readings). To start with cultural transmission: it is easy to imagine mechanisms underlying the learning of guitar chords, as revealed in the Buccino et al. (2004) study, transposed to the learning of how to knap a core stone into a useful blade. Instruction in this then vital skill would have surely, particularly in prelinguistic ancestor species, depended on such observational instruction in which novices practised their skills alongside accomplished knappers. Adaptive refinements of the MNS in successive hominins would have ratcheted up the effectiveness of the skill training and the ability to transmit increasingly complex technical skills across generations. Such effects, then and now, are greatly amplified by the unusually long postnatal maturation period, during which the impact of skill training is at its greatest, of, at least, recent hominins, in part necessitated by their having a big brain and relatively small birth canal (Smith and Tompkins, 1995). In addition, at some point in hominin evolution the further adaptation of a lifespan extending beyond a reproductive phase occurred, providing further scope for the transmission of complex technical skills by 'learning at the knee' of grandmothers and grandfathers (O'Connell, Hawkes and Jones, 1999).

Meltzoff (2005: 55) points out that 'imitation evolved through Darwinian means but achieves Lamarckian ends'. Meaning that it provides a basis for the inheritance of acquired characteristics. The characteristics will be the habitual ways of doing things and behaving towards others that constitute a given culture. So, to use his example, human toddlers will hold telephones to their ears and babble into them without any need for explicit instruction or training or explicit understanding.[6] But he further claims that imitation is not just a means of cultural transmission, it forms the basis for the development of a theory of mind in human infants, that is the growing awareness of the intentional states of others. Imitation is present at birth: a neonate will tend to copy an adult protruding their tongue for example. Older infants will readily imitate a novel action, as demonstrated by Meltzoff (1988) who had 14-month-old infants observe a series of unlikely actions on a set of objects, such as pressing a switch with the forehead. One week later the infants were reintroduced to the same objects and showed a strong tendency to perform the same actions on the objects which they had witnessed earlier.

This innate tendency to imitate, it is claimed, provides the bedrock for building a system to infer the mental states of others. As the child begins to act on the world, it can associate its own actions with its own bodily and mental states, for example the emotional states associated with the failure

---

[6] Whether such imitation is seen in other primates remains unclear. It is often claimed, as we have already mentioned, that there is a fundamental difference between human and ape learning, in that apes tend to emulate an action, that is, achieve the goal of the action by other means, whereas humans imitate (Tomasello, Kruger and Ratner, 1993, and Tomasello, 1996 are examples). More recently others have argued that apes also replicate the means of achieving goals they have witnessed. For example Whiten, Horner and De Waal (2005) 'seeded' two captive groups of chimpanzees with a different novel technique for foraging by training one member of each group. Most members of each group consequently adopted the new technique, so that it became the new cultural norm. Despite such observations there is a consensus that there is a marked difference in the extent of imitation in human and other primates, with the frequency in humans being far greater.

to achieve a concrete goal and the facial expressions associated with those emotions. Seeing another acting in similar ways elicits an inference or prediction or assumption that the other shares the associated mental states also, that the other is 'like me'. Also human infants can recognise when an adult is imitating them, looking longer and smiling more at imitators than non-imitators (Meltzoff, 1990). A consequence of these latter arguments and data is to acknowledge that, contrary to our earlier thought, our responses to other human bodies are very different to our responses to other objects, right from the start. The thought is that innate imitation is the means of forming connections, including affective bonds, with others on which will be built the skills associated with a given culture during development. For the developing human, there are two distinct classes of object in their world: things like me performing similar acts to me and the rest.

But Mirror Neurons Do Not Just Mirror

The foregoing discussion of imitation has regarded the MNS as a mechanism that just reflected specific bodily movements of another in the motor system of an observer. This is far from the case. The early findings, in monkeys, distinguished between classes of mirror neuron in terms of the specificity of their responses. Rizzolatti et al. (1996) reported responses in F5 when an experimenter performed a range of actions on food items: grasping, placing on a surface before a monkey, and manipulating. The majority of neurons responding to action observation were indeed highly specific and described as congruent. Congruent mirror neurones responded to a similar, very specific action when performed and witnessed, for example the monkey grasping a raisin with a precision grip and the sight of an experimenter grasping the raisin with the same grip. Another example the authors classified as congruent was a neurone that responded when the monkey saw the experimenter rotate their hands in opposite directions around a food item, as if breaking or tearing it, but only for one direction of rotation: clockwise or anticlockwise. The same neurone responded when the monkey rotated its own wrist in the same direction so as to take the food being grasped by an experimenter. This same neurone did not respond when the monkey observed or performed a grasping action. Other neurons, in contrast, were described as broadly congruent, responding to a range of movements, associated with a particular class of actions such as grasping, with a range of grips, an object.

Subsequent work has revealed a rich taxonomy of neurones within the monkey MNS. That at least some neurones were responding to a type of action, and not a, more or less, similar movement, is plainly demonstrated by the observation of neurones, in monkeys trained to use tools, which respond to both the grasping of a food item with a pair of pliers and inverting pliers, in which an opening of the hand was required to grip an object. Also neurones have been identified which respond to a particular grasping action when embedded in one intentional activity but not another, grasping to eat versus grasping to place for example (Fogassi et al., 2005). This and similar findings have led to the conclusion that it is the goal of the movement that is being responded to, or, in a different vocabulary, coded.

Other categorical differences between neurones within the MNS are suggested by observations of modulations by additional factors other than movement or goal. Spatial aspects of the actions have already been mentioned, such as the tuning to specific hands and direction of wrist rotation. But also the location of an action determines the response of some neurones. Caggiano et al. (2009) demonstrated distinctions between actions within and outside of the reaching space of rhesus monkeys. They measured the activity of neurones in F5, which had been previously identified as involved in the performance of monkey hand actions, while an experimenter performed the same actions either within or outside of the monkey's reaching space. About one-quarter of the neurones responded specifically to actions within reaching space, about one-quarter to actions outside of reaching space, and the rest were indifferent to location. An elegant extension of this finding investigated the effects on the location specific neurones of a physical obstacle to the monkey's reach within its normal reaching space. When prevented from reaching in this way, a large minority of the neurones changed their preferences. Some tuned to the space beyond the monkey's reaching space began to respond to actions within its (blocked) reaching space, while some neurones that had previously responded to actions beyond its reaching space now ceased to respond. The authors note that where in space an actor performs an action does not change its meaning for an observer. These neurones are therefore unlikely to be involved in action understanding. Rather, they appear more suited to coordinating responses to another agent, which clearly differ according to where the latter is in relation to the observer. This observation is important for our later arguments.

Another dimension that some MNS neurones are sensitive to is the perspective from which an action is observed. Caggiano et al. (2011) identified mirror neurons in F5 of two monkeys and recorded their responses while the animals observed video clips of actors reaching towards objects,[7] depicted from a variety of perspectives. A majority of the neurones tested in this way showed a viewpoint preference: some responding to an action depicted from the point of view of the animal, others to lateral views of the action and others to frontal views. Only 26 per cent of the neurones were viewpoint independent.

Clearly, on the basis of this evidence, the MNS does more than just mirror. It is probably a mistake to conceive of it as having a single function, such as the basis of action understanding or the basis of imitation learning. It probably participates in multiple types of overt behaviour with no precise mapping between the categories we use in 'folk' psychology and its responses. Also, importantly it adapts during an individual's lifetime, given that it is involved in the execution of hand actions on objects which must adapt in their range and deftness during individual development. It is shaped by the cultural history of the individual. The responses in monkey MNS to tool use after training, mentioned above, can only be the result of such adaptation.

A possibly fruitful way of explaining what the MNS does is to regard it as a brain network involved in coordinating actions on objects within toolspace which takes account of the action possibilities of other agents. There are some hints in the data just reviewed supporting such a notion. An example is the neuronal response to the direction of a wrist rotation in monkey MNS: Rizzolatti et al. (1996) suggests it is implicated in the efficient passing of an object from the hand of one agent to the hand of another. The next section further explores this way of understanding the MNS.

Cooperation in Joint Action on Objects

As we have seen, at least some neurones in the MNS of monkeys change their responses dynamically according to the behavioural possibilities that confront them, and are not a simple reflection of observed movements: whether the observed actions occur within or outside of reaching space, whether it occurs in a location to which a reach is blocked by an obstacle, whether the object acted on is held at an orientation which would allow the observer to make a grasp on the same object with an optimal rotation of their wrist, are all factors which modulate the activity of some neurones in the MNS of monkeys. It is therefore very tempting to interpret these neurones as tuned to the affordances for reaching into three-dimensional space towards objects and the collaborative or competitive

---

[7] Prior testing had established that these neurones fired to both the observation of an actual reach and a video of it.

potential for interacting with other agents. Before we elaborate on this theme we must take note of the existence of other classes of neurons within the MNS.

It has long been established that some neurones within the core F5 region of monkey MNS do not mirror in any sense, but respond just when the animal grasps an object and when they simply passively observe the same object. Murata et al. (1997) measured activity in F5 of a monkey while it grasped an abstract, geometric object or just looked at it. About half of the neurones examined were found to be visuomotor, in that they responded to the mere sight of the object and when grasping it. Moreover, the majority of these were highly specific, responding to only one or few of the six different objects tested. These F5 neurones are referred to as canonical and seem obvious candidates for the neural mechanism under-lying some of the object micro-affordance effects we discussed earlier. In the stampede to account for the mirroring properties of F5, the role of these canonical neurones, and their possible interaction with the mirroring neurones with which they are collocated, has been relatively neglected. In fact, if, as suggested here, the human MNS is best understood as a mechanism for the coordination of the joint action of agents on objects a close interaction of mirror and canonical neurones would be expected.

Adult humans are remarkably, and uniquely, good at the cooperative use of objects with their hands. The simple act of fluently passing a cup to another person requires a degree of coordination in space and time that defeats other primates: non-human primate tea parties tend to be very messy affairs. Consider (yet) again what is required for the simple act of passing an object between agents. Not only does the receiving hand need to arrive at a location adjacent to the hand that is holding the cup, but both hands must also have complementary orientations and grips. The giver of the cup must grip it in a way that allows the receiver to share the holding of the cup momentarily. The complex kinematic adjust-ments needed: the accelerations and decelerations, the opening and clos-ing of grips, the rotations of the wrist, elbow and shoulder may be likened to a dance. And notice that a purely mirroring response in either party would be likely to disrupt the dance.

In fact, the human MNS does appear capable of responding in an appropriately *complementary* manner. Newman-Norlund et al. (2007) measured brain activity with fMRI while their participants viewed images of a human hand grasping a device constructed so as to be compatible with either a precision or power grip. The participants were required to make either an imitative or complementary response. The latter would be a power grip when observing a precision grip and the converse; analogous to taking a cup with a power grip or precision grip depending on whether the giver was grasping it around its handle or body. Brain activity in areas identified with the human MNS was actually greater during the complementary response than the imitative action. Newman-Norlund et al. (2008) extended their investigations to joint actions which require a continuous and dynamic adjustment on the part of both agents in order to achieve a cooperative goal. Moving a heavy piece of furniture together would be a real-world example. Brain activity was recorded by fMRI as participants lifted, by using force pads, a virtual horizontal bar while balancing a ball which rolled on the top of the bar. When each participant controls one end of the bar the task clearly requires rapid, complementary actions with each actor having to compensate for errors introduced by their partner. Their actions cannot mirror each other: they are in effect mostly uncorrelated, with errors introduced by one having to be corrected by movements in the opposite direction by the other. In these circumstances enhanced activity was again observed in the MNS. Moreover when compared with arrangements for controlling the bar which required less cooperation (a condition where a participant controlled the bar without a partner and another in which both collaborators controlled the bar with their hands at the two ends of the bar) the only regions positively correlated with the increasing demand for complementary actions were components of the MNS in the right hemisphere only. It is also important to notice that the MNS activation occurred in the brain of a participant who was not actually observing the actions of their collaborator. They were in fact lying in the fMRI scanner observing just the consequences of the other's actions for the bar and the balancing ball.

So we know that elements of the human MNS appear tuned to aspects of the dynamics of joint action which include the movements of objects caused by other agents. Our sensitivity to, what might be termed, the 'behavioural network of agents and objects' is illustrated in a series of studies that investigate imitation and affordance in response to observing other agents acting on objects. Behavioural network refers to the dynamic relations between agents and objects, and their appearances, that are correlated with actions. The responses of the agents in such networks depend on the overall configuration of the network. Bach, Bayliss and Tipper (2011) showed that observations of a leftward or rightward reach towards an object produced a benefit in an imitative response of a leftward or rightward lever movement only when the reaching hand was depicted as having a grip appropriate for grasping an object visible in the scene, but incidental to the task. Vainio et al. (2008) showed that affordance effects are similarly modulated by relations between objects and agents in the network. Their participants viewed animations of a human hand forming a precision or power grip, after which they classified objects, which were precision and power grip compatible, by making precision or power grip responses. Only when the incidental seen hand formed a grip compatible with grasping the object were the typical micro-affordance effects observed.

Ellis et al. (2013) postulated that rather than mirror and canonical neurones having different functions, they are actually different aspects of a neural system that coordinates the actions of multiple agents within a material culture. Behavioural outcomes depend on a dynamic network of agents and objects that simultaneously constrain each other. Accordingly, perturbations in one element change the others. Interactions of this sort were demonstrated by their investigations of the effects on the responses of an observer of video clips of arm and hand moving towards an object. In a first experiment the clips began by showing two hands resting on a table viewed from the perspective of the participant. One of the hands then lifted and moved forward with the camera tracking this motion. About 3 seconds into the sequence an object came into view, resting on the table. The object was a graspable, common object with a handle that was oriented towards the right or left. The final phase of the video clip showed the hand closing in on one side of the object but not actually grasping it. The task for the participant was to press a key with their left or right hand to classify the object as a tool or a kitchen implement. There are two sources of implicit influence on the viewer's left- or right-handed responses in these scenes: the movement of the actor and the orientation of the handle of the object. Both influences are, of course, well established when investigated separately. Observing a moving arm and hand facilitates imitative (same limb) responses; and seeing a handled object affords a grasp compatible limb.

Combining these two sources of influence in fact produced rather complex and very different outcomes. Responses with the hand *opposite* to the actor's side of reach were facilitated compared to same-side responses. The affordance effect depended on the reach of the actor. If the actor reached with their right hand, the normal affordance effect was observed; whereas if a left-hand reach was observed the converse was found: with responses corresponding to the non-handle side being facilitated. One tempting way of making sense of these data is to suggest that the observers' motor systems were being primed to make complementary responses. That observers found it easier to respond with the hand contralateral to the actors reaching hand, suggests facilitation of a reach to a location on the object that would not be occupied by the end state of the actor's reach. The finding that when the actor reached with their left hand, responses with the hand optimal for reaching to the non-handle location on the object were easier is consistent with the right hemisphere specialism for complementary actions in the human MNS we described previously (Newman-Norlund et al., 2008).

Such data, revealing a radical reversal of, what were supposed to be, reliable effects of the MNS suggest an intricate interplay between its elements, such as mirror and canonical neurons, which is modulated by relations between objects, agents and presumed intentions.[8] It also suggests that the actions of another can be 'read' so as to predict their likely purpose, whether the other agent is grasping the object to use or to pass to someone for example.

Ansuini et al. (2014) similarly argue that the intentions of an agent are visible in the kinematics of their movements and so can be 'picked up' by an observer of them. That the intentions and goals of an action influences its kinematics is well established. Marteniuk et al. (1987) measured the trajectory of an arm movement towards a small disk which was to be grasped with a precision grip, revealing that the movement varied according to what the participant was to do *after* the grasp. If the intention was to fit the disk into a relatively small opening there was a longer deceleration phase in the movement, compared with when the intention was to throw the disk into a relatively large container. Similar differences in kinematics have been observed between grasping an object to place in a receptacle and grasping to place in the hand of another person (Becchio et al., 2008); reaching to grasp an object so as to place it compared to grasping to eat (Naish et al., 2013); and reaching to grasp objects within a competitive versus a cooperation context (Georgiou et al., 2007). Not only are there these intention-based differences in arm and hand movements, but, at least some, have been shown to be readable by observers so that the intentions behind them can be detected. Sartori, Becchio and Castiello (2011) demonstrated that observers of a reach to grasp could judge whether an agent was intending to cooperate, compete or act individually and Cavallo et al. (2016) that observers could discriminate the difference between a reach to grasp a bottle to drink from and a reach so as to pour the contents into a glass.

---

[8] These surprising interactions of imitation and affordance were confirmed in González-Perilli and Ellis's (2015) study which also further revealed the extreme sensitivity of motor responses to the precise kinematics of another's actions. Using the procedure described in the Ellis et al. (2013) study they compared the effects of viewing a reach towards an object when the action was completed by an actual grasp of the object, with the viewing of an incomplete reach, as in the original experiment. Outcomes were strikingly different in the two cases. The earlier results were replicated: when witnessing just a reach towards an object they were faster to respond with a hand opposite to the actor's side of reach. In contrast when an actual grasp was seen there was no such affect, in fact a non-significant tendency to imitate emerged.

This work on joint action, in summary, suggests that others are ready-to-hand in the same sense as the artefacts which we skilfully employ in our coping in the world. We are immersed in a world of agents and objects by virtue of an extensive development phase within a given material and social culture, and in most of our interactions we have an unmediated access to it. So that:

In most of our everyday interactions, we have a direct, immediate understanding of other persons' intentions because their intentions are explicitly expressed in their embodied actions. As a consequence, when observing another person's action, we do not only see a physical movement, but we 'see' an intentional action. (Becchio et al., 2008: 563)

A question which follows immediately from these findings is: how are these, often culturally specific, sensorimotor skills acquired?

Associative Learning within a Material and Social Culture

Why are there neural structures in the primate brain that respond to sensory events with motor activation? They may be part of their genetic heritage. Imitative responses, for instance, might confer sufficient advantage for natural selection to favour brains adapted for imitation. A genetic predisposition is suggested by the fact that human infants appear to imitate when only a few days old (Meltzoff and Moore, 1977). But a genetic account for the ability to detect in their movements whether someone is about to drink or pour from a bottle, for example, is not plausible. A more reasonable possibility is that an embryonic MNS is sculpted by subsequent learning processes. But, again, how?

An alternative to a genetic origin for the MNS is an associative learning account, so that the MNS is the product of individual adaptation to a material and social culture, in which brain responses to sensory and motor events become conjoined. So, on such an account, even imitative responses may be learned, the outcome of observing others imitate you: the parental smiles in response to the infant's smiles for example. Or observations of one's own actions: seeing your hand adjust its grip while grasping an object may conjoin the sight of the grip (and the object that is gripped) with the execution of that action. Cook et al. (2014) argue that:

the associative hypothesis implies that the characteristic, matching properties of MNs result from a genetically evolved process, associative learning, but this process was not 'designed' by genetic evolution to produce MNs. Rather, it just happens to produce MNs when the developing system receives correlated experience of observing and executing similar actions. When the system receives correlated experience of observing objects and executing actions, the same associative process produces canonical neurons. When the system receives correlated experience of observing one action and executing a different action, the same associative process produces logically related MNs. (182)

Associative learning has spent several decades as an outcast, condemned as impotent in any attempt to account for the representational and symbolic capacities of human cognition (as famously in Chomsky, 1959, for example). Its revival is underway, partly as a consequence of the growth of embodied cognition, but also on account of recent developments in machine learning and theories of brain function. We will say more about these developments shortly.

Some characteristics of the MNS certainly point to a far more adaptive system than might be expected from a fully specified or hardwired origin. As previously noted, neurones in the MNS of monkeys experienced in tool use have been found that had a greater response to the observations of tool use, such as grasping a food item with pliers, than when the same action was performed with hands or mouths . The implication is that these tool-responding mirror neurons are the result of the animal's immersion in a culture that includes artefacts such as pliers. They cannot possibly be hardwired. Direct evidence of this sort in the human case is not readily available, but there are indications of the malleability of the human MNS also. One example has already been described above: Buccino et al. (2004) showed activation in core areas of MNS as novice guitarists watched skill guitarists play chords. Generally human adaptation to novel sensory and motor associations is quite remarkable. Novice pianists acquire an association between the sound of a chord and its motor execution on a keyboard within about 20 minutes' practice, as Bangert and Altenmüller (2003) demonstrated by measuring EEG components evoked by listening to chords before and after practice. As Wilson and Knoblich (2005) point out:

Whereas the link between seeing a hand movement and planning a hand movement might plausibly be hard-wired, the link between hearing a diminished seventh chord and planning a hand movement is clearly not. (462)

There have also been explicit tests of an associationist account. Catmur, Walsh and Heyes (2007) demonstrated that relatively brief training of human adults could effectively remodel their MNS. Participants were required to make an index finger movement when observing a little-finger movement and the converse. Before training mirror-like responses were confirmed by measuring MEPs, in response to TMS of motor cortex, in the little and index fingers while observing little and index finger movements. After training, the responses were reversed: MEPs were produced in the little finger when observing index finger movements, and in the index finger when observing little-finger movement. Catmur et al. (2008) confirmed this counter-mirror learning using fMRI. Participants either trained to make foot responses when observing hand actions and the converse, or to make congruent responses. Subsequent observation of these actions showed increased activity in similar MNS brain areas in the two groups of participants, with counter-mirror responses in the brains of those trained in the incongruent condition. As Cook et al. (2014) point out this is rather good evidence against a strictly genetic specification of the MNS: one would expect a sensorimotor system configured genetically to be immune to contingent associations so as to ensure the benefits that had been selected for were preserved in the individual.

How is the apparent conflict between a genetic origin of the MNS and its adaptability to be resolved? Actually, there may be no conflict. A good analogy may be language acquisition in which genetics prepares a brain for language use but the specific form of what is acquired is determined by the local culture in which the individual develops. We return to this issue in Chapter 6.

A Predictive Brain?

At this point there is an important and unresolved tension in our account of the human MNS and canonical neural system. The claim that they are the outcome of immersion in a material and social culture, and that associative learning has adapted these sensorimotor brain networks to allow *skilful* interactions with the agents and objects that constitute that culture, accounts for many aspects of mundane, human behaviour. Much of the time we are 'lost' in our social and material world that is ready-to-hand, easily engaging in dance-like exchanges with those around us. We shuffle our way forward in the coffee queue, avoiding colliding with others in the queue (a slow dance) and find the coins which we pass to the barista in exchange for the container of hot coffee (a tango) and then navigate the crowded space and take a seat (a square dance, perhaps). The level of skill required is not noticed because almost everyone can do it most of the time, unlike, say, play a Bach composition for solo violin. Yet both performances depend on the same intense and extended practice that adapts the brain to allow the performance to become 'ready-to-hand'.

But *why* did you get to this point in the queue or the violin sonata, and how do those reasons elicit the flow of skilled behaviour? Where is the place for goals and intentions in this story? A zombie-like dance with other elements of the material and social world is not an adequate depiction of our lives. One way of introducing intentions and goals into the account is, as we have discussed earlier, to adopt the idea of motor simulation, in which the MNS in reflecting what others do provide a first-person understanding of what it is that the other intends to do (Rizzolatti and Sinigaglia, 2010), but we have also raised doubts about this version of a mind–brain identity theory. Also, how are our own goals and intention to engage with the skilful actions?

Another solution is to locate understanding outside of these brain systems and allow top-down modulations of them by this understanding or interpretation (Csibra, 2008). On this account, the mirror-like activation in an observer's MNS is the result of a prior understanding or interpretation of an action that is then emulated in their MNS. The emulation is constituted by motor activations that would achieve the same goals as the observed, interpreted, actions, rather than their mere duplication. Indeed, exact duplication is not possible because of muscular and skeletal differences between agents. So why emulate an action that is already understood? In order to coordinate actions between agents by allowing the observer to predict what the other is going to do next, given their goal, is one answer. And, for some, prediction is the primary function of the brain, about which we will say a lot more shortly. That the MNS is emulating rather than mimicking seen actions is certainly consistent with several of its properties described in the foregoing discussion. Most of its responses are not strictly congruent with the observed action. At least some are sensitive to the goal of an action rather than its actual physical manifestation, for example distinctions between responses for a grasp-to-eat and a grasp-to-place (Fogassi et al., 2005). Csibra (2008) proposes that activity in the MNS is, at least in part, a prediction of subsequent elements in an observed action, and the prediction is driven by a prior understanding of the goal or intention of the actor. He notes that often MNS activity precedes the observation of the action it is said to mirror: grasp mirror neurons in monkeys, for example, begin to discharge before the observed hand executes the grasp (Gallese et al., 1996)

Predicting the physical actions of others, in real time, is particularly important for humans because of our extensive social interactions involving physical exchanges, which involve high levels of mutual dependencies between the agents, such as when an object is passed from one to another. Wilson and Knoblich (2005) have described this MNS function as perceptual emulation. That is, it may extrapolate from sensory inputs so as to project a short distance into the future, allowing our hand, for instance, to anticipate where a proffered object will be.

The theory of perceptual emulation implies we, paradoxically, see the future actions of others, a possibility which is confirmed by studies of 'representational momentum', a phenomena first reported for the case of moving objects. That is when observers view successive images of a moving object, then are subsequently asked to judge whether a test image matches the final position of the object, they tend to detect fewer mismatches when a position is shifted forward compared to those shifted backwards (Freyd and Finke, 1984).[9] Hudson et al. (2015) demonstrated that similar effects occur during the observation of biological motion and, moreover, are modulated by what the observer takes to be the goal of the motion (see also Hudson et al., 2016). Their participants viewed videos of a hand reaching towards or withdrawing from an object after hearing the actor say either 'I'll take it' or 'I'll leave it'. They then viewed a probe consisting of a single frame of the video and had to decide whether or not it depicted the hand in its final position in the movement sequence. The representational momentum effect was replicated: probes showing the hand further along its trajectory towards or away from the object tended not to be distinguished from the actual final position. But also, importantly, the stated intention of the actor affected these judgements. Intentions to take the object increased the momentum effect for movements towards it, and intentions to leave increased the momentum in withdrawal movements. The authors conclude that knowledge of the intentions of other agents is integrated with sensory information, and extrapolations form the basis of the perception of unfolding action sequences. Events that do not conform to these extrapolations are detected more readily than those that conform: when surprised, 'readiness-to-hand' becomes 'presence-at-hand' perhaps.

This way of describing the relationship between brain events and sensory events is consistent with, so-called, hierarchical predictive coding (for general discussions of this notion see Rao and Ballard, 1999; Hohwy, 2007, 2013; Clark, 2013). This theory revisits old ideas that the brain is an inference-making mechanism for interpreting 'sensations' as 'perceptions' that account for the causes of the sensations. Helmholtz (1860) is a very prominent example of such thinking. The predictive coding approach reinforces Helmholtz-like assumptions with modern statistical and machine-learning insights that provides a plausible model of how

---

[9] It may be argued that the momentum effect is not truly a perceptual phenomenon. Rather it may be a judgement bias introduced by the viewer's interpretation of an action. Several findings support a perceptual interpretation however. For instance, it has been demonstrated that TMS disruption of brain areas involved in motion detection disrupts the momentum effect (Senior, Ward and David, 2002).

brains might actually 'infer' the causes of their sensory inputs, and also how they may adapt to a material and social culture.

A key element of the theory is that there is a level of brain architecture which is best described as a hierarchical network of specialised neural areas of increasing abstraction, with sensory data flowing forward (from bottom to top) and, very importantly, with rich backward flows from higher to lower levels. Aspects of the visual system as conventionally conceived, for example, seems to fit this general organisation: retinal responses feed forward, via the lateral geniculate nuclei, to V1 in the cortex, whose neurones respond to low-level features in the retinal input and broadcast forward to other cortical areas each seemingly having a specialised function, visual motion in V5 for example. In addition to the forward connections, there are interconnections at each level of the hierarchy, and, critically for the theory of predictive coding, there is extensive connectivity from higher levels to lower.[10]

The function of this overall brain organisation is to predict[11] the external, world states that have produced its responses by facilitating interactions between the levels of the hierarchy. Higher levels feed backwards an estimate of what the activation state of the lower level would be given the prediction of the higher level. The difference between the actual values at a level and the estimate of it by the higher level, carried by the backward projection, is therefore a measure of error in the prediction. If there is no error, the prediction is satisfied. If the prediction is not satisfied, two consequences are likely. One is that the higher-level units will adjust their activations so as to reduce the error. This might be described as a perceptual inference. The second consequence might be that long-term changes in connectivity occur which adjusts the 'model' embedded in the connections so as to (iteratively) reduce the error. This might be described as perceptual learning.

The behaviour of such networks has been characterised as Bayesian. That is, it conforms to Bayesian statistical procedures that estimate the probabilities of the truth of a hypothesis.[12] In the case of perception, the difference between the current state of the sensory system and what is expected, given a set of expectations or 'priors', is likened to 'Bayesian surprise' (where 'surprise' is a statistical term, not the mental state of an

[10] It is perhaps a measure of their significance that on some estimates backward connections far outnumber forward (see, for example, Chen et al., 2009).

[11] The sense of 'predict' is clearly not intended to refer to an explicit mental state, nor the earlier use of the term 'infer'. The intended sense is that the brain networks are sufficiently sensitive to the correlations among sensory and motor events to be able to extrapolate.

[12] Bayesian approaches are now abundant in the cognitive sciences. Here we are focusing on a particular variant or elaboration that is usually termed the 'free energy' approach.

agent). Critically, in order for a comparison between expected values and encountered values to be possible, an internal model is required that generates the expected values. This generative model specifies both the probability of sensory data given an event or object in the world and the prior probability of the occurrence of that event or object. Perception entails the inverting of the model so as to estimate the probability of the event or object being the actual causal account of the current sensory data.

Within a hierarchical network of this sort a hypothesis of the source of the sensory signals of events outside of the system is used to predict the activity states of the lower levels in the hierarchy, with the predictions cascading back down the network to the earliest sensory pathways. A prediction error may be determined at each level, with the predictions from the higher acting as priors for the level below. The networks are adaptive, as we shall see shortly, so it is possible that learning may occur over multiple timescales. Crucially they are able to refine their generative models by progressive reduction of the error terms that result when their predictions are compared with sensory data. It is important to note that this adaption is the result of mere exposure to the sensory signals. Immersion within a world will yield, given sufficient exposure, models of objects and events in that world that have causal effects on the sense receptors.

This result may appear slightly magical; a sense that can be partly dispelled by consideration of closely related models of learning in artificial neural networks. These highly simplified cases are described here so as to give the reader a better grasp of the gist of the mathematical results that underpin these recent findings in theoretical neuroscience. Artificial neural networks (simulated on conventional computing architectures) are intended to be brain-like in that they consist of simple processing units, that are richly interconnected (see Ellis and Humphreys, 1999; and McLeod, Plunkett and Rolls, 1998 for introductions to, and illustrations of, these ideas). Each unit has an activation state, determined by inputs from other units on weighted connections, and in turn modulate the states of other units via similar weighted connections. The systems adapt as a result of learning procedures that change the weights on the connections. One class of model of this type investigates unsupervised learning. That is, precisely, the ability attributed to Bayesian models of the brain: to extract representations of significant aspects of the external world (words, objects, actions and so forth) by mere exposure to examples, without those examples having to be named or labelled in any way. To understand how this is possible we need to consider first a particular type of artificial neural network: the Boltzmann machine.

A Boltzmann machine is an artificial neural network that seeks states of minimum energy where energy is defined as a function of the activation values of all the units. This global minimum can be regarded as an 'attractor' in that activation patterns will tend to be captured by an energy minimum and fall into the corresponding activation state. Boltzmann machine units are probabilistic and their activation is adjusted randomly over time. An activation rule turns a unit on with a probability that is function of the change in global energy that would result from the change and a 'temperature' term. The temperature adjusts the scale of energy change: at high temperature big increases are possible, at low temperatures only small increases. It has been shown that running such a network at high temperatures initially and then gradually reducing it, results in the network settling to a global energy minimum with a probability approaching one (Kirkpatrick, Gelatt and Vecchi, 1983). This process is termed annealing because of its analogy to the processes employed in the hardening of metals.

Boltzmann machines can be configured so as to learn the high-order statistical properties of sets of inputs (Ackley, Hinton and Sejnowski, 1985; Hinton and Sejnowski, 1986). To do so the units are divided into hidden and visible units. The visible units are either inputs or outputs (hence visible in the world), and the hidden units (within the 'black box' of the artificial brain) are 'representational' in that they have the potential to learn an efficient code to represent the statistical regularities in large sets of inputs. A small-scale demonstration of a Boltzmann machine solution to a tricky problem is learning to solve the shift-register problem (Hinton and Sejnowski, 1986). That is, to classify two horizontal arrays of eight binary units in which one array is a copy of the other but shifted to the right or left, with wrap-around. As an example 01100101 is a right-shifted twin of 11001010. The network trained on this problem had three sets of visible units: a set of eight for array 1, eight for array 2 and a set of three to signal whether array 2 was left- or right-shifted or the same, compared to array 1. There were, in addition, twenty-four hidden units, which after training would collectively code the relations between the sets of inputs and their classification. The problem is hard because pairwise comparisons will not suffice, at least third-order relations must be extracted.

The shift-register Boltzmann machine was trained by fixing or clamping all the visible units so as to represent an example of the two arrays of binary inputs and their shift and then annealed until a thermal minimum was arrived at. Co-occurrence statistics were collected, that is the frequency with which two connected units were both active. This process was repeated for twenty different sets of clamped units, yielding average co-occurrence statistics for the sample. The network was then allowed to run freely with no clamping of any of its units, while repeating the annealing process. This was also repeated twenty times and the average co-occurrence statistics derived. After this single 'sweep' of forty annealings the weights were adjusted in proportion to the differences between the co-occurrences when clamped and free running.[13]

The performance of the trained network was described as 'far from perfect' and the training highly laborious, with thousands of sweeps being required. It is a very long way from a network coding for shift detection to a system that can learn representations of, say, three-dimensional visual objects based on the hugely varying sensory events they give rise to. Yet, more recently, a system using Boltzmann-like networks has been demonstrated that may have the potential to do so and thereby contributed to a new wave in artificial neural networks, which is often referred to as 'deep learning'.

Hinton, Osindero and Teh (2006) describe an example in which importantly, given our description of hierarchical predictive coding, the success of learning depended on having multiple layers within the network, and that it could form generative models of inputs. Learning proceeds one layer at a time, and each layer is a variant of a Boltzmann machine referred to as a stacked restricted Boltzmann machine. A restricted Boltzmann machine (RBM) has no connections within a layer, but has symmetrical connections between visible units and a layer of hidden units. Once trained, the hidden units may then be used as inputs for another RBM, and so on to form a stack of hidden layers. This decomposition of the problem by having multiple layers turns out to be effective, perhaps surprisingly, in that learning is tractable. In this example the network was trained to represent the digits 0 to 9 by exposure to handwritten examples. This is a far more difficult task than solving the shift-register problem, and obviously closer to a real-world problem of the sort that confronts the black box that is our brain. The network was trained using (low-resolution) images of highly variable handwritten digits. Ten units, each standing for a digit, were initially combined with a set of input image pixel values to train an array of 500 hidden units in a similar manner to that described for the Boltzmann machine. The trained hidden units were

---

[13] Using the difference between the two runs provides important information for the system. How can a unit deep within a black box separate out signals from other units that result from the statistics of sensory inputs, from those that are a happenchance result of the current state of the network? One answer is to use the difference between clamped (sensory determined) and free-running cases. See Hinton et al. (1995) for another discussion of this issue.

then, when activated by image inputs, used as training data for a higher-level RBM of 500 units, which were in turn used to train a top level of 2,000 units. This latter group was to form an associative memory, thus the activation for the digit units were included in its training data. After training the network was tested on 10,000 novel images of digits, and made just 1.25 per cent errors.

This work is, no doubt, representative of important advances in machine learning, demonstrating a scaling up of the size of network in which effective learning can be achieved. Also it should be apparent that two aspects of these approaches, which we will examine more closely shortly, may make broad sense of some of the experimental findings we have discussed. Affordance would arise as a result, during skill acquisition, of the constant pairing of visual and motor responses. Mirror-like responses may reflect the requirement for a generative model of an input. However, it should be remembered, the model is several order of magnitudes smaller than real neural networks. As the authors confess, their network is of a scale roughly equivalent to about 0.002 cubic millimetres of mouse cortex! Yet it may offer a good model for understanding and testing some important recent developments in brain science theory which share several of its properties. In particular three common features should be noted between the model and the previously mentioned theory of 'free energy' which we will now describe in more detail.

First, a deep hierarchical architecture is identified as a necessary condition for deriving efficient 'representations' of the causes of sensory stimulation, allowing high-order statistical regularities to be extracted from the sensory flux by decomposing the problem into a number of simpler steps. Second, generative processes are posited as a solution to a number of otherwise intractable problems. Hinton (2014) notes that learning in a Boltzmann machine does not require labelled data precisely because it takes each input exemplar to be an *output* of a probabilistic generative model which is encoded in the weight matrix which is refined during learning. Thus, perhaps counter-intuitively, a good way to discover labels for, or 'features' within, a set of input data is to reconstruct the inputs. Also, he remarks in passing, for dynamic data, such as a video stream, a powerful method for reconstructing the inputs is to predict the next frame. The third characteristic shared by these artificial neural network models and the free-energy theory of real neural networks is that both posit processes akin to energy minimisation to mould neural networks into associative memory systems, within which representations of objects in the world are minima in a multidimensional surface or manifold.

The 'free energy' theory of real neural networks ties together these insights from statistics and machine learning with brain science in an attempt to produce a unified theory of brain function (Friston, 2005, 2009, 2010). Its core idea is that brain changes over a range of time scales will minimise free energy, where free energy is understood as the upper bound of a measure of the (statistical) surprise between a model of the causes of a set of data and the data. In the case of perception, for example, the generative models allow a measure of prediction error by comparison with forward flows of sensory-driven activation, at each level of the hierarchy in a deep network. These errors approximate to free energy and may be reduced in different ways. Learning, such as the adaptation to sensory data of an agent immersed within a material culture, as modelled by the stacked RBM perhaps, will develop and refine the generative models. Free-energy reduction can, in fact, be shown to be formally equivalent to Hebbian associative learning. Perception itself is the result of fitting a model, or representation, that minimises the real-time errors between the model's prediction and sensory data.

Another source of error reduction, which is close to the focus of our concerns here, is action. Simply put, another way of reducing free energy is to change the sensory input by actions such as moving eyes, heads and bodies (Friston, Kilner and Harrison, 2006; Friston et al., 2010). Under this formulation the perceiver may be regarded as an open system having sensory *exchanges* with the world, and so both impacted by and affecting, via actions, sense data. The point is that both action and perception can now be regarded as processes of energy minimisation, with internal states and behavioural responses both contributing to the same core purpose of reducing prediction error. Showing them to be dual aspects of free-energy minimisation in an open, dynamic biological system unifies action and perception, to a degree that was previously difficult to conceive of. Moreover, the control of action itself may obey the same logic as perception.

The goal of an action might be regarded as the generator of a hierarchical set of predictions of the sensory and motor consequences of the intermediate states of the real-time action which must unfold to achieve the goal. The predictions can be compared at all levels so that adjustments can be made as the action unfolds. For instance proprioceptive information allows the derivation of an error measure which serves as a motor command for its reduction (Friston, 2011). From this perspective, therefore, the actor predicts their own behaviour and its consequences in the same way they predict the actions of others, as described previously in this text. Again, the goal and the predictions are not, necessarily at least, intended to be explicit mental states of the agent;

rather, it is as if the agent were entrained as a consequence of learning which generate expectations which generate error terms which control perception and action.

These models do seem to provide plausible accounts of how humans might be immersed in their world, with objects and other agents ready-to-hand, but as Clark (2013) notes this seemingly takes us back to a zombie-like image of human behaviour, or, as he prefers, a desert landscape:

> In this desert landscape vision, there are neither goals nor reward signals as such. Instead, there are only (both learnt and species-specific) expectations, across many spatial and temporal scales, which directly enslave both perception and action. (20)

It is not clear how the ideas can be related to other forms of engagement such as when aspects of the world are present-to-hand.

What is more certain is that the free-energy theory makes specific sense of both mirror neurons and affordance, in that both would be a consequence of its suppositions about brain architecture and functions. Take mirror neurons: within the free-energy scheme the apparent mirroring of observed actions is assumed to arise because of the dynamics within a predictive coding neural network (Kilner, Friston and Frith, 2007). Given what we expect of another person's goals, we can predict their likely actions based on our own motor system. Such a prediction generates a model of an unfolding action at each level of the neural hierarchy including the kinematics of the expected movement. The error between the predicted and the observed kinematics propagates forward so as adjust the generative model at all the levels in order to reduce the corresponding error terms, including adjustments to the inferred goal of the agent so observed. The further pertinent assumption is that the neural networks that predict the likely actions of others also control the execution of those actions when executed by the observer. So, the same brain networks do the work of producing and predicting an action, hence the mirror-like properties of some neurons. In summary:

> the MNS is best considered within a predictive coding framework. One of the attractions of predictive coding is that it can explain how the MNS could infer someone else's intentions through observation of their movements. Within this scheme the most likely cause of an observed action is inferred by minimizing the prediction error at all levels of the cortical hierarchy that is engaged during action-observation. This account specifies a precise role for the MNS in our ability to infer intentions and formalizes the underlying computations. It also connects generative models that are inverted during perceptual inference with forward models that finesse motor control. (Kilner, Friston and Frith, 2007: 622–623)

The fit between affordance and the free-energy idea is also good. Friston et al. (2012) suppose that higher-level amodal neural networks form an attractor landscape, presumably sculpted by associationist learning procedures of the sort already discussed here, in which attractors provide predictions of unfolding sensorimotor events and so might be said to be 'representations of affordance'. The selection of a particular attractor state, which is the generator of particular sensory and motor predictions, depends on ascending prediction errors. The attractor state that best reduces the errors, that is, best accounts for the sensory data, including proprioceptive, would tend to be selected.

Taken together these are very powerful ideas offer novel insights into, and perhaps solutions for, several of the problems considered central in this text. Recent developments in associative learning demonstrated how it might be possible for a neonate human to adapt, as it develops, to its specific material and social culture. The free-energy theory of brain architecture and function suggests the general principles by which the encultured agent maintains homeostasis within its world. These principles reveal perception and action to be necessarily entwined: both are means to minimising the free energy in the brain of the agent. They also make sense of many of the empirical properties of the primate MNS.

Naturally we are left with important unresolved problems. Ghosts of the 'hard problem' continue to haunt. At several places we have noted the ambiguity in terms such as 'inference' and 'prediction' and 'goal' and 'intention' and 'understanding'. In fact, there are many layers of ambiguity here. A system that gets an agent's hand to the correct location and adopting the correct posture to receive an object proffered by another agent might be said to predict what action is needed based on an understanding of the intentions or goals of the other agent. But this language is surely that of an observer of those interactions. There is no explicit representation of those mental terms in the heads of the actors. They just get it done.[14]

In summary, the models we have described in this section provide plausible accounts of agents coping in their world, with objects and other agents ready-to-hand. Yet they fail to satisfy in the sense that something is clearly missing: it is a zombie or desert-like image of human behaviour. There needs to be an account of how the actor embedded in a world makes sense of what is happening and applies that

[14] Some have argued that free-energy formulations do not even imply a weaker sense of inference or prediction as intended by the (Helmholtzian) notion of unconscious inference (Bruineberg and Rietveld, 2014; Bruineberg, Kiverstein and Rietveld, 2016). In this revised version energy minimisation is extended beyond the brain of the agent to the agent–world system.

explicit understanding to what they do. The free-energy account makes only vague gestures to amodal representations at high levels in the hierarchy. We will sketch a potential solution to this impasse in the final two chapters, the essential idea being that we can view our own coping behaviours from a third-person perspective. Part of enculturation for the modern human is the adoption of methods of accounting for the behaviour of others and oneself by commentaries using language. We say, truly, that 'I took the glass of water because I was thirsty and needed to drink'. It will be claimed that these beliefs and goals exist in the world of the agent but not in their brains.

The sense of 'understanding' upon which these ready-to-hand interactions depend is procedural. I know how to pass the cup of water to my thirsty partner in the same way I know how to ride a bicycle. But 'knowing' or 'understanding' that my partner is thirsty because she said, 'I'm thirsty' is a different sense of 'knowing' and 'understanding'. It will be the work of the final chapters to convince the reader that explicit understandings of this sort arise, and perhaps only arise, in a community of agents which have become adapted to a material and social culture that has developed forms of symbolic representation, most notably of course language. When external, symbol systems acquire the power to control the generative models of our sensorimotor systems, then everything changes.

But before we get to that discussion we will complete this chapter with a focus on an aspect of human cognition that may be a prerequisite for external symbol systems such as language.

Actions, Intentions and Others: Dancing Again

We have argued that the human MNS, including the various classes of mirror neurons and canonical neurons, are adaptations to a culture that includes objects and other agents. The adaptations have provided for the particularly rich exchanges that occur between human beings, compared to, even, other primates. The brains needed for dextrous hands, the learning of skilled uses of those hands and their use in collaborative acts with others bring with them a particular mental attribute: shared intentionality.

Tomasello has marshalled powerful evidence and arguments to the effect that shared intentionality is unique to humans (examples are Tomasello et al., 2005; Tomasello and Carpenter, 2007). While chimpanzees show clear evidence of knowing what other chimps see and understand the intentions of others,[15] by attempts to conceal food from

---

[15] Again, the terms are ambiguous. In the context of our recent discussion they are third-party perspectives on the behaviour.

their competitors for instance, they do not appear to *share* intentions. Whereas humans begin to show an impulse to share attention, goals and actions with others when only around 1 year old. This impulse to collaborate, it is argued, has driven the culture accumulation that has taken us from simple stone tools to the space station, including the development of languages.

Discussing developments in the manner in which infants actively engage with others at around their twelfth month will perhaps clarify the notion of shared intentionality. Declarative pointing is one. That is when the infant points at an object with the aim of simply jointly attending to it, as suggested by the fact that they are not satisfied by an adult's response unless it consists of looking back and forth to the object and the infant, accompanied by positive comments (just looking at the object is not enough). It is at this time also that evidence of attempting to help others first emerges: pointing to an object simply to inform an adult. Very quickly these achievements are elaborated by developing motor and language skills to allow the child to engage in complex collaboration with others in actions on objects, say, taking it in turns with their parent to build a tower of blocks. This is in sharp contrast to all other primates. Chimpanzees, for example, do not point to objects to indicate things of common interest, or carry objects together, or cooperate to construct simple tools.[16] This difference may be vital for understanding why creatures that differ so little biologically diverge so enormously in their social and material cultures. The argument is that shared intentionality provides the foundations of efficient cultural transmission (Tomasello, Kruger and Ratner, 1993), which, given its ratchet-like accumulation, has given us cultural norms, religion, monetary systems, art, science and, of course, language.

Consider now in a little more detail the typical development of a human infant as they grow into their world and its material culture. Critically at around 9 to 12 months they begin to be capable of sharing or collaborating with others in actions on objects. Significant elements include following the gaze of a parent, imitating a parent's action on an object and attempting to direct a parent's attention. Taken together these behaviours may be described as the growing ability to share attention with others so as

---

[16] It is well known of course that chimpanzees collaborate in hunting. But here their collaboration appears to consist of group interactions among individuals pursuing their own ends but taking into account what the other individuals can see and are doing. See Chen et al. (2009) for an experimental comparison of children and captive chimpanzees that supports the individualist account of chimpanzee collaboration. Also *captive* chimpanzees do point, but seemingly only in an instrumental manner as in pointing to an out-of-reach piece of food so a human experimenter could retrieve it (Leavens and Hopkins, 2005). They do not point to indicate an object that would be of concern for another.

to collaborate in physical activity. Children as young as 12 months appear to understand roles in a cooperative task, so, for example, after being encouraged to place a toy in a basket held out by an adult, they would pick up the basket to take a proffered toy from an adult, while looking at the face of the adult (Carpenter, Tomasello and Striano, 2005). When about 18-month-old children are able to participate in cooperative activities in which they must play a specific role and imitate specific activities. Significantly if an adult collaborator attempts to withdraw the young child will often attempt to persuade them to re-engage, for example by grabbing an arm and dragging them back to the objects they were jointly acting on (Warneken, Chen and Tomasello, 2006). Also at 18 months active helping of a partner is seen, for example by removing obstacles hindering an adult's completion of a task (Warneken and Tomasello, 2006). We seem to be the only primate to have what has been termed 'we-intentionality' (Moll and Tomasello, 2007); that is the abilities just described to attempt to achieve a joint goal with others by engaging in reciprocal actions and helping others in their roles, based on an understanding of those roles.

It may be supposed that this early joint activity, during the period of maximum neural plasticity, leads to some of the properties of the human MNS which we have described earlier. In so doing it effectively shapes human cognition during ontogeny. Moll and Tomasello (2007) describe this as the 'Vygotskian intelligence hypothesis' so as to acknowledge the earlier insights of the soviet psychologist Vygotsky into the interaction of a developing child with its social and material environment and this interaction's role in transforming cognition (see Vygotsky, 1967 for an illustration of his perspective). One very important outcome of this joint activity with others is the ability to understand the perspective of others, as illustrated in studies in which 12- to 18-month-old infants played with toys together with experimenters. Tomasello and Haberl (2003) had an experimenter play with two toys before leaving the room, whereupon another experimenter handed the infants a third toy and played with the infant. Upon re-entering the room, the first experimenter expressed excitement and indicated they wanted a toy (without indicating in any way which toy). The infants selected the new toy. This is a very impressive act of perspective taking by such young children: they interpreted the experiment's excitement as directed at the novel object and had kept track of which of the three objects this was for another person.

It is important to see, that on this account, shared intentionality is a culture product. A human infant develops this, for Tomasello and his colleagues, uniquely human capacity because they participate in joint actions on the objects in their world. The possibility of such activity is of course a consequence of their sensorimotor endowments from previous generations. It can be further argued that this shared intentionality is the foundation of human communication and ultimately language, a possibility that we will consider in detail in Chapter 6.

Experimental cognitive psychology has tended to be individualistic, in that it has investigated the responses of single agents in interaction with, typically highly abstracted, elements of their world. It is only relatively recently that there has been a turn to the experimental study of social cognition in collaborating human adults acting on the world. In some of this work it is possible to catch glimpses of shared intentionality. Sebanz and her colleagues have, for instance, described studies of human joint action in which agents appear to form shared representations of actions and effects. In one such study Sebanz, Knoblich and Prinz (2003) had participants perform a version of the stimulus–response compatibility procedure which was introduced here in earlier chapters . Three conditions were compared. In one condition, participants responded individually by classifying the colour of a ring on a finger in an image of a hand which was pointing to the left or right, responding with their left or right hand. The usual compatibility effect was observed in that responses were facilitated for responses on the side cued by the pointing finger. In two further conditions, participants performed a go–no go version of the procedure, in that they responded by pressing just a single key to a single colour. They did this either alone or while sitting alongside another participant who was responding with the complementary response mapping. No compatibility effect was observed when acting alone, but the joint action condition essentially matched the condition in which one person responded to both colours. A subsequent study (Sebanz et al., 2006) measured ERPs while participants performed the go–no go version of the Simon procedure, either singly or in pairs. Electrophysiological responses were similar at frontal sites for both go and no-go trials for both participants when they worked in a pairs. Also a response taken to reflect inhibition of an action (the P300) had a greater amplitude on the no-go trials when they worked in pairs. These data suggest that two agents working together, on complementary tasks, spontaneously generate matching representations of the tasks. Each represents the same set of stimulus–response rules so that when a stimulus that signals an action for their partner appears, they prepare a sub-threshold response to it. Such synchronous coordination between agents is not obligatory however; that is, it has been shown to be modulated by the social context of the collaboration. Hommel, Colzato and Van Den Wildenberg (2009) found that the shared stimulus–response compatibility effect only occurred when participants worked with a collaborative partner, not when faced by a negative and competitive one. Costantini and Ferri (2013) found that participants who had been seemingly excluded from a virtual ball passing game also did not subsequently produce the shared effect, whereas those participants that were included did.

Costantini, Committeri and Sinigaglia (2011) demonstrated similar entrainment by the action possibilities of others using a micro-affordance procedure. Participants were required to perform a right- or left-handed reach to grasp action when presented with a go signal consisting of a computer-generated image of a room containing a table upon which appeared a handled mug. The depicted mug was oriented with its handle to the left or right and within or outside of the reaching space of the participant. The usual affordance effect of the facilitation of the responding hand compatible with the handle was obtained only when the mug was depicted within reaching space. In an additional set of conditions a human was depicted in the image, sitting at the table located so as to be able to reach either the near or far mug. In the presence of the avatar an affordance effect was obtained for both mug locations. Seemingly the affordances available to the other and those available to the observer have similar effects on the motor responses of the observer.

The foregoing suggests a quite remarkable connection between interacting humans when sharing a common toolspace. The notion of a toolspace was introduced in an earlier chapter as referring to the space around an individual within reach of their hands, extended by the observation that holding a tool effectively expands toolspace, and now, it is suggested, expanded again by the synchrony of the motor systems of agents within sight of each other.[17]

A further insight into this synchrony is provided by work that reveals our ability to infer the intentions of others within sight from a range of enmeshed sources. We have already discussed, and questioned, the role of the MNS in understanding the intentions of others (Iacoboni et al., 2005). The doubts about the precise role of the MNS in intention understanding do not undermine the observations that we can and do infer intentions from observing the movements of others. Our sensitivity is such that the initial stages of a reach to an object tell us what the agent intends to do with it: drink from it, or throw it or scrutinise it, as we have already shown. Sartori, Becchio and Castiello (2011) revealed how the kinematics of a reach to grasp action reveals information rich enough to

---

[17] The sense of 'within sight of each other' may be elaborated to within perceptual contact perhaps, and perceptual contact may be expanded by communication devices. There is clearly a lot more to say about this.

make judgements of this sort about the collaborative intentions behind the action. Their participants viewed videos of an actor grasping a toy wooden building block to either cooperate with another to build a tower of blocks, to compete with another to place the block or to perform an individual act (at either a fast or slow speed). Participants viewed only the initial phase of the reach, from lift off to first contact with the block, and the presence of another agent in the scene was not visible. Participants had to perform a series of pairwise discriminations after viewing a video: competitive versus fast, competitive versus cooperative and so forth. They could readily judge which acts were cooperative, collaborative or individual. A second experiment in which aspects of the reach were occluded revealed that seeing arm movements and the agents face contributed to the judgement, with the latter being more important whenever distinguishing a social action from an individual one, in which the latter was enacted at the speed associated with the social act (fast for competitive, slow for cooperative). Manera et al. (2011) showed that purely kinematic information is sufficient. They replaced the videos with point-light displays constructed by extracting the three-dimensional position of the wrist, index finger and thumb during the action and representing just these positions with a white dot against a black background. Even this sparse information was sufficient for reasonably accurate intention judgement.

It seems clear that humans are highly adept at both detecting the intentions of others and integrating those action intentions into their own unfolding behaviour so that we can, in a collaborative context, essentially synchronise our sensory-motor systems with others to achieve a precision and fluency in cooperative acts greater, surely, than any other species. We positively seek and thrive on such synchronous behaviour. Tarr et al. (2015) note that all human cultures appear to enjoy a form of dancing, which is essentially synchronised movement. One account of this is that dancing *together* enhances social bonding by rewarding those who engage in it by triggering the release of endorphins. Of course dancing involves exertion which also triggers endorphin release, so to separate out these factors the authors examined the effects of highly and partially synchronised movements under high- and low-exertion conditions. Groups of school students performed either identical or different movements to the same music and movements were either whole-body dance movements or small hand movements. Synchrony independently increased pain thresholds (a proxy for endorphin increases) and measures of in-group bonding.

In summary, this chapter sought to convince the reader that our responses towards our co-species has some important similarities with our responses to objects in general. Many of these responses are implicit responses of the agent's motor system in response to the seen actions of other agents. Just as our implicit responses to inanimate objects and artefacts are often the product of an intense learning phase consequent on our immersion in our material culture, responses to other agents are often those learned as the result of an immersion within our social culture. Our implicit understandings of the intentions of others and the consequent ability to predict their actions as they unfold allows us to interact with others in skilful, fluent collaborative acts. Of course, nearly always, we act on objects with others so the material and social influences on our actions are entirely enmeshed. Just as we forget ourselves in a world of objects, so we lose sight of others in negotiation of our social world. Both objects and agents become ready-to-hand.

5   Material Cultures

This chapter will discuss in more detail the consequences of material cultures for humans. It will suggest that they have been every bit as significant in shaping us as our social culture. Indeed, the two are not easily separable. The emphasis will be on the relationships between human capacities and artefacts. The results of these processes, accumulating over epochs, endowed humans with sensorimotor capacities in which, it has been argued here, the advantages bought by skilful manipulation of objects with the hands were critical. Towards the end of Chapter 3 we discussed the effects on the brain of tool use by an individual human. These affects seem to be both immediate and long-term. It is difficult to exaggerate the importance of these observations. They suggest a dynamic interaction between human material culture and human capacities. We construct artefacts that fit our capacities but, as shown by the examples discussed in Chapter 3, these new combinations lead to adaptations in human capacities, which in turn create new niches for the development of our material (and social) culture. Chapter 5 will also challenge the seeming common sense notion of a clear division between agents and the objects they act upon. There are some who regard this dichotomy between us and our artefacts as a 'tyranny' (Latour, 1999).

Attempts to interpret the culture of others by studying their artefacts are not new but a discipline of 'material culture' as an independent branch of anthropology is recent.[1] Its growth has highlighted a contrast between 'material culture' as the study of artefacts so as to infer a culture, with the impact of artefacts in the *making* of a culture. We will consider this latter idea through an examination of varieties of so-called materialism, both old and new versions.

---

[1] And like any academic discipline is often busy with the definition of its key terms such as 'culture', 'material', 'object', 'thing', 'artefact'. This text will ignore these issues in the hope that useful work can be done with their common usage.

Old and New Materialisms

Marx and Engels were among the earliest thinkers to attempt to construct a materialist account of human societies. In their conception of a science of history (see Marx and Engels, 1970, for instance) they famously argued that the material circumstances of producing the means of subsistence was the key to understanding the diversity of premodern and modern human societies. In any given society, an individual would be faced with material conditions made up of a historic endowment from their forebears and conditions created by their own actions. These material circumstances would constitute the individual's mode of existence to which they would adapt.

The impact of the means of subsistence ('the mode of production') is felt at multiple levels within a society, with Marx and Engels paying most attention to the 'relations of production'. That is the forms of social organisation that a particular way of producing things entails. Such things as property rights, political and belief systems together constituted the 'superstructure' that facilitated the ways of producing. Changes in human productive powers, from hunter-gatherer to mass producer and consumer, necessarily provoked the, discontinuous, changes in superstructures evident in the history of those societies.

Consequent on these macro-scale effects there are also micro-scale effects on the behaviour and capacities of individuals within these societies, which of course is our focus here. For Marx and Engels these effects were profound. In a very real sense individual are made by their material conditions:

The way in which men produce their means of subsistence depends first of all on the nature of the actual means of subsistence they find in existence and have to reproduce. This mode of production must not be considered simply as being the production of the physical existence of the individuals. Rather it is a definite form of activity of these individuals, a definite form of expressing their life, a definite mode of life on their part. As individuals express their life, so they are. What they are, therefore, coincides with their production, both with what they produce and with how they produce. The nature of individuals thus depends on the material conditions determining their production. (Marx and Engels, 1970: 42)

Consider the world, described earlier in this text, of rushing to meetings using taxis, lifts and smartphones, followed by note taking on laptops. The reader and author share this world, probably. Now notice how different this must be from the world of a hunter-gatherer deep in a rainforest or a metal worker in the bronze age. The differences are not just a matter of changes in technology that build on a fixed human capacity so as to transform their material environment. In addition, the members of these different societies differ profoundly because of, it is argued, the variation in their ways of engaging with their environment.

It is this idea that we will pursue further in this chapter: that in making and doing humans make themselves. The reader will probably have already noticed that several of the recent insights provided by cognitive neuroscience, described in earlier chapters, provide some understanding of how such a process is actually realised. We will now view similar processes from an anthropological perspective. Contemporary anthropology contains several theoretical perspectives which could be seen as materialist in the sense just described, in that they attempt to illustrate and explain how making, and how the objects which are made are used, have impacts on the agents. One theme is concerned with how variations in skilled action underlie cultural variation. A second constructs a way of conceiving of agency in which artefacts are seen as sharing agency with humans.

Ingold (2000) has focused on the particular importance of the development of skills transmitted down the generations, which are literally incorporated into the individual by producing shifts in perceptual and motor abilities. An illustrative example concerns the making of string bags, called bilums, by the Telefol people in New Guinea. Their children will begin helping their mothers with this task when 2 years old with tentative attempts to combine shredded fibres to form the string that will be intricately looped into bilums. For Ingold the skill and its transmission have important characteristics that are not readily apparent when viewed from an orthodox perspective in which skill depends on the acquisition of rules and knowledge. The actions of a highly skilled bilum maker cannot be formalised as a description of a sequence of fixed behaviours. It is more akin to a conversation between the materials and the maker's body, into which the tools, such as a needle, are incorporated. Constant adjustments are required to allow for the inconsistencies in the materials. The makers themselves liken the fluency required to the flowing of a river. Of course, it is not just a question of dextrous fingers: the perceptual system must become tuned to the requirements of the task. Visual and haptic information must be attended to at a scale appropriate to the toolspace-centred activities, and in doing so toolspace is adapted.

The transmission of these skills is equally not the transmission of fixed motor programmes; it is, Ingold claims, more akin to *growing* into the skill. The novice is provided with extensive exposure to skilled making by observing and working alongside skilled makers. The latter are seen to nurture the growing skills by exposing the novice to the sensorimotor context of the task through countless repetitions of elements of it. These activities occur at the same time as the novice's body is also growing to maturity so critically:

These skills, then, far from being added on to a preformed body, actually grow with it. In that regard they are fully part and parcel of the human organism, of its neurology, musculature, even anatomy, and so are as much biological as cultural. (Ingold, 2000: 360)

Learning to make balims for the Telefol is like learning to talk or walk, as is learning to use smartphones and tablets for the next generation of skilled users across the globe. Experiences which we assume will begin to sculpt the apprentices' mirror neurone systems (MNSs) in accord with their material culture of birth. Gamble (2007) speaks of the 'childscape' which includes parents and kin, but also the artefacts which make up a material culture. The childscape will determine the developmental trajectory of an individual.

It is easy to miss how radical a proposal this is. That the skills developed in a particular human culture are constituted by changes in the biological properties of the individual challenges the widely held notion of there being a common biological endowment for a species, its genotype, and variation in its expressions, the phenotypes, reflect the impact of environ-mental influences on this fixed capacity. If the phenotype is properly seen as including the developments in individuals as they respond to the material and social culture inherited from previous generations, plus the effects of transformations they bring about themselves, then the genotype–phenotype distinction is blunted. The notion of a modern form of human that has remained biological fixed throughout its history is challenged. As we have already noted in earlier chapters there are measurable and permanent changes in the sensorimotor systems of indi-viduals when they become users of tools. These changes are passed on to future generations who inherit their ancestors' tool set in the form of a material culture. Viewing human development in this way may solve what Renfrew (1996) has called the sapient paradox. That is the likely fixing of the human genome at the latest some 60,000 years ago, marking the completion of the speciation phase, contrasted with the more recent breath-taking acceleration in human capacities in the last 10,000 years. The paradox can only be solved, surely, by reference to the plasticity of the young human brain and its immersions in a culture which stamps its impression on the developing organism.

An individual human's biological development can now be seen, from the viewpoint just described, as modulated by the material and social culture that surrounds them at birth and as they develop within it, con-forming to the habitual ways of acting within that culture. We have only just begun to understand these interactions from the perspective of cognitive science, but some anthropologists have long discussed their behavioural consequences, pointing out that each of us is born into such a *habitus*. This term is used by many, and in a variety of ways, but, in its most relevant sense for our concerns here, was introduced by Mauss and elaborated by Bourdieu (1977, 1990). Mauss had observed, even in relatively similar societies, the marked differences in the ways individuals used their body. When serving with the British army during the First World War he noticed that the digging of French and British troops was so different that neither could use the others' tools effectively, so 8,000 spades had to be changed every time a division from one nation replaced the other in the trenches. He also noted changes over time within a society, even within the span of a human life, citing swimming techniques as an example:

here our generation has witnessed a complete change in technique: we have seen the breast-stroke with the head out of the water replaced by different sorts of crawl. Moreover, the habit of swallowing water and spitting it out again has gone. In my day swimmers thought of themselves as a kind of steam-boat. It was stupid, but in fact I still do this: I cannot get rid of my technique. (Mauss, 2006: 79)

Like digging and swimming, even walking is not simply a biological given, it is shaped by the material and social culture in which it developed and is immersed. Mauss claimed, for instance, to be able to detect that a young woman had been convent educated by the fact that she would walk with her fists closed. Others, of his acquaintance, were said to be capable of distinguishing between a French person and an English person just by scrutinising their gait.

Mauss's intriguing, but sketchy, description of *habitus* and its effects was greatly extended in Bourdieu's theory of practice (1977, 1990), work which is hugely influential in the humanities, but less so in the life sciences. The *habitus* is said to arise as the result of a particular set of material conditions of subsistence and to consist of:

systems of durable, transposable *dispositions*, structured structures predisposed to function as structuring structures, that is, as principles of the generation and structuring of practices and representations which can be objectively 'regulated' and 'regular' without in any way being the product of obedience to rules, objectively adapted to their goals without presupposing a conscious aiming at ends or an express mastery of the operations necessary to attain them and, being all this, collectively orchestrated without being the product of the orchestrating action of a conductor. (Bourdieu, 1990: 72)

While, once again, this work tended to focus on the level of the social and institutional dispositions that constitute a *habitus*, such as marriage traditions, systems of power, it was also intended to account for the dispositions of individuals in their mundane actions. Body *hexis* was used to refer to the pattern of body postures that are transmitted down the generations as a result of imitation by children of the actions of adults. These include the ways of walking, holding the head, facial expressions, the use of tools and, of course, ways of talking. Ideas such as these are, of course, entirely consistent with the phenomenology of Merleau-Ponty, as sketched in the first chapter. His notion of an intentional arc is meant to capture the coupling between an actor and their world which skill acquisition produces, and which ensures a 'maximal grip' on the world. The skill consists not in a set of learned rules, but in dispositions to respond to the behavioural possibilities that become apparent as a result of the tuning or refinement of the agent's perceptual and motor abilities. Thus, purposeful behaviour does not necessarily require the actor to have an explicit inner representation of this purpose, rather, to use Merleau-Ponty's metaphor again, it is akin to a soap bubble resolving the various forces acting on it by forming a sphere without in any sense having a model of that sphere. Dreyfus (2002) points out that this notion has a resemblance to the neural networks, which we discussed earlier, that form basins of attraction in an energy landscape.

There is some empirical support for broad differences in material cultures producing differences in the cognitive architecture of their populations, including differences in the allocation of visual attention to objects. Uskul, Kitayama and Nisbett (2008), for example, compared communities of herders, fishermen and herders in a region of Turkey (so they had a common language, ethnicity and nationality). These three groups differed in the degrees of social dependency necessitated by their ways of living. It was claimed that both farming and large-scale fishing, as practised by the two Turkish communities, required a high degree of coordination and hence social interdependence. In contrast, the herding practices were said to require less social collaboration leading to greater independence or individualism in social norms. Perceptual and cognitive testing revealed broad differences between the groups. The farmers and fishing community tended to adopt 'holistic' styles of processing while the herders were more 'analytic' as revealed by tests of visual discrimination. So, for example, they viewed a line drawn within a square frame, after which they drew a line within a frame, of the same or different size, which was required to be either of the same absolute or relative size. The idea being that an absolute judgement required the viewer to ignore the contextual information provided by the frame whereas the relative judgement dependent upon holistic attention to both line and frame. The herders were more accurate than the farmers and fishermen in the absolute condition, and the farmers and fishermen were more accurate than the herders in the relative condition. Similar outcomes, revealing a holistic versus analytic contrast, were obtained for grouping pictures of common objects and making similarity judgements. The authors conclude that occupying different ecological niches, requiring different economic activities, entails differences in cognitive style.

Broad differences in child-rearing practices between East Asian and Western cultures have been repeatedly observed. The differences are said to reflect a rearing for interdependence compared to a rearing for independence respectively (Nisbett and Masuda, 2003), which are said to be reflected in differences in the manner in which individuals in those cultures direct their attention to objects and events. Adults in the United States when observing visual scenes, for example, are found to direct greater attention to objects, while adults in China and Japan tend to focus on the context and events (Nisbett et al., 2001). Such differences can be detected in infancy. Waxman et al. (2016) measured eye movements as 2-year-olds viewed videos of adults engaged in actions on objects. Infants raised in the United States applied more attention to the objects than the actions, while infants raised in China paid more attention to the actions.[2]

These findings suggest a network of mutual influences within a given culture. The ways of organising the provision of the economic needs of a community condition or constrain social relations creating the *habitus* or set of dispositions that characterise the behaviour of individuals within the community. The enculturation of a young child involves the acquisition of these dispositions, ways of seeing and acting included, as a result of joint action with others. The role of others in providing a model and 'scaffolding' in this process of enculturation is very obviously essential, much investigated, and was discussed earlier in this text. Less clear is the part played by objects and artefacts. As we will find in the next section anthropologists have some relevant and surprising claims about the 'agency' of objects.

Objects and Agency Again

The things we make are a very salient indication of human capacities and the variations in these artefacts, over time and across cultures, can be used

---

[2] These biases in attention were assessed indirectly by examining subsequent responses to novel stimuli in which the novelty was a new action on a previously viewed object or a previously viewed action on a new object. Whether novel actions or objects produced longer looking times, for instance, indicated which category had been most attended to during their first encounter.

to interpret the nature of the societies in which they were produced. The power of objects to record in this manner was graphically illustrated in a recent collaboration between the British Museum and the BBC which sought to chart a history of the world, from 2 million years ago to the present, with a choice of just 100 objects chosen from a collection of 8 million (MacGregor, 2011). The objects ranged from a stone axe to a credit card, and in simply having those two objects named the reader will, probably, gain an immediate insight into the distance between the two societies that made and used them. The two, very different, worlds are encapsulated in their objects. This history of humanity told through the 100 objects was widely seen as a huge success.

Yet such critical regard of our artefacts is rare. The material objects that surround us go largely unnoticed. Normally they are ready to hand, and are rarely scrutinised in our moment-by-moment interactions with them. Miller (1987) has described this as the 'humility of things' because actually they profoundly affect us, yet remain in the background, as he writes elsewhere:

objects are important, not because they are evident and physically constrain or enable, but often precisely because we do not 'see' them. The less we are aware of them the more powerfully they can determine our expectations by setting the scene and ensuring normative behaviour, without being open to challenge. They determine what takes place to the extent that we are unconscious of their capacity to do so. (2005: 5)

Objects are then very powerful and can affect us both when scrutinised and when ignored. Their impact on what we do is such that it leads some to regard them as having agency, in a variety of senses, two of which we will now briefly focus on.

Certainly, we routinely ascribe agency and intentionality to our arte-facts, particularly perhaps when they go wrong and emerge from their place in the background. Basil Fawlty's beating of his car with a piece of shrubbery when it 'refused' to start, in a memorable episode from the television comedy *Fawlty Towers*, captures this tendency to see our arte-facts having consequences for us independently of any human agency. Or are we laughing at Basil's stupidity in treating the car as if it had agency? Gell (1998) has argued that we routinely anthropomorphise artefacts in this way and it is not stupid or a confusion to do so, since the intentionality of the maker or creator is embedded in the artefact. His analysis focused on the effects of works of art on those who viewed them. A work of art is appreciated as resulting from the application of technical processes or activities by another agent; it is the product of the ingenuity of another. When confronted with an artefact we face a social entity which links us to

its creator or creators. Gell (1992) discusses 'technologies of enchantment', noting the real power of some human constructions to 'dazzle'
others. He describes the elaborate prows of Melanesian trading canoes:
far larger than their functional requirements and adorned with elaborate
carving. Their purpose was to unsettle trading partners and thereby
dominate them in the trading process. Analogous powers might be associated with the cathedrals of medieval Europe: gigantic displays of craft
and engineering prowess which would have been an overwhelming
experience to those who encountered them.

At a lesser scale, even mundane objects can have potent affective
powers, as shown vividly in this example:

Daily, I slice bread with my maternal grandmother's bread knife. Neither beautiful nor valuable – its handle scored white melamine, its wide serrations still sharp –
it connects me to my mother's hands (that used this knife) and to my grandmother's hands (smaller than my mother's, arthritic already when I was born); to
my grandmother's kitchen, beloved in my childhood; and to the long-ago morn-
ing light that filtered through the sunroom into that kitchen, in a long-sold house,
in a far-off city. All this is present when I take it up and tackle a loaf. (Messud,
2017)

These remarks illustrate that social relations are not just about person-to-
person interactions, but can also include objects and artefacts, which
therefore might be said to have a social life. This idea may be broadened
to include commodity exchange within which the independent power of
material objects can be glimpsed (see Appadurai, 1988 and Malafouris,
and Renfrew 2010 for discussions of the notion of a social life of things).

These examples of putative agency in objects depend on scrutiny of the
object: its emerging from its background because it stops fulfilling its role
or because of its overwhelming salience, perhaps because of its value, or
because the object itself is intentionally the focus of attention. But we
have noted that typically we do not see the objects that constitute our
material culture, despite our dependence on them. How can objects be
said to have agency in these circumstances? One way of answering this
question is to consider the distinction between a human agent and a tool,
a distinction we have already questioned. Where is the agency in this
pairing?

Let us turn our attention back to the, so-called, hand-axes of the
Acheulean epoch we discussed earlier. These have been discovered in
Europe, Africa, the Near East and South Asia, and dated from nearly
2 million years ago to as little more than 100,000 years ago. They are often
associated with *Homo erectus*. These tools are not axes in the modern
sense, but handheld blades that could have been used for a variety of

cutting and scraping tasks. Their form was very consistent over the epoch in which they were made, being roughly pear shaped with two convex faces forming a sharp edge. Many fit near perfectly into the palm of a human hand. This final form was achieved by the progressive flaking of a suitably sized and shaped piece of flint by striking it with a hammer stone, and, possibly further refined by the use of wood or bone implements.

Our previous discussion of toolmaking such as this included claims that the making reveals glimpses of the mental processes of those who made them. Some pointed to the need for a hierarchical plan of work, with the use of recursion, as the flaking proceeds from rough outline to the final shaping. Elsewhere others have pointed to the regularity in the form of the tools over epochs as indicative of a passing down of a design, and described their making in terms of the design's implementation, using a mental template and plan of action sequences (for example Pelegrin, 2005). But might it not be more like the making of balims by the Telefol? That is a process of skilled and fluent adjustments to the unfolding demands of the task with the materials exerting their unpredictable influences in the making, rather than a sequence of planned actions applied to an inert object generated from a blueprint. Ingold, again, provides a vivid, and poetic, description of this possibility in the actions of a skilled knapper:

the essential characteristic of his activity is not that it is concatenated but that it *flows*. In the hands of the skilled knapper, brittle flint becomes liquid, and is revealed as a maelstrom of currents in which every potential bulb of percussion is vortex from which fracture surfaces ripple out like waves. The knapper follows these currents in the rhythmically percussive movement of detaching flakes. If there is regularity in the form of the artefact, it comes from the fluent rhythmicity of the movements that gave rise to it. (Ingold, 2013: 45)

The agent–object distinction is blurred in this way of describing a skilled activity. The object is not passive in the process and guides, to some extent, the toolmaker who, if truly skilled, is not applying a set of fixed actions derived from a blueprint but *noticing* the responses of the material to their blows and modifying their actions appropriately. The noticing is a vital part of the skill involving modifications in sensory mechanisms in the progression from novice to virtuoso. While describing the core stone as having agency is stretching the use of that term beyond its common language use, it does not seem accurate to regard it as inert in the process of making either. The final form of the artefact is the result of this dynamic relationship between the core stone and the knapper equipped with a hammer stone, depending on the range of grips and rhythm of blows made possible by the human hand and the fracturing characteristics of the material (Davidson et al., 1993).

The actual use of the axe introduces another sense in which the agent–object distinction may be diluted. Notice how well it fits the hand; as Ingold points out, if you cup your hands together you enclose a space that is a good approximation to the three-dimensional shape of some of the axes. The hand-axe could be conceived of as an extension of the skeleton of its user, thus abolishing the distinction between body and tool. We discussed in Chapter 3 the immediate effects of tool use on sensorimotor systems and also the long-term adaptations that result from skilled tool use. These findings seem to support the anthropological conjectures of those such as Leroi-Gourhan (1993) who regard early tools as being 'secreted' by the brain and mind of early humans, co-evolving with the human body and brain. The very same observations might be made of contemporary tool use. Think how comfortably a smartphone fits into the hand and how its use is facilitated by our evolved toolspace: nestling in our two hands as we type a text message with our thumbs, monitoring the effects of our touches on the screen. As with the making and use of stone axes, smartphone use is undoubtedly also producing adaptations to that toolspace. Gindrat et al. (2015) measured the cortical potentials, by EEG, in response to touches on the fingertips of the thumb, index and middle fingers of touch-screen phone users and non-users. All three digits had enhanced responses in the users group, compared to the non-users. Moreover, these enhancements occur over a range of time scales: the thumb and index finger potentials were correlated with the intensity of use over the previous ten days, and the thumb even fluctuating according to the pattern of daily use, matching the fluctuations day by day in use as measured by phone battery logs. Similarly Bassolino et al. (2010) showed how toolspace was modified as a result of using a computer mouse: with it being extended to incorporate the screen whenever the mouse was merely held.

So where does the subject end and the object begin in these cases? Is the subject–object distinction valid at all? Where is the agency? Does the use of the adjective 'smart' in describing an artefact imply that Gell was right to claim that humans habitually regard objects as social entities which embed agency? These questions will continue to exercise many, but no answer will be attempted here, other than to observe that the issue may be a matter of decision rather than dis-covery. The terms we use to describe the world are, after all, conven-tions, are they not? Perhaps we will get a clearer grasp of this issue when we discuss language in the next chapter.

The Loop: Making Things, Niche Construction and Remaking the Species

The things we make are potent in a variety of ways then and their effects go far beyond the interactions, between individuals and artefacts, sketched in the previous section. As we have suggested a number of times in this text phenotype adaptation to a niche which we have constructed has driven human development and continues to.

The dominant contemporary view of evolution, referred to as the standard evolutionary theory (SET), has natural selection as the driver of adaptation to an environment, with beneficial random gene mutations being passed on to descendants through DNA. In recent years a variety of additional factors driving adaptation have been included in what has been termed an extended evolutionary synthesis (ESS) of standard models with other modern insights (Laland et al., 2014, 2015). These additional factors include the shaping of an organism by the environment in which it develops, the shaping of the environment by the organism itself and the transmission across generations by non-genetic influences such as culture. Their inclusion in accounts of human capacities tends to dilute the notion of the capacities being 'programmed' by genes or their being an expression of a genetic 'blueprint'; rather a central notion is that of reciprocal causation.

A particularly important factor of this sort, that is germane to the issues before us here, is the Baldwin effect, actually first described at the end of the nineteenth century (Baldwin, 1896) but now receiving renewed attention as the debate around the need for an ESS and the inadequacy of SET has grown. The effect refers to the impact of learning, or adaptations, during the lifetime of an organism on its descendants. Given that the environments of any organism may change, slowly or suddenly, the ability to adapt to these changes has survival value. Baldwin (1896) therefore proposed that phenotype adaptations, or learning, during development could itself be selected. Organisms which generated novelty in their phenotypes in this way increased the probability of hitting on a way of prospering in response to the changing environment. Subsequent selection may then both favour those organisms which could adapt in this way and those specific adaptations which were most successful. A consequence of such a process would be an acceleration of evolutionary change as illustrated in a computer simulation described by Hinton and Nowlan (1987) in which they consider the extreme case of an organism with a neural network having many potential connection patterns for which there is only one good solution, that is one possible set of connections that enhances reproductive fitness. Searching for the solution without constraints would be laborious in the extreme and would not scale for any network large enough to be biologically plausible. But if just some of the connections were to be genetically determined and the others set by a learning process the search problem is greatly reduced.

In their simulation, a population of reproducing organisms was modelled with a simple network having just twenty connections that were specified by twenty 'genes' having three alternative forms (alleles). One specifies a connection is present, a second that it is absent, and the third specifies a switch that is set by learning to present or absent. An initial generation of 1,000 organisms was created by random assignment of each allele but constrained so that the switch variant had a probability of 0.5, and the present and absent variants each had a probability of 0.25. As a consequence, the initial genotype typically had half of its connections genetically determined and half could be set by learning during a phase of about 2^{10} learning trials. Each trial was simply a random setting of the switchable connections. Connection change was halted whenever the combined fixed and adapted connections arrived at the single solution. The organisms adapted in this manner then 'mated', with mating pairs being selected at random, but those that had discovered the good solution having a greater probability of being selected as a parent, with the probability being a function of the speed of their learning. After about twenty generations the population had evolved the genotypes from which it was possible to learn the correct set of connections, obviously far faster than the random search through the 2^{20} combinations of alleles which would have been required had all the connections been set by genetic endowment. While the simulation is not intended as a realistic model of an evolutionary process, it does illustrate the massive benefits to be derived, in principle, from the neural plasticity which accounts for the Baldwin effect.

Badyaev (2009) has described a real example of such accelerated evolution as a consequence of the Baldwin effect. The house finch has, in just seventy years, colonised all of continental USA, expanding from its native region in the south west. This spread was accompanied by morphological changes in new populations of the birds, over just a few generations,[3] as they adapted to novel environments, with ranges of

---

[3] With new populations differing, in under ten generations, by around two standard deviations of the mean in some morphological features. Analysis of the factors associated with these changes, by experimental and statistical control, established their likely causes as, one, a biasing of the sequencing of male and female progeny (by variations in a number of factors involved in sex determination, such as the onset of incubation) and, two, male progeny being more affected in their morphology during development by the environmental conditions.

climate and ecology diverging from their original habitat. The subsequent generations of the new populations were of course the descendants of the survivors, those that were preadapted to exhibit adaptive responses to the new environmental challenges, thus amplifying those responses, over generations, as they assist in winning the selection battle.

Kuzawa and Bragg (2012) point out that the human lifespan is highly unusual in that weaning is relatively early, allowing high rates of reproduction, and the period of infantile dependency is long (considerably longer than other primates) but survival rates are high. Among the consequences of this pattern is a long developmental stage and the involvement of the extended family (older siblings and grandparents) in childrearing. When combined with human plasticity these circumstances will tend to supercharge human adaptations. The unusually long childhood, the period between weaning and juvenile independence, is characterised by somatic growth and sexual immaturity. In this interval, the child's body is being literally shaped by its *habitus*. These ontogenetic changes can be profound. This is illustrated by the changes in visual function found in the children of human groups who forage for shellfish and sea cucumbers on the seabed without modern diving aids. The human eye is of course adapted for land dwelling and therefore our underwater vision is poor. Because water and the fluid between the lens and the cornea have roughly the same refractive index, the refractive power of the eye is reduced underwater and the image is severely blurred. Gislén et al. (2003) found that the children of the Moken, who dive for food in coastal regions of South East Asia, have unexpectedly high-resolution underwater vision: being able to resolve spatial frequencies twice as high as nondiving European children. It is thought that the difference is due to the Moken's habitual constriction of pupil size and accommodation of the lens while underwater. We can assume that equally profound changes occur in other human groups, so that variations in their bodily capacities correlate with differences in their material cultures.

It is clear then that evolutionary changes in an organism may be accelerated by the entrenchment of adaptive responses to environmental change. But what if the organism is itself responsible, at least in part, for those environmental changes? Such a feedback loop has the potential to further speed and shape the trajectory of the development of a species. The shaping of an environment by an organism is usually referred to, in discussions of evolutionary influences, as niche construction and is one of those factors that some say does not receive sufficient attention within SET (Odling-Smee, Laland and Feldman, 2003). In the case of humans, niche construction might be said to operate at a variety of levels including the physical, social and cultural environments, with the latter including symbolic systems (see Kendal, Tehrani and Odling-Smee, 2011, for an overview). In the remainder of this chapter and the next we will shift focus a number of times so as to consider the effects of niche construction at all these levels. We will eventually conclude however that these analytic distinctions are just that, in fact they operate together and are interdependent (see Fuentes, 2015, for an overview of their interdependence in the case of human evolution).

Simply put, niche construction is the modification of an organism's adaptive environment as a consequence of its activities, so that natural selection and niche construction enter into a reciprocal relationship. Subsequent generations inherit a modified material culture and thereby a novel selective environment which has the potential for affecting which genotypes are passed on to subsequent generations. The most commonly referenced example in the case of humans is lactase persistence (Gerbault et al., 2011). Lactase is an enzyme produced during weaning to aid the digestion of milk, and in most humans its production decreases after the weaning phase. In some however production persists into adulthood. The genetic mutations which account for its presence in modern populations have been dated to the origins of animal domestication, and, obviously, in particular the production of dairy products, with substantial associations between the frequency of the alleles for lactase persistence and those activities in space and time.

The profound changes in human capacities and characteristics that are associated with changes in a material culture are not confined to biological adaptations. Our interests here are more to do with cognitive adaptations, and specifically with the elaborations that become possible as the result of new forms of scaffolding. These changes do not occur in a social vacuum, of course. Human action depends on already existing social networks, in many cases the existence of a developmental environment that transmits the practical skills. As is clear in our earlier discussion of balim making, many of our adult capacities depend upon an apprenticeship in skilled actions as a child within a social group. Sterelny (2011) argues that this apprentice model is a key to understanding the development of the behaviourally modern human and thereby solving the sapient paradox we mentioned earlier in this text. In particular the apprentice model is said to explain the reliable transmission across generations of technical skills and elaborations in material culture, so that innovations are preserved. Such elaborations have depended on the construction of learning environments that facilitate the fidelity of their broadcasting down the generations, rather than reflecting just cognitive adaptation. In effect, this aspect of niche construction constitutes an engineered developmental environment and thus:

identifying the ways humans organize the developmental environment of the next generation helps explain the fidelity and bandwidth (the volume) of cultural inheritance, the features that make it central to human evolution. (Sterelny, 2011: 810)

Apprentice learning similar to the balim makers has been the dominant form of teaching the young until very recently in human history. In the case of spoken language, it arguably still is. A critical feature is that the adults actively structure (engineer) the learning environment, so that skill acquisition is not just imitation. The young are encouraged to participate in adult activity and given subtasks appropriate to their abilities that allow the incremental learning of the skilled actions, while simultaneously driving the consequent adaptations in neural and skeletomuscular systems. The new generation of artisans reared in this manner thereby become a repository for their material culture and are the key to its further transmission. They also provide for the possibility of technical innovation within generations. Such a process of cultural transmission and elaboration also required, if it was to be sustained, a population size that could buffer the embodied culture in the event of environmental challenges and consequent losses of experts. Together these circumstances provided the possibility of locking in cultural practices leading to modern forms of human behaviour:

This combination, and only this combination, allowed cognitive capital to be accumulated and behaviourally modern cultures to emerge. (Sterelny, 2011: 818)

This approach can be clearly distinguished from one in which modern behaviour[4] reflects just purely cognitive gains, locked in by natural selection. It should be clear that, again, the relationship between these elements is entirely reciprocal: changes in the material culture will allow adaptations in cognitive capacity which will allow further innovations of the material culture. Some of the elaborations of a material culture are also the results of, what elsewhere, have been described as scaffolded cognitive powers and the social organisation of skill acquisition during the developmental period is part of this, as will become clearer when we discuss material symbols in the next section of this chapter.

---

[4] 'Modern behaviour' here refers to a constellation of traits that is generally regarded as being associated with human populations of about 50,000 years ago at the beginning of their expansion into Asia and Europe. Evidence for modernity of this sort include: burial, art and self-adornment, blade and composite toolmaking, hearths and increases in the spatial range of human groups.

Material Symbols, Networks and Symbol Systems

A critical further aspect of human material culture is the use of physical objects for purposes not directly concerned with the provision of material needs. One mark of behaviourally modern human societies (that is those from about 50,000 years ago) is the symbolic use of physical materials. Is it possible that the origins of symbol systems in general began with the attachment of non-utilitarian significance to physical objects?

As group size and, consequently, social complexity increased so the need to mark distinctions between groups and within groups arose, with paints, jewellery, carved or incised objects, physical relics and their like being potential markers of place in a social hierarchy (see Sterelny and Hiscock, 2014, for archaeology's insights into these developments). We have already discussed the potency of objects as vessels of human agency. Their use as tangible symbols for human power and status is entirely consistent with such observations. Hiscock (2014) argues that one early example of a class of material symbols may have been stone tools themselves. They are undoubtedly the product of highly skilled artisans and their production constituted an enormous investment in gathering the materials and fashioning them into tools, as well as learning and transmitting the techniques. The makers and their products would have been highly valued given their enormous contribution to the capacities of their social groups. For such reasons:

Artifacts and their manufacturing processes probably acquired functions as social signals – as honest signals of valuable capacities. (Hiscock, 2014: 27).

An indication that this may be true is that some such tools appear to be unnecessarily elaborate, given their assumed function as a tool. It is claimed that some Acheulian hand-axes, for example, are made with such high craft values that their purpose was to convey the skill of the maker. Can these very earliest, putative symbols[5] be the basis of the symbol systems associated with the modern behaviours of *Homo sapiens?*

Certainly some forms of what might be termed the symbolic behaviours that are taken to mark the beginning of modern behaviour include the use of objects to denote status, rather like the accomplished stone tool is read as an indicator of the skill, and hence value, of its maker. In these cases the interpretation or reading of the material symbol might be said to be dynamically linked to its actual making. Its intrinsic properties

---

[5] Words such as 'symbol', 'sign', 'read' and 'interpret' are being used in a very loose sense in this discussion of material symbols, it has to be admitted. The intention is to sketch a conjecture of a link between actions which are currently regarded as barely connected: making things and communicating.

demonstrate it to be the result of highly skilled actions. Can this notion be extended to symbol systems generally, including language? Or should material symbols be distinguished from linguistic forms?

Godfrey-Smith (2017) discusses a way of understanding the link between the maker of a material symbol and its reader which *might* be usefully generalised to symbolic communication in general. That is to regard the roles of the maker and the reader as an example of a 'sender' and a 'receiver', with the sender having the intention of eliciting a response in the receiver. In the case of a symbol of status this would be to recognise and accept the place in the social hierarchy of the sender. There is also an implicit assumption that senders and receivers share common purposes; that, broadly, they aim to cooperate and a primary purpose of communication is the coordination of actions. Importantly the communication may span time and space. Godfrey-Smith illustrates this model with a highly speculative account of some forms of early art. One such is so-called cupules that are found on most continents, can be as old as several 100,000 years and consist of sets of small, concave hemispheres hammered out of rock. These, it might be assumed, were constructed with the purpose of being seen (there is evidence that they may have been painted with ochre to heighten their salience) and it being noticed that they were not features of the natural world but artefacts made by co-species and thereby signalling their joint presence in the locations marked in this way.

There are interesting differences between these two putative examples of object as symbols: the hand-axe and the cupule. In the former it is its intrinsic properties of being a fine example that signals the status of its maker. In the latter, the signal appears to depend on a joint understanding between the sender and receiver, that is they are co-adapted to produce and interpret these material symbols so that their *full* significance is established by convention. They would have been taken as evidence for the presence of others as a consequence of their clearly being made by others. But their geometric form was, probably, a sign intended to mean something like 'this is our place'. Is there a route from these material symbols to symbol systems, such as language, in which the symbols have an entirely arbitrary relationship with the things they denote, and therefore depend upon the sender and receiver jointly adapting to the rules of association? The answer must be: only in a very hazy sense. All such systems depend on there being a conduit between sender and receiver, and this immediately suggests a role for the MNS. The MNS, we have already suggested, was elaborated in response to the needs of skilful and cooperative actions on the material world. That is it coordinates the dynamics of joint action on objects, and makes it possible to predict the actions of others. We will discuss this in greater detail in the next chapter which examines sensorimotor accounts of language evolution, in particular spoken language. In this chapter we conclude with a discussion of other symbol systems which have a clearer connection to the early use of material symbols.

In fact the development of elaborate material symbol systems arrived after spoken language. Renfrew (2008) notes it was during the 'tectonic phase', beginning about 60,000 years ago, that artefacts came to have great symbolic importance in human societies. It was during the first part of this period that the glorious cave paintings and stone carvings, such as the Venus figures, appeared. Subsequent elaborations of human material culture resulted in a massive increase in the symbolic significance of the artefacts associated with those societies, particularly with the beginning of agriculture towards the end of this period. Renfrew discusses two cases. The first is the notion that some material substances, gold for example, or objects have an intrinsic value, and this becomes an established 'fact' within a society. The second is concerned with sacred objects, that is artefacts or material remnants that are accorded great power within a group of adherents to a belief system. Each of these 'new' developments had profound importance in the establishment of modern human societies: intrinsic value makes it possible to massively expand commodity exchange and wealth accumulation and the sacred provides the means to mobilise ever larger groups around a common 'ideology'. Both then underpin modernity. Yet neither can be associated with either the human genome, given they arise long after the speciation phase was complete, or the intrinsic properties of the materials concerned. Their potency is to do with their place within a network of agents and objects.

This way of viewing agents and objects and their role in establishing social orders has been elaborated in actor-network theory (ANT), one of whose founders is Bruno Latour (see Latour, 2005, for example), mentioned at the outset of this chapter. According to ANT such networks, made up of objects, signs and actors, constitute society and the dynamics of the networks *fully* account for a given society or social situation. No one sort of entity in the network is privileged. Thus, it might be said that actors share their agency with objects and signs and concepts. Imagine a convivial meeting of friends sharing conversation and cups of coffee. The cups are not, as (modern Western) common sense would suggest, passive entities in this particular network. As was shown extensively in Chapter 2 the cups are powerful in this situation: they summon very precise forms of behaviour from the actors and could be said to be control devices for arm extensions and hand posture and so forth. The cups also embody human agency and skill in their design and form, and so are themselves enmeshed within far larger scale systems of artefact design and making. But the principles remain the same at all scales of network.

Latour (2007) invites us to consider the explosion of the Space Shuttle *Columbia* on re-entry in 2003 and the subsequent events. In the following two years, during which the shuttle was grounded, a huge effort investigated the technical and *organisational* failings leading to the disaster. Numerous failings were identified, including for example in the chain of communications between engineers and project managers preventing important information entering into decision making after the realisation that the craft had been damaged on takeoff. The implication for Latour is that *Columbia* cannot be fully understood as just a physical object, fully described in a set of technical drawings say. In fact:

after the explosion of the shuttle Columbia, hundreds of hitherto-unknown actors had to be drawn into the discussion – a legal dispute, a 'thing' in the etymological sense. Suddenly, everyone discovered that the shuttle was actually encased in an organization, NASA, and that many 'parts' of Columbia could not be seen in an ... exploded view of the shuttle. And yet those parts were indeed elements of the process of assembly necessary for the final assemblage of parts to function safely. (Latour, 2007: 141)

The progression from makers of stone axes to makers of the space shuttle is a huge development in human capacity and agency. This is a consequence of cumulative elaborations of social and material culture, of the sort sketched in this chapter. Central to this has been innovation in symbol systems which have effectively extended human cognition and the scope of human collaboration. In the next chapter, we turn to consider language, which seems to be a special case among symbol systems. Spoken language predates the systems of material symbols whose origins we have discussed here, and orthodoxy has it as a unique genetic endowment. It is the (biological) key, perhaps, to human cultural evolution, not the assembly of human actors and objects as ANT claims.

6   Language

As is often said, language changes everything. A spoken language massively amplifies the direct, person-to-person transmission of skills from the expert to the novice and the opportunities for cooperation in general. A written language massively amplifies the transmission of a material and social culture across generations. The passage from stone axes to the space station would not have been possible without language. But surely language itself must have been part of this cultural evolution. It did not, it will be argued here, arrive ready formed but developed intertwined with developments in social and material culture over eons. It is therefore not surprising that it is characterised by being the product of highly social and especially dexterous primates.

Before we examine the detailed claims about how language came into being as successive adaptations to increasingly sophisticated social and material cultures, we need to face up to the size of the challenge confronting such accounts. Two huge issues immediately arise. First, given the uniqueness of human language and it being, seemingly, an instinct (Pinker, 1995) which is acquired, almost, irrespective of the developmental context, it is surely a genetic endowment of a process of natural selection acting on random gene variations in earlier hominins. Second, the structure of human language is very special and it demands an internal cognitive structure that mirrors this structure (Fodor, 1975). We will attempt to deal with each of these issues in turn.

First, language must be a genetic endowment. In the last chapter, it was pointed out that more recent models of evolutionary processes allow scope for factors other than natural selection on gene populations to account for human development. Cultural inheritance and niche construction strongly influence the capacities of future generations. Although it is a long stretch indeed from lactose tolerance to language use, the arguments employed and reviewed in what follows will often assume that successive adaptations in hominin communication in response to their changing developmental niche led to language. A strict genetic account is unlikely and unneeded. Rather evolutionary processes, as understood within the ESS, led to a 'language-ready' brain. These processes included exaptation (Gould and Vrba, 1982) in which current capacities or features of an organism, previously evolved for one particular function (or not having a function) are now used to support another, perhaps very different, function. An example would be dextrous hands, evolved to grasp and manipulate objects effectively, becoming the means by which, the members of a highly social group begin to communicate with a protolanguage of gesture. This 'culture' of signing by hand gesture would then be transmitted to subsequent generations.

The second issue that we must face in attempting to explain language evolution is the orthodox claim that language is very special. It is a unique communication system because of its principles of organisation which make it effectively limitless. It has a hierarchical organisation of its elements, and a set of rules of combination (a syntax) that makes it possible to generate an effectively infinite set of sentences, of potentially infinite length, from a finite set of parts. Recursion is central to this unbounded power of expression (Hauser, Chomsky and Fitch, 2002). Informally, recursion is a rule which includes itself, and in the case of language an example would be a sentence that includes another sentence as one of its components, as in: 'Chomsky believes that syntactic recursion in language is uniquely human'. Such an embedding of phrases within phrases entails that the key relationships are not between adjacent elements in a sentence, and that the architecture of language can only be captured by a hierarchical 'phrase–structure grammar' which reflects the relations between widely separated elements in an expression. Hauser, Chomsky and Fitch (2002) distinguish between this 'Narrow Language Faculty', which is uniquely human, and other aspects of the 'Broad Language Faculty' which includes aspects shared with other human behaviours and other species. This idea of recursion being central to human languages (and accounting for their uniqueness) has been referred to as the minimalist program (and remains fiercely contested, as in Pinker and Jackendoff, 2005). At the conclusion of this chapter even this minimal argument for language having universal properties will be questioned.

Having clarified the exceptionalism of language and having suggested an appropriate model for its evolution, we now consider the details of how this evolution was the result of refinements to the sensorimotor system that allowed progressive refinements to the social and material developmental niche within which further sensorimotor developments were facilitated. In order to better understand the influences of material and social cultures on the evolution of language three accounts of its origins will be described, each of which identifies a different key aspect of the capacity for action of earlier hominins as the foundation on which language was built. The first account (the mirror hypothesis) claims that the MNS for grasping in primates led to the development of a language-ready neural network that was elaborated during the evolution of *Homo sapiens*. The second account (the toolmaker hypothesis) draws attention to the specific requirements of toolmaking and use, in particular the need for hierarchical and recursive 'mental' operations in the construction of artefacts having multiple elements. The third account (the joint action hypothesis) seeks the origin of language in the requirements of agents engaged in acting together on objects, with some properties of language having their roots in the requirements of physical object exchange and bodily interactions. We will consider each in turn before attempting a synthesis from their insights.

The Mirror Hypothesis

As we discussed in Chapter 4 mirror neurones in the F5 region of monkey brain fire when the animal forms a specific grasp or observes the same action in another agent. It has been argued that the elaboration of this system in hominins and perhaps their immediate forebears provided the basis of early gestural languages (Rizzolatti and Arbib, 1998; Corballis, 2003, 2010; Arbib, 2005, 2011). That is language was first a system of signs constructed by nimble-fingered hominins from sequences of hand gestures, probably augmented by vocalisations and facial expressions. On this sort of account language is a cultural adaptation, rather than a genetic endowment, of which we will have more to say shortly.

The power and efficiency of a gestural communication system is, of course, demonstrated by modern sign languages, which can be shown to be linguistically equivalent to a spoken language, in the sense of obeying the same organisational principles, differing only in modality specific characteristics (Neidle, 2000; Stokoe, 2001, 2005). American Sign Language (ASL) combines gestures that mimic the things denoted, so for example the sign for bicycle is a peddling motion with the two hands, with gestures that have only an arbitrary association with the thing referred to, established by convention. The sign for wrong, for example, is a hand, shaped with the thumb and little finger extended and the middle three fingers clenched, moved towards the mouth. Importantly for a central element of the thesis of this book, the gestures should be made within a 'signing area'. The signing area is the space in front of the signer, from their head to their waist, and between their shoulders. That is the space which we have previously in this text designated the toolspace and for which our brain has been specifically adapted. The conjecture is that the sensorimotor adaptions which provided for the skilled actions needed in toolmaking and tool use, *and the transmission of those skills*, also provide the foundations of an embryonic communication system. The neural networks dedicated to the control of hand shape and movement in response to visual objects, to the allocation of visual attention to locations and objects, to perceiving and imitating the movement of the hands of other agents, and to predicting the actions of others based on their intentions, all within reaching space, are the mechanisms on which language has been built. The human brain was made language ready by the brain adaptations necessary for sophisticated toolmaking and tool use. Embryonic communication systems were exaptations of these evolved brain structures.

Obviously, were this conjecture about the gestural origins of language true, there needs to be an explanation of how it evolved into a vocal system. Arbib (2005) describes the stages by which the language-ready brain might have become the basis of spoken language. He identifies the MNS as the key mechanism allowing a largely gestural language to become largely vocal. Specifically, the primate mirror system for grasping was colonised by a language system as a consequence of an infant and child brain growing towards maturity in a language using community. These adaptations would have presumably been progressive and synchronised with the developing material and social cultures of the communities in which the child developed.

A critical stage in the development of a gestural language, according to Arbib, is the adaptation of a MNS for grasping, which is assumed to have been present in early hominins, so as to extend its functions to allow explicit imitation of the actions of others. The capacity to imitate, after prolonged exposure, the skilled grasping and use of objects was elaborated so that an individual could recognise and repeat an action *sequence*, including novel elements, performed by another in a single trial. This complex imitation system subsequently formed the basis of a communication system using pantomime. One can imagine a progression from the pantomiming of an object directed action, such as a hammering motion, to instruct a novice in a task to the mimicking of the behaviour of other moving things, such as the undulations of a fish or the sea, in order to communicate an idea. A subsequent stage could be the disambiguation of the meaning of a pantomime, fish or wave, say, by the use of an accompanying manual, vocal or facial gesture. Such a system, which combines pantomime with gestures that are established by cultural convention, marks the emergence of protosign; that is, again according to Arbib, a set of actions that are defined by their communicative intent rather than their relationship to skilled actions in the world. His important, further claim is that a system of protosigns was the foundation for so-called protospeech.

Protospeech was constructed on the 'scaffolding' of protosign in a process in which conventional or iconic gestures, within a particular culture, came to replace pantomime. As demonstrated by sign languages, this conventionalisation of pantomime could have been, in principle, almost entirely gestural, but the advantages of vocal signs are surely obvious. It allows communication over distance, without the need for direct lines of sight between the communicating individuals and enlarges the potential repertoire of signs. The auditory–vocal system co-evolved with the developing protospeech, making possible the production, and comprehension, of ever more complex vocalisations, including ones critical for a fully formed human language, such as consonant and vowel alternations. The neural adaptations underpinning these refinements led to the increasing involvement of F5-like regions in the control of vocalisation. The end point of this trajectory was Broca's area in *Homo sapiens.*

These are intriguing and strong claims. They challenge the long-held orthodoxy that language is a unique genetic endowment entailing the development in the human brain of the regions specialised for language production and comprehension,[1] in particular its syntactic properties.

Rather:

no powerful syntactic mechanisms need have been encoded in the brains of the first *Homo sapiens.* Rather, it was the extension of the imitation-enriched mirror system to support intended communications that enabled human societies, across many millennia of invention and cultural evolution, to achieve human languages in the modern sense. (Arbib, 2005: 123)

What empirical support is there for these speculations and conjectures? Two sources, which we will discuss here, are the evidence for strong associations between speech and hand gesture, and evidence for shared brain mechanisms for action (in particular grasping) and language.

First, consider gesture and language. There does appear to be close, and necessary, links between gesture and speech (Goldin-Meadow, 2005). Human speech is almost always accompanied by simultaneous body movements: swaying, grinning, grimacing, winking, arm waving and, most importantly, hand gestures. Some of these gestures are conventional, having a meaning established by cultural transmission. When saying 'that's OK' an English speaker might rise their thumb and position

---

[1] A standard account of the brain architecture supporting language use now extends far beyond the classic Broca and Wernicke distinction as we make clear shortly (also see Pulvermüller and Fadiga, 2010 for a detailed discussion).

it vertically, while their fingers are clenched. An Italian speaker might accompany the same expression by forming a circle with the thumb and forefinger touching and extending the other fingers. Gestures not only reinforce the spoken message. They may also nuance it: when, for example, I say 'I am certain to finish that task today'; while simultaneously displaying crossed fore and index fingers.

There is growing experimental evidence that such connections between gesture and speech are intrinsic and obligatory. Bernardis and Gentilucci (2006) investigated whether simultaneous production of speech and gestures by their participants had reciprocal effects. Gestures could either be meaningful, a raised arm with the hand extended and the palm facing forward meaning stop for example, or meaningless. The speech was also either meaningful, the word 'stop' for example, or not, the letter string 'lao' for instance. The spectrograms of the spoken words were analysed both when uttered alone and when combined with a gesture. Concurrent gestures which signalled the same meaning as the spoken word modulated formants (energy peaks) in the spectrogram compared to the word spoken alone, whereas the meaningless gesture had no such effect, nor did a concurrent meaningful gesture affect the pronunciation of the meaningless word. Reciprocal effects of the spoken word on the kinematics of concurrent gestures were detected. That is parameters such as their duration, height of the hand, the amplitude of the oscillation of the hand, and velocity were affected by the pronunciation of the meaningful words but not the meaningless case. The meaningless gesture was not affected in this way by simultaneous spoken words.

It is probably not surprising that behaviours commonly associated together impact each other in this way, but Vainio and his colleagues have demonstrated, in a series of experimental studies, that the relationship between gesture and vocalisation runs deeper than the mere association of particular gestures with particular words. Vainio et al. (2013) tested the idea that even at the level of articulatory feature speech and hand gestures are linked. Articulatory features are the state of the vocal apparatus associated with different speech sounds. So, for example, to produce the sounds of [b], [p] or [m] the lips must be brought into contact at some point during their execution. Vainio et al. (2013) conjected that some features of hand grasps might be shared with such features of the vocal mechanisms when making some speech sounds. Making sounds that required restrictions in the vocal track, the [i] sound when saying 'pit' for example, compared to those that depended on an open vocal track, as in the [a] when saying 'father', could perhaps be likened to closed and open precision and power grasps. Similarly, the placement of the tip of tongue on one's teeth when sounding the consonant [t], compared to the moving of the back of the tongue towards the roof of the back of the mouth to say [k] was likened to the posture of the hand digits in a precision and power grasp.

Unlikely as the conjecture of articulation mimicking grasping may appear on first acquaintance, the authors demonstrated that the act of making a precision or power grasp was facilitated by saying a syllable string composed of precision or power-like articulatory features. Participants were faster in making precision grips while saying [ti] and [pu], compared to saying [ka] and [ma], while the converse was true when making power grips. A subsequent study (Vainio et al., 2015) demonstrated that the forward and backward movements of the tongue involved in saying [te] and [ke] facilitated congruent forward and backward movements of a joystick. Moreover, the influence was mutual: congruent limb movements speeded vocalisation. Wikman, Vainio and Rinne (2015) further showed that motor acts modulated brain responses in what is regarded as classic auditory cortex. Responding to visual and auditory targets with precision and power grips decreased activation, measured by fMRI, in auditory cortex, with the change being affected by grip type only in the case of auditory targets.

Given this close association of gesture and the phonetic expression of language it might be expected that the speakers of different native languages have different repertoires of gesture. Which they do, as the earlier example of the English and Italian gestures for something like 'that is good' illustrated (see Kita, 2009, for more examples). This is not surprising perhaps, just another aspect of culture difference, acquired in development by members of a particular culture based on their observation, and imitation, of other members of their culture. Some gestures appear to be language specific however. This is demonstrated by their being acquired by blind speakers of that language. Özçalışkan, Lucero and Goldin-Meadow (2016) compared congenitally blind native speakers of English and Turkish, and these two groups with sighted speakers of the two languages. An analysis of gesturing while talking about motion (which is known to differ markedly across languages) revealed that the blind speakers used similar gestures to the sighted speakers of their language. It follows that the association between speech articulation actions and the hand gestures does not depend upon the imitative learning of cultural conventions. Rather it suggests that the two share a common mechanism at some point in their generation.

The second source of data pertinent to the mirror hypothesis concerns the claim that progressive adaptations to primate brain area F5 are the basis of spoken language and culminated in Broca's area in *Homo sapiens*. Certainly, there are a variety of demonstrations of shared brain mechanisms for language, hand grasps, pantomime and gesture. More specifically there are many studies that show activation in 'language areas' of the brain in response to observing and executing hand actions,[2] and related action deficits resulting from brain injury in those areas, but before discussing examples of these we should pause to consider what actually a language area is taken to be. The early identification of regions of the brain that, when disrupted, led to specifically linguistic behavioural deficits encouraged the notion that the architecture of the brain was highly modular. The standard model of language (probably best represented in Geschwind, 1970) had Broca's area, in the left inferior frontal gyrus, responsible for speech production, and Wernicke's area, in the left, superior posterior temporal lobe, responsible for comprehension. Language, it was thought, was dependent on this left hemisphere network and damage to the regions or the connections between them produced the variety of language disorders seen in brain-damaged patients.

More recent work has expanded language's supposed territory in the brain, as a result of new findings but also, probably, because the strong brain modularity concept is under general challenge (and of course these two factors interact). So, for instance, what is actually regarded as Broca's area differs quite widely, according to how it is assessed: by anatomic feature, neuropsychological test or functional assessment (Hagoort, 2005). In fact, elements of language processing are thought to involve extensive portions of the left prefrontal cortex, and Hagoort (2005) suggests the term 'Broca's complex' to refer to this extended language network. This notion will be used here as we consider the overlap between language and hand actions in the human brain, in both brain-damaged patients, and in intact brains.

So, what specifically is the evidence, in support of the mirror hypothesis, that human brain areas, previously regarded as the neural basis of language use, also participate in, or are active during, the execution and observation of hand actions? One source is found in a set of studies that investigate the relations between monkey F5, associated with grasp sensitive mirror neurons, and Broca's, a selection of which we will now consider. The bold claim that often arises in this work is that Broca's is the homologue of monkey F5 (Rizzolatti and Arbib, 1998). A powerful case for the homologue claim was the demonstration that this so-called speech centre also responded to grasp actions (Rizzolatti et al., 1996). The study used positron emission tomography (PET) to image cerebral

---

[2] Some of which should be treated with caution as not all rule out the possibility of the participants engaging in subvocal commentaries on the actions they are seeing. In general however the converging evidence for a link between 'language areas' and action is good.

blood flow to compare the effects of participants observing another agent, the experimenter, grasp common objects with those of the participants performing the same grasp actions themselves. Both these conditions were compared with a baseline of passive observation of the objects. Two regions in the left hemisphere showed a significant increase in activation during action observation: one in the temporal lobe the other in the caudal part of the inferior frontal gyrus (Ba 45). This portion of the left inferior frontal gyrus is part of classic Broca: the brain region that Paul Broca identified as implicated in speech production; when damaged the patient's speech becomes effortful with disruptions to its rhythm, articulation and grammar, a condition known as Broca's aphasia. The authors concluded that the activation of a speech area during the observation of another agent grasping an object supports the idea that language and gesture recognition share an evolutionary mechanism.

Grasping an object is not communicating however. A gesture has communicative intent, and thus a number of studies have sought a link between language areas and gestural actions. A link between *gesture*, not just grasping, and Broca's complex was confirmed by Grèzes, Costes and Decety's (1998) demonstration of similar brain responses to purely gestural hand actions. They used PET to assess brain responses to the observation of a variety of hand actions. One comparison was between meaningful gestures, a pantomime of opening a bottle for example, and gestures drawn from ASL (of which the participants were ignorant). The meaningful actions provoked activity in, among other regions, the inferior frontal gyrus of the left hemisphere (Ba 44 and Ba 45, again part of classic Broca), whereas the meaningless actions did not. Króliczak and Frey (2009) used fMRI to assess brain activity in participants who were required to plan and execute hand gestures. That is, they responded to the presentation of a word by performing an appropriate hand action. Two types of gesture were elicited: transitive actions pantomiming the use of a tool, in response to the word 'writing' for example, and intransitive actions that did not involve an object, in response to the word 'hitchhiking' for example. In both cases, and for responses with either hand, an extensive left hemisphere network was active during the planning phase for the actions. This network included the inferior frontal gyrus as in Grèzes et al.'s (1998) study. A reasonable conclusion of such work is that pantomime and conventional gestures elicit, when seen and planned, activity in left hemisphere regions which overlap with those involved in speech production.

Another route to understanding the relationship between gesture, or action in general, and language use is to assess the degree to which both are affected by injury to the putative common brain areas. Deficits in tool use and pantomime in patients with left-side brain damage is well established. Pantomime performance is particularly significant for the mirror hypothesis of language evolution because such actions have a communicative intent, unlike mere imitation. Accordingly Goldenberg et al. (2007) sought to isolate effects of brain damage on pantomime from those on imitation. Patients with aphasia resulting from a left-side cerebrovascular injury were examined by fMRI and their pantomime and imitation abilities assessed. They were asked to mime the use of familiar tools and objects, and imitate meaningless gestures performed by an experimenter. Those with defective pantomime abilities consistently had damage within their left inferior frontal gyrus, and the adjacent areas on the insula and precentral gyrus. An additional analysis of all those with intact imitation confirmed the involvement of the Broca's complex in pantomime and revealed that, in this subgroup of patients, all those who exhibited a form of global or Broca aphasia had a pantomime deficit, while none exhibited both Wernicke aphasia and deficient pantomime. The implication is clear: pantomime by hand gestures and speech production are associated with common brain regions.

In sum, there is a reasonable body of evidence to demonstrate the obligatory association between pantomime, gesture and speech, even at deep levels such as phoneme production. Such connections are confirmed by the involvement of parts of the Broca's complex in deficits in the behaviours. In this regard, the mirror hypothesis for language evolution is supported. But as noted at the beginning of this chapter, language is more than an arbitrary sequence of pantomimed or conventional signs. It is generative on account of its hierarchical and recursive organisation. How is this to be explained as the outcome of adaptive pressures, or cultural influences, on dextrous primates? The next account of language evolution, the toolmaker hypothesis, has more to say on this.

The Toolmaker Hypothesis

Other accounts of how language developed from actions on objects focus on what some have termed 'technological praxis'. One general claim, again touched on in earlier chapters, is that some of the requirements of early toolmaking are echoed in some of the properties of human languages. These are particularly concerned with the hierarchical organisation of sequential behaviours, about which the mirror hypothesis was largely silent. Remember that the so-called minimalist programme of language acquisition insists that recursion is a necessary element of all human languages. A second claim, about the role of toolmaking in the evolution of language, concerns the role of language in the transmission and coordination of increasingly sophisticated technical skills (Gibson and Ingold, 1994).

It has often been noted that manual actions on objects and spoken language production both involve hierarchical combinations of motor elements (Greenfield, 1991, 1998; Greenfield et al., 1994). The higher-level act of making a handled stone axe requires repeated lower level actions: a blade must be attached to a wooden shaft, say; to achieve this the binding, blade and shaft must be fabricated; the fabrication of each requires recurrent acts, such as the repeated striking of stone against stone to make the blades. A spoken sentence is a rule governed combination of words and the words are formed by combining phonemes. This common-ality in the organisation of utterances and action sequences has led some to suspect a common neural basis for both, again Broca's area and adjacent regions have received most scrutiny.

Brain imaging studies, using PET, confirm that Broca's area is active during action observation, as we discussed previously. We will now review subsequent work, some of it using fMRI, that has led to similar conclu-sions, but also provides the basis for a finer-grained analysis of the links between language and action, with some data suggesting that different regions in putative 'language' areas may be involved in what could be described as the syntax of action sequences at various levels of abstrac-tion. The implication being that the syntactic organisation provided by the brain mechanisms allowing these action sequences was exaptated by an emerging language facility.

Fazio et al. (2009) examined the consequences of damage to Broca's area for perceiving or understanding action sequences. The authors tested patients suffering from Broca's aphasia, carefully screening them to ensure they did not have any additional motor defects (apraxia) as a consequence of their brain injury. They viewed video clips of action sequences, such as a person reaching to grasp a bottle placed on a table, and physical events, such as an object falling. The patient was then required to order four single frames from the clip into their correct sequence. Their performance was significantly impaired for ordering action sequences compared to control participants, but not for physical events. Moreover, this deficit was significantly correlated with language deficits, specifically in sequencing words in sentences and syllables in words.

Koechlin and Jubault (2006) had their (neurologically unimpaired) participants perform sequences of key presses with their left or right hand or both, in response to a visual cue, under two experimental condi-tions. In the first simple condition participants responded with both hands each time a visual cue appeared until it changed colour, upon which they began a fixed sequence of five trials in which they performed a learned response sequence: both hands then both hands then right hand then right hand then left hand. The end of the sequence was signalled by a cue colour and the participant returned to the baseline responding with both hands on every trial. The second experimental condition, the superordinate condition, required key presses to letter cues with each of three letters indicating either a left or right-hand response. The mapping of letter to hand of response was varied and defined by a superordinate level of response to letter rules. The baseline response was the repeated application of rule1 until a change in the letter cue colour required responses following a fixed sequence of the rules: rule1 then rule 1 then rule2 then rule2 then rule3. Again, a colour change in the final item indicated a return to the baseline responding. The contrast between these two conditions is that between responding with an over learned chunk of behaviour, analogous to uttering a phoneme say, to responding with a set of chunks combined according to a rule, uttering a sentence say.

The analysis of the measurements of brain activity using fMRI, while the participants produced these behavioural sequences, focused on the transitions between motor acts, that is event related increases in activity. In the case of the simple condition an increase in activity, compared to the baseline fixed response, was observed for each response in the learned sequence of responses only in the premotor regions of both hemispheres. Whereas an increase in activation at the initiation and termination of each sequence, compared to the intermediate trials, was observed in the posterior region of Broca's area and the equivalent region in the right hemisphere. In the superordinate condition increases in activity in each of the simple chunks in a sequence, compared to the fixed rule baseline, were observed in the same posterior regions of Broca's area and its right hemisphere equivalent. In contrast, the initiation and termination of sequences of superordinate action sequences was associated with increased activity, compared to the trials within a sequence, in anterior regions of Broca's area and its right hemisphere homologue. The authors conclude that this pattern of activity is evidence for a network of brain areas involved in the control of action sequences organised as a set of hierarchical action plans, with the level of abstraction increasing from premotor cortex through posterior to anterior regions of Broca's area and its homologue.

The dependence of both forms of hierarchically organised behaviours, language and actions, on common or overlapping brain networks has been cited here as evidence for the toolmaking account of language evolution. The claim is that networks that evolved to support skilled, and hierarchically organised, actions was colonised by language facilities. But of course it could equally be the case that both facilities share brain networks that are best regarded as an inheritance of domain-general abilities in sequential behaviours (see Fedorenko, Duncan and Kanwisher, 2012 and Wilson et al., 2015 for such an argument, and the discussions here in the final chapter). Additional evidence is required if the specifically toolmaking account is to be sustained.

One strategy for seeking evidence that early hominin technology was responsible for some of the brain adaptions needed for language is to examine patterns of brain activation in individuals engaged in the making of early tools (Stout and Chaminade, 2007; Stout et al., 2008). This work has focused on the making of Oldowan stone chips and the subsequent Acheulean hand-axes, associated with a period from about 2.6 to 0.3 million years ago, and during which hominin brains are estimated to have trebled in size. Both technologies require highly skilled incremental working of a stone core, either to obtain a number of usefully sharp chips or, in the case of the hand-axes, the desired characteristic shape. Both involve strategic 'decisions'. Where to best strike the core so as to leave a residue optimal for extracting the next chip, or the, more demanding, need to 'plan' the sequences of strikes that yield the final shape of the hand-axe. The qualified use of 'decision' and 'plan' reflects the doubt we have concerning the internal or external origin of these achievements, given the description of this making ignores the active participation of the materials and objects which was suggested in our early discussions of skilled actions on objects. We will return to these and related issues shortly.

In fact, when brain activity in novice nappers making Oldowan flakes was measured by PET (Stout and Chaminade, 2007), no activation in the prefrontal regions associated with planning and decision making was detected. Rather the activity seemed to depend on the sensorimotor areas we have previously conjected underly the human toolspace. This study was extended to the case of *skilled* toolmakers (three archaeologists each with more than ten years' experience making stone tools) producing Oldowan flakes, but now also Acheulean axes (Stout et al., 2008). In the case of Acheulean axe making, as previously noted, it appears that the original knappers intended to create a particular final shape and to achieve this would have required more extensive hierarchical organisation of action sequences. Comparing these modern expert toolmakers making of Oldowan flakes with the novices in the earlier study suggests the development of a network, in the experts, extending across both hemispheres which the authors interpret as reflecting integration of the tools with the user's sensorimotor systems, with the bilateral organisation reflecting the bimanual demands of the task. The greater complexity of the Acheulean task was reflected in the PET data and notably, given our current concerns here, in the right hemisphere inferior prefrontal gyrus (BA 45), the right hemisphere homologue of Broca's area.

A more recent, and highly ambitious, study aimed to understand how the acquisition of toolmaking skills changed individual brains. Hecht et al. (2014) analysed changes in the brains of their participants as they underwent a two-year apprenticeship in Palaeolithic toolmaking. Their imaging techniques, MRI and diffusion tensor imaging (DTI),[3] allowed them to track microstructural changes in the brain's grey and white matter, in particular in the inferior frontal parietal regions. The six apprentices were trained to make Oldowan blades, Acheulean hand-axes and the later tools associated with Neanderthals and early *Homo sapiens*. Of course, the participants in this study had modern brains, already adapted to skilfully manipulate a vast range of artefacts. Therefore, any changes in the brain regions of interest, resulting from learning new Palaeolithic skills, would be particularly compelling evidence for a causal link between such activities and, specific, changes in brain architecture in prehistory. The thought is that if this moderate level of skill acquisition affects the structure of modern, adult brains the likely impact on the smaller brained hominins who were probably exposed to these skills in childhood is massively increased. Sufficient perhaps to have the consequence of these phenotypic adjustments to a material culture become selected as in the so-called Baldwin effect that we discussed in the introduction to this text. That is variations in the effectiveness of acquiring the phenotype for toolmaking will be selected for, and so the regulating genes are altered so that a predisposition for the behaviour becomes hardwired in subsequent generations.

In fact, changes in frontal parietal brain regions and circuits were observed during the skill acquisition. Changes in the connectivity, as measured by diffusion magnitudes, to the left parietal lobe (the supramarginal gyrus), to the ventral regions of the primary motor cortex in both hemispheres and to the right inferior frontal gyrus pars triangularis. An increase in grey matter was also observed in the supramarginal gyrus. These changes were correlated with both the intensity of the training phases and the skill level achieved (as measured by the accuracy of the hammer strikes on the core stone). Of these regions, the left supramarginal gyrus and the pars triangularis have been implicated in the extended language processing network we discussed above.

---

[3] DTI measures the diffusion of water within a bundle of axons, so can be used to trace white matter pathways in the brain.

In summary, the evidence for the toolmaking hypothesis of language evolution, which we have so far described, is substantial but far from conclusive. While there is compelling evidence for overlapping brain networks for action and language, particularly in the case of Broca's area, the evidence that this arose specifically because of the needs of early stone toolmaking is incomplete. Perhaps this not surprising. Contemporary models of brain function tend to prefer distributed processing account of behaviours such as language and action, with different regions contributing according to the specific task. Making a stone tool is a very complex task, involving many different brain areas, and determining with any certainty brain regions that might be responsible for a particular element of it, such as hierarchical coordination, is a huge challenge. At present, we probably know too little about how complex, real-world tasks map onto the brain and how acquiring the skills to perform such tasks modifies our brains.

At the outset of this section we referred to a second influence of a toolmaking culture on language evolution which concerned the role of language in the transmission of technical skills (Gibson and Ingold, 1994). Recently an experimental study has illustrated how this may have worked. Morgan et al. (2015) investigated the transmission of Oldowanian toolmaking skills among groups of (obviously modern) human participants. Each group had to learn the toolmaking techniques in different ways. The first group was just given the appropriate tools and examples of the flakes they were to reproduce; another group had to recreate the toolmaking by simply observing a tutor, with no interactions; a third group allowed the tutor to interact by actively demonstrating the techniques, such as adjusting their pupils' grasps; a fourth group allowed gestures between the tutor and pupils, but no vocalisations; and the fifth group were allowed to talk. Transmission chains were created for each group by having a pupil become the tutor for the next pupil. Six measures of performance revealed that merely imitating another produced little benefit compared to the first untutored group, while most improvement occurred in the gesture and verbal groups. This experimental procedure is not of course a realistic simulation of skill acquisition, which would typically require several years of tutored practice. Nevertheless, it does illustrate the manner in which a group who employ even a rudimentary gesture system would gain a competitive edge over those who did not, and thus how protolanguage systems would have turbocharged the transmission of a material culture.

Discussion of the transmission of a material culture highlights its collaborative nature. A focus on the effects of the technical practices within a culture on the brains of individuals within it tends to conceal the essential collaborative nature of the practices. The next section discusses how the organisation or coordination of joint action on objects may have provided another possible route to language.

The Joint Action Hypothesis

The aforementioned orthodox view of language, that it is a genetic endowment and a feature of individual brains, reflects an individualist tendency in cognitive science but is, perhaps paradoxically, particularly prevalent in accounts of language use. It is paradoxical because language makes no sense outside of a community of language users; yet the focus of attention is often on an individual's comprehension and production of language and their consequent mental capacities. As Clark (1996) has pointed out, a spoken conversation is, intrinsically, a form of joint action, having a lot in common with other joint activities such as dancing and playing music (see also Garrod and Pickering, 2009). Some of the capacities that underpin our ability to participate in such joint activities in general might be expected, therefore, to have contributed to a language-ready brain.

We have already established that humans have extraordinary capacities for engaging with other humans without recourse to formal language. One form of connection, which we have only touched on so far, is revealed in the synchrony that can be observed among humans moving together. The effect can be powerful: London's Millennium Bridge had to be closed and extensively re-engineered soon after opening because it developed an extreme lateral 'wobble' as a consequence of the synchrony in the gaits of those crossing it (Strogatz et al., 2005). Such synchronous behaviour extends beyond imitation of the movements of others. Agents become entrained during social interactions and networks of agents have global properties that appear to be those of a single entity, so well integrated is it. In a simple example Schmidt, Carello and Turvey (1990) showed that when two participants were instructed to each swing one of their legs with the same tempo, their joint behaviour mimicked that of a single agent swinging both their legs. So as the tempo increased a change occurred from a pattern in which the two legs were swung in parallel to one in which they swung synchronously in opposite directions.[4]

---

[4] This work belongs to a variety of ecological cognitive science which applies ideas drawn from the formalisms of dynamic systems theory to human behaviour and development (for an example see Smith and Thelen, 2003). We will not further consider this approach in this text, but it should be obvious that it has great potential in making sense of the sensorimotor interactions, both within and across individuals, that have been our focus here.

Entrainment of this sort occurs during language use: Shockley, Santana and Fowler (2003) showed that participants engaged in a conversation about how to solve a puzzle synchronised the swaying of their bodies. The authors speculate that speech is a mechanism for, among other purposes, entraining the bodies of those engaged in joint action so as to weld them into a collective organism. Is it possible therefore that the vocalisations that were, we presume, an element of protolanguages had, in addition to their evolving communicative function, a role in directing or coordinating collaborating bodies? That they were in effect a form of work song, uttered to synchronise the bodily movements of groups.

Other forms and mechanisms of social engagement that may be more obviously linked to language use are those required to jointly attend to and act on objects in the world, such as a simple act of picking up and passing something to another person. Studies of infant development of such joint action skills have shown them to be important factors in the development of language in an individual and it seems reasonable to suppose that in this case ontogeny does recapitulate phylogeny.

Typically, infants of around 4 months will begin to respond to seen objects with hand actions, and by 6 months can coordinate a reach for objects within their effective reaching space (Rochat, Goubet and Senders, 1999). Critically for the present discussion at around 8 months they will begin to reach for objects outside of their reaching space whenever an adult sits alongside them (Ramenzoni and Liszkowski, 2016). This 'social reach' clearly depending on the child having expectations of the role of another person in achieving the goal of an action. Around this time an infant will begin to follow the gaze of others. Among an extensive literature, Brooks and Meltzoff (2002) established that from about 12 months an infant will follow a head turn more often when the head turner's eyes are open than when they are closed. Thus, establishing that the infant appears to 'understand' that there is something to be seen, and is not merely imitating the other. In a subsequent study (Brooks and Meltzoff, 2005) they revealed that this capacity developed towards the end of the child's first year: at 9 months old their participants did not differentiate between head turns with closed and open eyes, they seemed to imitate the head turn per se, while at 10 and 11 months old they more frequently followed the looking of another whose eyes were open. Moreover, gaze following at 10 and 11 months was strongly correlated with their subsequent language scores at 18 months, with, among several measures of language, word comprehension being markedly better for those children who tended to follow gaze earlier.

By the beginning of their second year children are beginning to coordinate their actions with others in joint actions on objects and have developed an awareness of the objects which, specifically, they have shared with others in those activities. Moll et al. (2008) showed this to be the case with 14-month-olds. Their participants jointly engaged with an object with an adult and subsequently would more likely select the object from a set of distractors when the same adult made an ambiguous request for one of the objects but did not if a different adult did so. It seems that such infants have developed a sense of shared knowledge arising from shared activities. Also, around this age, children become active in helping and encouraging joint activity, as we touched on previously, for instance dragging an adult back into engagement with an object. Importantly for the present discussion this helping and encouraging can take the form of communicative gesture. Pointing may be used to indicate something that is wanted or to which they wish to direct attention. But also, as Liszkowski et al. (2006) have shown, 12- and 18-month-olds will point to an object to inform a person who they 'know' is looking for it. This is a particularly interesting case because it is, as the authors describe it, informative pointing, requiring an insight into the intentions of another and their consequent informational needs. Behne, Carpenter and Tomasello (2014) show that this is extended in older children to the creation of iconic gesture. That is, 27-month-olds who had learned to solve a manual puzzle which required a variety of actions to solve, such as twisting and pushing on components of a novel apparatus and were required to explain how to do it to a glove puppet were observed to use gestures to communicate what was needed. For instance, they would gesture the need to push a component upwards by an upward movement of the hand with the palm facing upwards.

The conjecture is that this progressive development of a system of communication in an individual human, captures some of the stages of its evolution over the eons; as was said ontogeny recapitulates phylogeny. The driver of the developments of a communication system in both cases is the need to act with others on objects in their world. Our links with others are visceral and largely not reflective. An understanding of the intentional states of others is not the result of passive observation but arises from becoming engaged in activities with them. The sharing of such activities is thereby the basis of communicative exchanges.

A Synthesis: Language as a Remarkable Confluence

A search for a single factor to account for the evolution of human language is of course probably futile. All three possible routes to language described here are probably better viewed as entangled, with their relative contributions varying over time. The data on modern toolmakers demonstrating changes to brain areas which have been previously linked to language use, the left ventral and parietal regions, support the conjecture that the structural brain changes invoked by the requirements of stone toolmaking were co-opted by the evolving communications needs of hominins, but as was shown the toolmaking skills themselves would have benefited from the elaborations in communication that were co-occurring. Similarly, the need for joint activity in the increasingly complex social orders made possible by growth in technical mastery might well have provided the substrate for communication in the form of the MNS. But the joint activity would have been enhanced by the emerging means of coordination through manual and vocal gesture. Language is thus a confluence of adaptive responses to a changing material and social culture, and is itself part of that culture, contributing to the driving of adaptation.

This account of language as a cultural artefact, originating in the practical activities of a society, rather than a modular mental faculty gifted by gene mutation, is consistent with the many recent findings of it seemingly being built from, and grounded in, sensorimotor elements (see Fischer and Zwann, 2008 for a review). Here are just a few examples. The silent reading of action words such as 'kick' and 'lick' elicits brain activation in the motor cortex regions that are involved in the execution of those actions, and listening to sentences describing hand or leg actions modulates TMS induced motor responses of those body parts (see Pulvermüller, 2005 for a summary of these and related findings). There have been repeated finding of various kinds of action to sentence compatibility effects. For example, the participants in Glenberg and Kaschak's (2002) study had to judge whether a sentence made sense or not and signal their judgement by pressing a button which required a movement of their hand towards or away from their body. The button presses were facilitated whenever the sentence described a compatible action, such as an inward movement to 'open the drawer' or an outward movement to 'close the drawer'. This compatibility effect was also found with abstract exchanges, so 'Liz told you the story' was easier to respond to with an inward movement than 'You told Liz the story'. Neurological disorders of the motor system have impacts on language use. Most strikingly motor neurone disease produces language deficits, in production and comprehension which are more pronounced for verbs than nouns (Bak and Hodges, 2004). Conceptual knowledge appears to be modality specific, at least in the case of concrete concepts, as evinced by studies in which participants report on the content of concepts by various means (Barsalou, Solomon and Wu, 1999; Barsalou et al., 2003). When required to verify if a property belongs to concept for example, they are facilitated if they had earlier verified a perceptually similar property compared to a dissimilar one: verifying that a pony has a mane is easier after verifying that a horse has one than after verifying that a lion has one. Understanding spoken language appears to elicit complementary motor responses: for example listening to the description of a visual scene which contains directional information such as 'You are standing across the street from a 40 story apartment building ... on the 10th floor, a woman is hanging her laundry out the window' results in a tendency to make corresponding eye movements in the listener, in this case upward (Spivey et al., 2000). Even abstract concepts have been related to actions in the world, first in terms of the extensive use of metaphor in the use of abstract terms, as when spatial terms are used in expressions like 'Things are looking up' (Lakoff and Johnson, 1980). But also, more recently an extension of the sentence compatibility effect demonstrated that the motor system is engaged when abstract terms are understood. Guan et al. (2013) used ERP measures to show that the precision and speed of a hand movement up or down was increased after the comprehension of the compatible terms 'more and more' and 'less and less' respectively.

These data suggest that language and its understanding is drenched in sensorimotor allusions. This is not to say that it is confined to sensorimotor simulations. The claim that it is a cultural artefact entails it being the product of continuous refinement and elaboration across generations. It might be expected that the development of formal representational systems such as written language would have had profound effects on spoken language, including its formalisation. An effect which would have been massively amplified by the introduction of institutions of education within which the young are drilled in the rules of this now formalised language system. It seems possible that the orthodox view of language has been seduced by these, actually recent, aspects of its development. The assumption that language is so unique and special that it must have arrived fully formed as a consequence of a genetic mutation ignores the interplay of culture and the brains of individuals within it. Crucially it has underestimated the plasticity of the developing brain and its capacity for it adapting to its material and social culture.

The adaptation of an individual brain as it develops within a language using community may be regarded as a process of internalisation, thus inverting the causal logic of the 'language of thought' approach. Rather than human languages reflecting an internal mental architecture, the latter comes to reflect some aspects of the formal systems employed within a society, including its language. Language provides the basis for or at least conditions some mental processes in the sense of providing it with a system of arbitrary reference and combinatorial rules (see Clark,

2008; Vygotsky, 2012; and Dove, 2014 for similar arguments). Given that linguistics and psycholinguistics have tended to study language in populations of the WEIRD, that is in western, educated, industrialised, rich and democratic societies (which Henrich, Heine and Norenzayan, 2010, have claimed are actually highly atypical compared to our species in general), it is perhaps not surprising that they have tended to assume these formal properties are necessary and universal features of all human languages. Also, their focus on written language (Linell, 2004) has reinforced the view of language as a formal system. In fact, studies of the diversity of languages do not offer strong support for there being only surface differences among them, with their deep structure sharing a set of universals.

Evans and Levinson (2009) argue that cognitive science in general has failed to appreciate the diversity of the, estimated, 5,000 to 8,000 human spoken languages, of which only a fraction have been fully described. Their survey of those reveals little of the uniformity predicted by language being a genetic endowment and reflecting the architecture of a 'mentalese'. There is a huge range of morphologies among those languages, ranging from isolating languages which lack affixes for person, number and tense to polysynthetic languages which combine many morphemes so as to create entire sentences within a single word. Some languages do not have some of the major grammatical classes which are found in the most extensively studied language groups, such as adjectives and adverbs. Others have classes of word not, commonly, found in the dominant languages, such as ideophones that, in a single word, combine all the sensory associations of an event or actions of a person. For example, in Nupe, an African language, there is a single word for the throb or beat of the heart as felt in a sore finger (Blench, 2010). In some languages, this class is as large as nouns and verbs. The semantics of languages differ hugely and the variations seems to be associated with the practical and cultural concerns of the speakers. The importance of kinship in some Australian populations is reflected in their languages having a particularly rich vocabulary for expressing complex family relationships. Importantly constituent structure and recursion are not quite the essential features of all languages that orthodoxy claims. Many languages have few restrictions on word order, Latin being an example of one with free word order, and recursion is often restricted, in the aforementioned polysynthetic languages, for example, in which almost all the structure is within words and there is little at the clause level. The authors conclude that far from human language having a set of core universal features, close examination of a range of our languages reveals that:

We are the only known species whose communication systems varies fundamentally in both form and content. (Evans and Levinson, 2009: 431, their emphasis)

A reasonable conclusion here is that language is a cultural artefact, constrained of course by earlier adaptations of the sensorimotor systems to the need for coordinated actions in social groups, but shaped by the material and social cultures of its users. It is thus to be seen as an important element in the human niche, external to the individual but shaping each of us so as to tune and equip us for a place in the world. It is one among several such representational symbol systems which arise within a community of dextrous and social agents.

7 A Synthesis: Networks of Human Agents as Physical Symbol Systems

This final chapter will attempt to draw together the various insights arising from our discussion of an embodied framework so as to create a synthesis of its conceptual and empirical understandings of cognition. In particular, it will attempt to unify embodied accounts of cognition, which reveal its sensory-motor basis, with symbolic exchanges, which arise within networks of agents acting together in a material culture. It will conclude that this critical interface between the ready-to-hand world and the presence-at-hand world is sorely neglected within the mainstream and hence poorly understood. First, we will summarise the major conclusions derived from our discussions thus far.

Sensorimotor Embedding: the Empirical Case for Our Place

In the first chapter, we discussed the notion of 'place' as used in various contexts and in various intellectual traditions. Like all animals we are born into a niche, or perhaps better put a range of niches, for which we are adapted in the traditional biological sense, which defines the limit of our unaided capacities, in that, under normal circumstances a fertilised human egg produces an adult who is bilaterally symmetrical, having two eyes, two ears, two legs and two arms with five-fingered hands. The sensory system is adapted in a similar sense also. It is responsive to only a limited bandwidth of the electromagnetic and sound spectrums, for instance. The skeletomuscular system and the sensory system have coevolved to mutually serve each other. In very gross terms the sensory system responds to those properties of the world that the skeletomuscular system is capable of exploiting. But of course, they are not actually two systems. To separate them is an analytic abstraction. When we move our bodies we systematically transform our sensorium and this very tight coupling provides an unmediated access to the world in which we are thereby embedded.

As was pointed out this conception of being embedded in a world, that is being-in-the-world rather than being an external observer of it, has philosophical roots, notably in the phenomenological tradition. Remember Merleau-Ponty's claim that we are 'geared into the world'. We have shown that this idea now has good empirical support. First, we now understand that human sensory processing involves multiple brain pathways, some of which appear closely tied to action. The phenomena of blind-sight and forms of visual agnosia, discussed in Chapter 2, are forceful demonstrations of direct sensory coordination of body movements. The evidence for a ventral–dorsal distinction, and more recent elaborations of it, refines such insights, and suggests ways in which visual responses control, or are coupled with, various classes of bodily responses. These include whole-body movements, but importantly also actions within the reaching space of an agent and provide broad empirical support for the notion of affordance. Objects do indeed solicit actions.

The evidence for sensorimotor networks specialising in the control of actions on objects specifically within reaching space, also reviewed in Chapter 2, provides a basis for understanding how objects could afford the actions associated with them. It also motivates an elaboration of the notion of affordance given the paradoxical findings that motor activation is observed in response to *depictions* of affording objects and scenarios, as when, as previously described, an image on a screen of a barrier to a reach modulates the effects of an object depicted behind the screen (Costantini et al., 2010). In such cases it might be said that the observer's motor system is responding *to* a representation, not as, one might be tempted to claim, that the observer is *forming* a representation. Whereas in other cases the affordance effects appear closer to the notion of an unmediated coupling of an object with a sensorimotor system, as evinced by the, also previously described, observation of motor-evoked responses for graspable objects presented during the attentional blink and therefore undetected (McNair, Behrens and Harris, 2017). It seems a variety of senses or classes of affordance must be contemplated. The two cases we are considering here might be said to correspond to, one, affordance arising in our engagement within a material culture with familiar objects that are ready-to-hand, and, two, affordance as a response to objects within our symbolic culture which are present-at-hand. We will have more to say of this distinction later in this final chapter.

Another aspect of earlier conceptual work, in both phenomenological and ecological traditions, which has found recent empirical support is, as discussed in Chapter 3, the idea that tools are incorporated into human bodies to such an extent that they can be regarded an outgrowth of the musculoskeletal system. As Gibson (2014) pointed out, a tool skilfully deployed is no longer an object in the world of its user but it becomes a part of the user's body and thereby illustrates that the boundary between an agent and their world is not the surface of their skin, thereby diluting the object–subject dichotomy. More profoundly the consequent adaptations in the sensorimotor system, over multiple timescales, that tool use brings, changes the individual agent's place, in the sense used here, in the world. Their reach is, literally and metaphorically, extended. But notice also in addition to the changes in the individual that the tool use brings, the world is also changed in that the elaborations of a material cultural are examples of niche construction. Again, more on this later in this chapter.

The world in which we are embedded is not just a material one, it is simultaneously material and social. As we noted previously the two are intrinsically entangled. Our artefacts, carry great social significance and our engagement with others originates, we have argued, from the requirements of joint action with others on objects. Much of this interaction, when skilful, consists of fluent, dance-like exchanges which are unmediated and synchronised in real time as the action unfolds. Other bodies may also, it can be argued, be ready-to-hand. The discovery of the primate mirror neurone system, and an increasing understanding of its elaboration in humans, has provided empirical support for this 'transparency' of the intentions and actions of other agents. It has been argued here, in Chapter 4, that rather than conceiving of the mirror neurone system as the basis of understanding others, it better conceived as a system, or part of a system, for the coordination of joint activity in real time. The issue of *explicit* understanding, as we will argue in more detail later, arises in the context of a commentary on such interactions. It is effectively post hoc to the actions themselves, when these occur in the context of our skilled coping behaviours.

We conclude that there is now good scientific evidence for humans being embedded in their material and social world in a manner that fits with the earlier analyses of some varieties of phenomenology. Such a viewpoint is provided with added weight by the fact that we now have, in addition, some understanding of the principles by which each of us becomes so embedded during development. The descriptions in Chapter 4 of the free-energy idea and of related mechanisms of unsupervised learning in multilayer neural networks appear to offer a contemporary version of associative learning sufficiently powerful to account for a mapping between a body and its world of the sort needed. That is, mere exposure to sensory events, as a result of immersion and activity in a world, will shape the sensorimotor system. Repeated exposure to actions, objects and others in the environment during development will build a body with the appropriate set of coping skills for that environment. During this development, the *effective* body and its world is constantly remapped. Also, it seems, such remapping continues throughout the lifespan, albeit at a slowing pace, as when elderly thumbs are trained by use of new tools such as smartphones.

Motor Geniuses and Toolspace

The conclusions of the previous section could equally apply to other animals, certainly most primates, which share the basic architecture of having a plastic central nervous system coupled to a sensory and motor system. What makes humans special in the sense of being the only species capable of such evident technical and cultural prowess? The most likely answer is, of course, a host of features and circumstances, but a primary factor, it has been argued here, is our sheer dexterity. The coevolution in our ancestor species of the musculoskeletal structures of the upper limbs and the neural systems, motor and sensory, required for their deployment gifted us an unmatched ability to manipulate objects within our reach. It should be clear enough following our discussions at several places in this text that the neural networks that support high fidelity and high resolution actions in our toolspace are extensive (see Perry, Amarasooriya and Fallah's 2016 review of near hand visual attention systems for other examples).

It is easy to neglect the fundamental importance of the ability to thread needles, wield accurate hammer blows, fluently pass an object to another and other similar apparently mundane manual skills, but such abilities have provided the foundations for three key capacities that together make humans unique. First, and most obviously, our ability to make things has meant that we have continuously reconstructed our niche so that our adaptations became predominately to a material culture rather than a natural environment. An effect boosted by the very long development phase for young humans. As Ingold (2000) points out, this means that the notion of a biologically modern species does not apply in our case; we are not done yet! Second, these adaptations were intertwined with social developments: the increasing mastery of the natural environment that was a consequence of increasing sophistication in our material culture provided the basis for larger social groups, which itself drove adaptations so as to allow the increasingly complex social coordination required. Included in these would be the transmission of the manual skills required within a particular culture which would have taken the form of joint activity between novice and expert. Third, and probably most significantly, our manual dexterity, combined with the transparency of human intentionality to another human that is a requirement for joint activity, has provided the basis of a communication system which became language. Manual dexterity made possible a rich vocabulary of gesture and panto-mime with which to construct a protolanguage. The mechanisms that underpin joint activity, such as the special purpose attentional systems and the MNS, would have facilitated the exchange of the gestures in a *dialogue*. At this point, skilful communicative acts now form part of the culture which may be transmitted to and elaborated by future generations.

Acting Together: Everything We Do We Do Together

As was suggested in the previous section a significant factor driving adaptations in early human societies was the increases in social complex-ity consequent on the increases in group size that were themselves a consequence of increasing technical powers. In fact, increases in tech-nical prowess and social sophistication are different aspects of a single process. Technical and social developments are mutual. The consequen-tial neural adaptations to these developments have led to what some have termed a social brain.

In Chapter 4 we suggested that the MNS in the primate brain should be regarded as a system, or part of a system, for the coordination of the joint actions of agents within their material culture. Given the social brain idea it is hardly surprising that the MNS in the human is almost certainly uniquely extensive: one recent estimate, as noted in Chapter 4, is of fourteen neural groups distributed across nine Brodmann areas. We also pointed out some of the behavioural consequences of these brain systems: humans find it very difficult not to become entrained by the actions of other humans, with a strong tendency to imitate. And imitation turns out to be very important. Imitation learning in which young humans learn 'at the knee' of mature and skilled members of their community has been, and is still in many instances, an important element of human enculturation. Some claim it is the prime, Lamarckian mechanism underlying the ratchet effect of cultural transmission, in which progressive refinements in material culture became the develop-mental environment for the next generation and were thereby locked in.

But, as we previously observed, mirror neurons do not just mirror. The MNS as a whole seems to be implicated in range of joint activities from simple imitation to complex interactions within a material culture in which objects and other agents afford responses in their observers. Recent single-cell investigations of the MNS in non-human primates have uncov-ered a rich repertoire of neuronal responses, with modulations according to: whether the observed events are within reaching space or not; the goal of an otherwise similar action; the hand used in the action; the direction of a wrist rotation in an action; whether an action occurs beyond or within a physical barrier; and the viewing perspective. Other, canonical neurons in the MNS respond specifically to the grasping affordance of seen objects and also when the animal makes the associated grasp. Some activity in the human MNS, as measured by fMRI, has been shown to be complementary to the actions observed in others as if preparing a cooperative response to the other agent. Behavioural studies with humans have similarly suggested a highly dynamic system in which object affordances together with the actions of other agents simultaneously modulate the responses of an observer. The kinematics of another's reach are included in this network of influences seemingly providing information about the goal and intentions of an action that can be 'picked up' by an observer. The theories of predictive encoding (Rao and Ballard, 1999) and the consistency of those with the free-energy idea (Friston, 2005) add to these empirical observations. We conclude therefore that our material and social cultures are utterly intertwined and we are we immersed in such a way that routinely allows an unmediated access. The notion of our place in the world is in this way elaborated, compared to the description in the first section of this chapter.

A further important conclusion is that the human MNS, as described, is not a fixed genetic endowment. Rather it unfolds in response to a specific developmental environment and so cultural variation would be expected. This was clearly illustrated by the observation of tool related responses in monkeys after training in tool use (Iriki et al., 1996). In humans, such effects will be profound, with the cultural heritage of each generation providing the development environment for the MNSs of the next generation. Part of which, as we noted above, have been systems of communication made possible by their colonisation of some of the functions of the MNS which allowed humans to 'read' the intentions and goals of others. It is hardly surprising, given this conjecture, that strong overlaps have been discovered between the human MNS and neural networks which have long been implicated in language use.

The Very Extended Phenotype and Cultural Toolkits

Human neural plasticity is profound and as a consequence, our effective bodies may undergo changes over a range of timescales, from evolutionary to lifespan to moment, as we have previously described. The adaptations to the changing developmental environment have been explained, in part, by exaptation. A previously evolved capacity is adopted to fulfil a new function. Neural networks allowing the handling of objects with others being recruited for communication is one example. At the neural level this is said to be consequence of a general principle of neural reuse (Anderson, 2010, 2014). That is brain organisation can be characterised by its reuse of neural networks for multiple cognitive purposes in evolutionary and individual development, rather than it being strictly modular. This is supported by evidence, collated from a meta-analysis of fMRI studies that shows that a typical brain region participated in nine of eleven different task domains, ranging from action execution to reasoning, that were investigated. We assume that the observation that the human brain can be remapped so that new functions can be built by assembling or reconfiguring existing neural circuits is related to the models of associative learning that were discussed in Chapter 4, in that they offer glimpses of how such processes might be implemented.

It follows that here is no fixed human phenotype. As noted in Chapter 5 the spectacular growth in human powers over the last 10,000 years postdates the fixing of the genome by about 50,000 years. This disconnect between a genetic endowment and human development across generations can be partly accounted for by the sorts of processes and factors discussed in relation to the MNS in the last section. That is adaptations during the lifetime of individuals can be selected for, along with the ability to generate such variations in phenotype (the Baldwin effect). In addition, and perhaps particularly important in the human case, are the transmission of a culture across generations and the transformations in that culture which constitutes a form of niche construction.

The human niche includes what might be regarded as a toolkit which each generation receives as an inheritance and is trained in its use. Critically, included in this toolkit are systems of communication or symbolic exchange which have be elaborated over eons from the first, gestural and iconic, protolanguages. Spoken language is properly conceived of as a set of skilled actions which can be read by other agents in a manner similar to their reading of non-verbal action during joint activity. It is acquired alongside such joint activity and exploits early gains that arise from cooperation with others. These include being able to take the perspective of another and subsequently the shared intentionality which is uniquely human. The speech sounds represent states of the world in a manner akin to pictorial representations, in that they are *taken* to refer to some state of the world rather like pictures of actions and objects on a display screen are taken to stand for such states in the real world.[1]

---

[1] Speech is usually contrasted with iconic forms of representation, in that language, in general, refers by convention. Here the discussion is about how the observer of a speech sound or picture regards it. Both are taken to refer to some state of the world.

As such they evoke neural responses which are shared with the responses to the real-world events, as in most of the affordance experiments described in this text. On this way of talking about the relationship between symbols, like spoken words and gestures, and a listener or an observer, the representation is in the world not the head. The agent is responding to a representation in the world, a thing in the world.

Notice also that symbols may be used like other tools to solve problems in the world. The architect Frank Gehry used freehand drawings in the early stages of designing the remarkable Guggenheim Museum building in Bilbao and described himself as a 'voyeur' of this process. His actions on paper revealed, he claimed, aspects of the early design that surprised him. If his intuitions are correct, the process was not one of problem-solving in his head translated into marks on paper, it was more akin to a physical manipulation of symbols in the world *revealing* a solution to the problem-solver. This example illustrates what is usually termed the extended mind idea, often associated with theories of embodied cognition. The claim is that much of human cognition is 'offloaded' to the world and therefore the mind is constituted by a coupling of events in the brain and events or objects in the world (see Clark and Chalmers, 1998, for an early discussion of this idea and Clark, 2008, for a more recent elaboration). The events and objects in the world are referred to as scaffolding for the events in the head. It should be obvious that much of our material culture can be regarded as scaffolding in this sense: my imperfect memory is augmented by the capacities of my smartphone.

Speech then is an early addition to the human toolkit and also serves as a scaffold in the sense just discussed. Notice that it can scaffold the activity of two or more people working together, with a constant dialogue facilitating the moment by moment adjustments in their actions that is required for successful collaboration. Here language is a public entity: the symbols are in the world not the heads of the actors. But, importantly, spoken language can also scaffold the actions of an individual. I can comment on what I am doing using speech. Rather like Gehry solving problems with pencil and paper, I can talk aloud as I struggle with a novel task and these marks in the sound spectrum guide me to 'seeing' a solution. And of course, this speech can be silent.[2] Like many of the features of our cultural toolkit we may adapt so as to internalise them, something we will discuss in more detail in the next section.

---

[2] These two uses of language, actual and silent speech, are, at least partly, responsible for a tangle of confusions around the language of thought controversy (see Fodor, 1975, for the seminal formulation of the case for and Searle, 1980, for a famous challenge to it, among the vast literature on this dispute).

Spoken language then is essentially an in the world, rather than in the head, representational system rooted in the joint activity of human agents in a material culture. Other symbol systems have been added to the toolkit in recent human history. Written language is one, versions of which are usually said to have begun about 5,000 years ago, with Mesopotamian cuneiform being a prime example. Its origins are relatively well understood (Thomsen, 1984). It developed from a series of physical tokens, in clay, needed to keep track of economic exchanges demanded of the expanding trade in agricultural products. Each token would be a physical symbol for a specific quantity of a specific commodity. This system of symbols was elaborated over the next few thousand years to arrive at sequences of symbols impressed on clay tablets, some of which may be described as phonograms, that is icons that stood for sounds. Again, the point is that these physical symbol systems are cultural inventions in response to the demands of an expanding material culture. It can be expected that written and spoken symbol systems will have had mutual influences during their further development into modern forms. The use of phonograms is an example. A consequence of such developments is a formalisation of language in general, a process which would have been accelerated by the increasing importance of systems of formal education.

Such a trajectory is very different from the orthodoxy that until recently dominated cognitive science's perspective on language. That is the view that language reflects an in the head formal system of representation that is specified in the human genome. A thought may be constructed in this 'mentalese' and expressed as a sentence, spoken or written, which reflects the structural architecture of mentalese. On the account developed in this text, this inverts the actual relationship, which is that language is a symbol system invented and elaborated to solve problems by augmenting the processes within and between individual brains. This reframing does nothing to diminish the importance and uniqueness of language in our species. The invention of the phoneme is at least as important as the invention of the hand axe in the human story.

Adaptation to a Niche: the Exocerebrum and Virtual Symbol Systems

Modern humans are born into a world drenched in symbols and formal systems for manipulating symbols. In addition to natural language, written and spoken, we encounter mathematical formalisms, computing languages, pictorial or iconic systems, art conventions, dress conventions, religious symbolism and so on. In some of these we become expert to varying degrees, which entails neural adaptation, as in any other skill acquisition. We can be said to internalise some of these systems so that brain processes come to reflect some of the properties of those formal systems. One way of seeing such adaptations is that the sensorimotor mechanisms of the primate brain can be 'programmed' to approximate the operations of or on symbol systems. Consider the case of arithmetic. This is typically introduced in school as a set of drills for manipulating physical symbols using pen and paper. Long multiplication for instance involves decomposing the problem into a set of steps which can be solved 'in the head', as a result of rote associative learning, with the results of each step being noted on a paper in a spatial arrangement which represents the order of the numbers (columns for units, 10s and so forth). Rumelhart et al. (1986) discuss how such a practice allows an essentially sensorimotor brain to implement a 'virtual' symbol system. They characterise the human brain in ways entirely consistent with the account developed in this text: it is built to excel at pattern matching, to predict states of the world consequent on the activity of self or others and, most significantly of all, to manipulate objects in the environment. The latter is crucial in building a culture which includes symbol systems:

Especially important here is our ability to manipulate the environment so that it comes to represent something. This is what sets human intellectual accomplishments apart from other animals. (Rumelhart et al., 1986: 45)

In the case of our example of long multiplication continuous practice at manipulating the symbol system in the world results in the ability to do so in the head by imagining the state transitions drilled into us at the school desk.

The claim here is that this illustrates a general account of how it is possible for so-called higher-level cognition to be implemented in human neural networks evolved for sensorimotor purposes. Many of what are commonly regarded as essential characteristics of human cognition, such as reasoning, deduction and decision making, are a cultural endowment not a biological one.

John Duncan and his colleagues have described some features of human brain organisation that appears to be consistent with this idea of the brain being effectively programmed to implement sequential mental processes (Duncan and Owen, 2000; Duncan et al., 2000; Duncan, 2010), and, it should be noted, is consistent with the idea of neural reuse mentioned earlier in this chapter. They identify a frontal and parietal region of the primate brain as a network for assembling sequential cognitive processes which they refer to as a multiple-demand system. Single cell recordings in monkey, brain imaging and neuropsychological investigations in humans have revealed its involvement in a range of tasks.

For instance, Duncan and Owen (2000) reviewed brain imaging studies of human participants engaged in solving various, very different problems: resolving response conflicts; learning a novel task; using working memory; and making perceptual discriminations. Despite the range of problems that the participants were dealing with the foci of activation in all cases were in a surprising confined region of frontal cortex. The conjecture is that this multiple-demand network allows an agent to assemble a set of subtasks into a sequence; from making a cup of coffee to solving a problem in logic. Central to problems of this sort is the issue of control: at each stage in a sequence the focus must be on the current subtask, but must then, on its completion, be shifted to the next subtask, with any results being passed from the one to the other. Such an idea is consistent with the some of the long-known consequences of damage to frontal areas. That is disruption to complex sequences of behaviour in the form of missing subtasks or the insertion of incompatible ones.

As with language then, other elements of the human cultural toolkit elicit adaptations that lead to a commonality of actions in the world and mental processes in the head. But, again, the former are the basis for the latter, rather than the inverse relationship that has tended to be the orthodoxy within cognitive science. Or perhaps a better way of conceiving of the relationship is to abandon the distinction between in-the-head and in-the-world in the case of symbol manipulation. Bartra (2014) has proposed something similar in advancing the notion of an 'exocerebrum', which can be regarded as a refinement or special case of the extended cognition school's use of the notion of scaffolding. That is, his idea that symbol systems are prosthetics for the brain, augmenting its biologically given[3] capacities so as to derive novel functions, in a manner similar to that of the sensory substitution devices we discussed in Chapter 2 that allow a user to 'see' the world as a result of tactile stimulation on the skin.

From Ready-to-hand to Presence-at-hand: a Spectrum or Two Routes?

At this point we need to return to important distinctions, which have been mentioned in several places in this text, but largely passed over. They involve some of the very hardest problems in cognitive science, as we have acknowledged. We must consider whether they can be made sense of in the light of our preferred accounts of human cognition, based on the

---

[3] The term 'biologically given' is perhaps misleading given we have argued earlier that culture is a driver of adaptations in the body. Perhaps 'sensorimotor core' conveys the intended meaning rather better.

evidence surveyed here. Consider these binary distinctions, which we seem drawn to, that have been applied to human mental processes and states: ready-to-hand and presence-at-hand; implicit and explicit understanding and processing; reflexive and reflective reasoning; early and late evolutionary achievements; fast and slow mental processes; low and high-level cognition; system 1 and system 2 mental processes;[4] direct and indirect perception; dorsal and ventral visual processing; and of course, non-conscious and conscious mental processes. These terms are related, and the relationship is often seen as to do with brain architecture, with the dichotomies reflecting basic divisions within the brain that were arrived at with the modern human. Broadly, the first term of each of these binary distinctions is associated with early phylogenetic features, and the second term with later features. Also, broadly, the second terms taken together are usually seen as constitutive of human uniqueness. We have arrived back at Rodin's thinker: the reflective, reasoning primate whose detached gazes on the world are intended to scrutinise it so as to understand it and who expresses those understandings in a language. As we have argued, in fact it is evolutionary forces acting on dexterity that created the basis for layers of cultural adaptations which we now refer to with terms such as 'thought', 'understanding' and 'language'. Psychology and cognitive science have often tended to conflate these and see the cultural adaptations as brain adaptations and, moreover, see them as core. This is a confusion that has seriously clouded our understanding of just what it is that human brains do.

As we pointed out in the early chapters, most of our actions are highly skilled and depend on a synergic coupling of a body with objects, including other bodies, and events in the world during development. We look, walk, reach, grasp, catch, talk, hear, because our growing body was trained to do so as a result of immersion in a material and social culture. Clearly such behaviours are likely to be classified as ready to hand, fast, implicit, low level, system 1 and so forth. Others, are equally obviously present at hand, slow, explicit, high level and system 2. Examples might be: solving a crossword puzzle, deciding which way to vote in a referendum and gazing at a work of art. Yet a great many other behaviours appear not to fit such a binary scheme. Moving a heavy piece of furniture with another person may depend on a constantly varying mix of skilled sensorimotor coordination with explicit decision making and joint problem-solving; such as will it fit through that opening if we tilt it slightly?

---

[4] A distinction made by Daniel Kahneman (2012) which broadly captures intuitive and deliberative mental processing.

The point is that any particular behaviour in the world depends on a variety of resources and their contributions will vary moment to moment and with skill levels. An alternative way of approaching distinctions between mental states and processes, which avoids the gross binary classification and is suggested by our discussions here, is to consider three fundamental and intertwined contributions to our behavioural capacities, combined with an understanding of their social context. These contributions are a core sensorimotor system, the agents' level of skill and the degree of dependence on in the world entities, including symbol and representational systems. Any particular act will depend on different 'mixes' and a taxonomy of actions based on analyses of these distinctions will yield a spectrum of mental states or processes rather than a stark binary classification.

A taxonomy of actions of this sort produces different ways of understanding brain architecture, particularly in light of our increasing awareness of its plasticity. Rather than a fixed architecture, perhaps with a distinction between early and late contributions from evolution, there must be multiple layers. These will include contributions from the deep history of our species, but also from far more recent times, as we adapted to new ways of, essentially, making our livings and also, most importantly, with contributions from the developmental history of an individual. A strictly modular organisation is not tenable given these insights, which appear to favour instead a highly interactive neural organisation with networks participating in many different mental processes and recombining in news ways to allow adaptations in response to changes in its milieu (Anderson, 2014).

A Research Programme for Embodied Cognitive Science

The stated original intent of this text was to describe a frame that captures a unified embodied theory of human cognition. Condensed to its essentials the view we have arrived at might be described as follows. Human cognition is best understood as the means by which exchanges within a constantly evolving network of skilful bodies and objects are regulated so as to further human interests. If this framework is adopted it follows that the questions that determine research programs will change. This final section will simply list what seem fruitful questions that need answers under our new frame and related changes required in our scientific practices so as to address them.

There are a huge number of unanswered questions about human sensorimotor capacities, largely because the recognition that perception and action are, effectively, inseparable is only just becoming widely accepted. What is happening in the human brain, for instance, when the person, whose brain it is, moves and acts on objects jointly with others? There are such enquiries (some of which we have described here, obviously) but they are rare compared with those investigating perception in empty handed and lone individuals. Also, studies of the human motor system are almost entirely segregated from work in the perceptual sciences. It should be obvious that participants need to be liberated from the psychophysics and motor control laboratories or the laboratories need to become immersive. Perception and action needs to be investigated in fully engaged agents, moving and acting in an ecologically valid environment. This is undoubtedly hard but becoming a realistic possibility given developments such as immersive technologies and wireless EEG devices that provide new opportunities for data collection in ecologically valid contexts.

We require a taxonomy of actions to replace our taxonomy of mental terms which are mostly folklore derived. The mental verbs remember, believe, decide, see, hear, feel, think, recognise, understand, know, imagine, aware and so forth, are examples of our cultural toolkit that allows us to comment on, and make sense of, our own and others' behaviours. Cognitive science has tended to purloin them, often regarding each as referring to a homogeneous mental phenomenon. Attempts to project some of them onto specific brain functions have repeatedly failed. At this point it is not clear what a taxonomy of human action would look like, but maybe a glimpse is offered by our discussions of whole-body and hand actions in the early chapters. The notion of toolspace could be regarded as an attempt to construct a category of action, being specific to actions undertaken, with or in the absence of others, on objects within the effective space of an agent. This is a particularly interesting case because the 'effective space' is constantly changing with technical innovations in our material culture.

Given that human bodies, brains and cultures co-evolve, understanding how and in what way they do so requires an ending of the demarcation of traditional scientific disciplines. In particular anthropology and cognitive science must talk more, to each other. This cannot be better expressed than in the following quotation:

I can see no further intellectual justification for continuing to separate these disciplines. For we now recognise that such processes as thinking, perceiving, remembering and learning have to be studied within the ecological contexts of people's interrelations with their environments. We recognise, too, that the mind and its properties are not given in advance of the individual's entry into the world but are rather fashioned through a lifelong history of involvement in relationships with others ... And the discipline that will be called into being ... will be the study of how people perceive, act, think, know, learn and remember within the settings of their mutual, practical involvement in the lived-in world. (Ingold, 2000: 171)

The power of the integration of anthropology and cognitive science was also glimpsed in this text in those descriptions of consequent brain adaptations in those learning to knap stone tools. Given skilled activity in general is a key to our unmediated access to the world and in understanding differences between cultures, far more attention should be devoted to how skills are acquired and how they expand the world of those who possess them. These are questions that cannot be answered from solely within any of the existing disciplines. Also, more generally, cognitive science has to stop investigating only populations of the WEIRD (Henrich, Heine and Norenzayan, 2010). If we now accept the co-evolution idea, it is clearly important that we ask questions about how human cognition varies across cultures. This seems particularly important in the case of language use, were the notion of it being a universal symbol system reflecting universal properties of the brains of *Homo sapiens* is rejected according to the new frame we advocate here.[5]

The growing realisation of the extent of neural plasticity, and its key place in the new frame, prompt questions about brain adaptations over a range of timescales: over generations, within individual development and moment to moment. We have little idea about how these, now key, processes work and to what degree they can be distinguished from each other or to what degree they are interrelated. For example, what are the origins of the multiple-demand brain networks that Duncan has described as implicated in multiple cognitive functions and allow an agent to assemble subtasks into sequences (Duncan and Owen, 2000)? Are they the outcome of being raised as a member of one of those WEIRD populations, and therefore drilled, during a formal education, in exercises that consist of tasks ordered into sequences of subtasks? Or do they have earlier origins in the brains of ancestors who mastered the skilful transformation of physical materials into artefacts?

Cognitive science has, almost, wholly ignored the role of affect in human cognition, as has, it must be confessed, this text.[6] Yet another key element of the new frame we have sort is that humans are uniquely, and necessarily, engaged with other humans. An ancillary element of the social brain hypothesis draws attention to the importance of the affective bonding that occurs between members of human groups. The role of

---

[5] Among the many implications it does suggest that the Sapir–Whorf hypothesis might be worth revisiting.

[6] Damasio (2006), Rizzolatti and Sinigaglia (2010), and Hufendiek (2016) are examples of exceptions to this tendency.

emotions in regulating relations among humans, and hence human cognition, has been largely ignored in cognitive science until recently. Even in simple shared tasks, however, one human being seems to have an emotional disposition to work with and help another, something that is largely lacking in other animals. Understanding the affective dimension of joint action and its role in cementing and regulating the 'network of skilful bodies and objects' must be added to the list of questions to be addressed.

One final remark: a consequence of the arguments and evidence offered in this text is that modern humans are not finished yet, in the sense they will continue to adapt to their material and social cultures. Moreover, many of the adaptations will be the result of elaborations of our developmental niche as a result of human technological and social innovations. It follows that we will continue to make ourselves. That we now understand this is the case is a profound insight carrying with it a huge burden of responsibility. Should we not now attempt to understand what the way-points of the trajectories currently open to us might be like?

References

All URLs accessed June 2018.

Abrams, R. A., Davoli, C. C., Du, F., Knapp, W. H., and Paull, D. (2008). Altered vision near the hands. *Cognition, 107*(3), 1035–1047.

Ackley, D. H., Hinton, G. E., and Sejnowski, T. J. (1985). A learning algorithm for Boltzmann machines. *Cognitive Science, 9*(1), 147–169.

Allport, D. A. (1987). Selection for action. *Perspectives on Perception and Action, 15,* 395–419.

Ambrose, S. H. (2001). Paleolithic technology and human evolution. *Science, 291* (5509), 1748–1753.

Anderson, M. L. (2003). Embodied cognition: A field guide. *Artificial Intelligence, 149*(1), 91–130.

(2010). Neural reuse: A fundamental organizational principle of the brain. *Behavioral and Brain Sciences, 33*(4), 245–266.

(2014). *After Phrenology.* Cambridge, MA: MIT Press.

Ansuini, C., Cavallo, A., Bertone, C., and Becchio, C. (2014). The visible face of intention: Why kinematics matters. *Frontiers in Psychology, 5.*

Appadurai, A. (1988). *The Social Life of Things: Commodities in Cultural Perspective.* Cambridge: Cambridge University Press.

Arbib, M. A. (2005). From monkey-like action recognition to human language: An evolutionary framework for neurolinguistics. *Behavioral and Brain Sciences, 28*(02), 105–124.

(2011). From mirror neurons to complex imitation in the evolution of language and tool use. *Annual Review of Anthropology, 40,* 257–273.

Bach, P., Bayliss, A. P., and Tipper, S. P. (2011). The predictive mirror: Interactions of mirror and affordance processes during action observation. *Psychonomic Bulletin and Review, 18*(1), 171–176.

Bach-y-Rita, P., Collins, C. C., Saunders, S. A., White, B., and Scadden, L. (1969) Vision substitution by tactile image projection. *Nature, 221,* 963–964.

Bach-y-Rita, P (1972). *Brain Mechanisms in Sensory Substitution.* New York: Academic Press.

Badyaev, A. V. (2009). Evolutionary significance of phenotypic accommodation in novel environments: An empirical test of the Baldwin effect. *Philosophical Transactions of the Royal Society B: Biological Sciences, 364*(1520), 1125–1141.

Bak, T. H., and Hodges, J. R. (2004). The effects of motor neurone disease on language: Further evidence. *Brain and Language, 89*(2), 354–361.

Baldwin, J. M. (1896). A new factor in evolution. *American Naturalist, 30*(354), 441–451.

Baldwin, T. (2007). *Reading Merleau-Ponty: On Phenomenology of Perception.* London and New York: Routledge.

Bangert, M., and Altenmüller, E. O. (2003). Mapping perception to action in piano practice: A longitudinal DC-EEG study. *BMC Neuroscience, 4*(1), 26.

Barsalou, L. W., Simmons, W. K., Barbey, A. K., and Wilson, C. D. (2003). Grounding conceptual knowledge in modality-specific systems. *Trends in Cognitive Sciences, 7*(2), 84–91.

Barsalou, L. W., Solomon, K. O., and Wu, L.-L. (1999). Perceptual simulation in conceptual tasks. *Amsterdam Studies in the Theory and History of Linguistic Science, Series* 4, 209–228.

Barton, R. A., and Dunbar, R. I. (1997). Evolution of the social brain. In A. Whiten and R. W. Byrne (eds.), *Machiavellian Intelligence II: Extensions and Evaluations* (pp. 240–263). New York: Cambridge University Press.

Bartra, R. (2014). *Anthropology of the Brain: Consciousness, Culture, and Free Will.* Cambridge: Cambridge University Press.

Bassolino, M., Serino, A., Ubaldi, S., and Làdavas, E. (2010). Everyday use of the computer mouse extends peripersonal space representation. *Neuropsychologia, 48*(3), 803–811.

Becchio, C., Sartori, L., Bulgheroni, M., and Castiello, U. (2008). The case of Dr. Jekyll and Mr. Hyde: A kinematic study on social intention. *Consciousness and Cognition, 7*(3), 557–564.

Beer, R. D. (2014). Dynamical systems and embedded cognition. In K. Frankish and W. M. Ramsey (eds), *The Cambridge Handbook of Artificial Intelligence* (pp. 856–873). New York: Cambridge University Press.

Behne, T., Carpenter, M., and Tomasello, M. (2014). Young children create iconic gestures to inform others. *Developmental Psychology, 50*(8), 2049–2060.

Bernardis, P., and Gentilucci, M. (2006). Speech and gesture share the same communication system. *Neuropsychologia, 44*(2), 178–190.

Berti, A., and Frassinetti, F. (2000). When far becomes near: Remapping of space by tool use. *Journal of Cognitive Neuroscience, 12(3)*, 415–420.

Binkofski, F., and Buccino, G. (2004). Motor functions of the Broca's region. *Brain and Language, 89*(2), 362–369.

Biro, D., Haslam, M., and Rutz, C. (2013). Tool use as adaptation. *Philosophical Transactions of the Royal Society B*, 368(1630) http://rstb.royalsocietypublish ing.org/content/368/1630/20120408

Blench, R. (2010). The sensory world: Ideophones in Africa and elsewhere. In A. Storch (ed.), *Perception of the Invisible: Religion, Historical Semantics and the Role of Perceptive Verbs, Sprache und Geschichte in Afrika* (pp. 275–296). Cologne: Köppe.

Borghi and Riggio (2009). Sentence comprehension and simulation of objects temporary, canonical and stable affordances. *Brain Research, 1253*, 117–128.

  (2015). Stable and variable affordances are both automatic and flexible. *Frontiers in Human Neuroscience, 9*, 351.

Bourdieu, P. (1977). *Outline of a Theory of Practice*. Cambridge: Cambridge University Press.

(1990). *The Logic of Practice*. Stanford, CA: Stanford University Press.

Brass, M., Bekkering, H., Wohlschläger, A., and Prinz, W. (2000). Compatibility between observed and executed finger movements: Comparing symbolic, spatial, and imitative cues. *Brain and Cognition*, *44*(2), 124–143.

Broadbent, D. E. (2013). *Perception and Communication*. Oxford: Pergamon Press.

Brooks, R., and Meltzoff, A. N. (2002). The importance of eyes: How infants interpret adult looking behavior. *Developmental Psychology*, *38*(6), 958.

(2005). The development of gaze following and its relation to language. *Developmental Science*, *8*(6), 535–543.

Brozzoli, C., Makin, T. R., Cardinali, L., Holmes, N. P., and Farnè, A. (2011). Peripersonal space: A multisensory interface for body–object interactions. In M. M. Murray and M. T. Wallace, M. (eds.), *The Neural Bases of Multisensory Processes* (pp. 449–466). London: Taylor and Francis.

Brozzoli, C., Pavani, F., Urquizar, C., Cardinali, L., and Farnè, A. (2009). Grasping actions remap peripersonal space. *Neuroreport*, *20*(10), 913–917.

Bruineberg, J., Kiverstein, J., and Rietveld, E. (2016). The anticipating brain is not a scientist: The free-energy principle from an ecological–enactive perspective. *Synthese*, 1–28.

Bruineberg, J., and Rietveld, E. (2014). Self-organization, free energy minimization, and optimal grip on a field of affordances. *Frontiers in Human Neuroscience*, *8*, 599.

Buccino, G., and Riggio, L. (2006). The role of the mirror neuron system in motor learning. *Kinesiology*, *38*(1), 5–15.

Buccino, G., Vogt, S., Ritzl, A., Fink, G. R., Zilles, K., Freund, H.-J., and Rizzolatti, G. (2004). Neural circuits underlying imitation learning of hand actions: An event-related fMRI study. *Neuron*, *42*(2), 323–334.

Buxbaum, L. J., Sirigu, A., Schwartz, M. F., and Klatzky, R. (2003). Cognitive representations of hand posture in ideomotor apraxia. *Neuropsychologia*, *41* (8), 1091–1113.

Caggiano, V., Fogassi, L., Rizzolatti, G., Pomper, J. K., Thier, P., Giese, M. A., and Casile, A. (2011). View-based encoding of actions in mirror neurons of area f5 in macaque premotor cortex. *Current Biology*, *21*(2), 144–148.

Caggiano, V., Fogassi, L., Rizzolatti, G., Thier, P., and Casile, A. (2009). Mirror neurons differentially encode the peripersonal and extrapersonal space of monkeys. *Science*, *324*(5925), 403–406.

Campbell, F. W., and Robson, J. G. (1968). Application of Fourier analysis to the visibility of gratings. *Journal of Physiology*, *197*(3), 551–566.

Carey, D. P., Harvey, M., and Milner, A. D. (1996). Visuomotor sensitivity for shape and orientation in a patient with visual form agnosia. *Neuropsychologia*, *34*(5), 329–337.

Carpenter, M., Tomasello, M., and Striano, T. (2005). Role reversal imitation and language in typically developing infants and children with autism. *Infancy*, *8*(3), 253–278.

Catmur, C., Gillmeister, H., Bird, G., Liepelt, R., Brass, M., and Heyes, C. (2008). Through the looking glass: Counter-mirror activation following incompatible sensorimotor learning. *European Journal of Neuroscience, 28* (6), 1208–1215.

Catmur, C., Walsh, V., and Heyes, C. (2007). Sensorimotor learning configures the human mirror system. *Current Biology, 17*(17), 1527–1531.

Cavallo, A., Koul, A., Ansuini, C., Capozzi, F., and Becchio, C. (2016). Decoding intentions from movement kinematics. *Scientific Reports, 6.*

Chalmers, D. J. (1995). Facing up to the problem of consciousness. *Journal of Consciousness Studies, 2*(3), 200–219.

Chartrand, T. L., and Bargh, J. A. (1999). The chameleon effect: The perception–behavior link and social interaction. *Journal of Personality and Social Psychology, 76*(6), 893–910.

Chen, C. C., Henson, R. N., Stephan, K. E., Kilner, J. M., and Friston, K. J. (2009). Forward and backward connections in the brain: A DCM study of functional asymmetries. *NeuroImage, 45,* 453–462.

Chomsky, N. (1959). A review of B. F. Skinner's *Verbal Behavior. Language, 35* (1), 26–58.

Clark, A. (2008). *Supersizing the Mind: Embodiment, Action, and Cognitive Extension.* New York: Oxford University Press.
  (2013). Whatever next? Predictive brains, situated agents, and the future of cognitive science. *Behavioral and Brain Sciences, 36*(03), 181–204.

Clark, A., and Chalmers, D. (1998). The extended mind. *Analysis, 58*(1), 7–19.

Clark, H. H. (1996). *Using Language.* Cambridge: Cambridge University Press.

Cook, R., Bird, G., Catmur, C., Press, C., and Heyes, C. (2014). Mirror neurons: From origin to function. *Behavioral and Brain Sciences, 37*(02), 177–192.

Corballis, M. C. (2003). From mouth to hand: Gesture, speech, and the evolution of right-handedness. *Behavioral and Brain Sciences, 26*(02), 199–208.
  (2010). Mirror neurons and the evolution of language. *Brain and Language, 112* (1), 25–35.

Costantini, M., Ambrosini, E., Sinigaglia, C., and Gallese, V. (2011). Tool-use observation makes far objects ready-to-hand. *Neuropsychologia, 49*(9), 2658–2663.

Costantini, M., Ambrosini, E., Tieri, G., Sinigaglia, C., and Committeri, G. (2010). Where does an object trigger an action? An investigation about affordances in space. *Experimental Brain Research, 207*(1–2), 95–103.

Costantini, M., Committeri, G., and Sinigaglia, C. (2011). Ready both to your and to my hands: Mapping the action space of others. *PloS One, 6*(4), e17923.

Costantini, M., and Ferri, F. (2013). Action co-representation and social exclusion. *Experimental Brain Research, 227*(1), 85–92.

Costantini, M., Frassinetti, F., Maini, M., Ambrosini, E., Gallese, V., and Sinigaglia, C. (2014). When a laser pen becomes a stick: Remapping of space by tool-use observation in hemispatial neglect. *Experimental Brain Research, 232*(10), 3233–3241.

Creem, S. H., and Proffitt, D. R. (2001). Grasping objects by their handles: A necessary interaction between cognition and action. *Journal of Experimental Psychology: Human Perception and Performance, 27*(1), 218.

Csibra, G. (2008). Action mirroring and action understanding: An alternative account. *Sensorimotor Foundations of Higher Cognition. Attention and Performance, 22*, 435–459.

Damasio, A. R. (2006). *Descartes' Error: Emotion, Reason and the Human Brain.* New York: Penguin.

Davidson, I., Noble, W., Gibson, K. R., Ingold, T., and Leavens, D. A. (1993). Tools and language in human evolution. In K. Gibson and T. Ingold (eds.), *Tools, Language, and Cognition in Human Evolution* (pp. 363–388). Cambridge: Cambridge University Press.

de Gelder, B. (2016). *Emotions and the Body.* New York: Oxford University Press.

De Vignemont, F., and Iannetti, G. D. (2015). How many peripersonal spaces? *Neuropsychologia, 70*, 327–334.

Dennett, D. C. (1993). *Consciousness Explained.* New York: Penguin.

Di Paolo, E. A., and Thompson, E. (2014). The enactive approach. In L. Shapiro (ed.), *The Routledge Handbook of Embodied Cognition* (pp. 68–78). Oxford: Routledge.

Dove, G. (2014). Thinking in words: Language as an embodied medium of thought. *Topics in Cognitive Science, 6*(3), 371–389.

Draganski, B., Gaser, C., Busch, V., Schuierer, G., Bogdahn, U., and May, A. (2004). Neuroplasticity: Changes in grey matter induced by training. *Nature, 427*(6972), 311–312.

Dreyfus, H. L. (1972). *What Computers Can't Do.* New York: Harper & Row.

(1992). *What Computers Still Can't Do: A Critique of Artificial Reason.* Cambridge, MA: MIT Press.

(2002). Intelligence without representation – Merleau-Ponty's critique of mental representation the relevance of phenomenology to scientific explanation. *Phenomenology and the Cognitive Sciences, 1*(4), 367–383.

(2007). Why Heideggerian AI failed and how fixing it would require making it more Heideggerian. *Artificial Intelligence, 171*(18), 1137–1160.

Droll, J. A., Hayhoe, M. M., Triesch, J., and Sullivan, B. T. (2005). Task demands control acquisition and storage of visual information. *Journal of Experimental Psychology: Human Perception and Performance, 31*(6), 1416–1438.

Dunbar, R. I. (2009). The social brain hypothesis and its implications for social evolution. *Annals of Human Biology, 36*(5), 562–572.

Dunbar, R. I., and Shultz, S. (2007). Understanding primate brain evolution. *Philosophical Transactions of the Royal Society B: Biological Sciences, 362*(1480), 649–658.

Duncan, J. (2010). The multiple-demand (MD) system of the primate brain: mental programs for intelligent behaviour. *Trends in Cognitive Sciences, 14*(4), 172–179.

Duncan, J., and Owen, A. M. (2000). Common regions of the human frontal lobe recruited by diverse cognitive demands. *Trends in Neurosciences, 23*(10), 475–483.

Duncan, J., Seitz, R. J., Kolodny, J., Bor, D., Herzog, H., Ahmed, A., Newell, F. N., and Emsilie, H. (2000). A neural basis for general intelligence. *Science*, *289*(5478), 457–460.

Edelman, G. M. (1993). Neural Darwinism: Selection and reentrant signaling in higher brain function. *Neuron*, *10*(2), 115–125.

Egly, R., Driver, J., and Rafal, R. D. (1994). Shifting visual attention between objects and locations: Evidence from normal and parietal lesion subjects. *Journal of Experimental Psychology General*, 123, 161–177.

Ellis, R., and Humphreys, G. W. (1999). *Connectionist Psychology: A Text with Readings*. New York: Psychology Press.

Ellis, R., Swabey, D., Bridgeman, J., May, B., Tucker, M., and Hyne, A. (2013). Bodies and other visual objects: The dialectics of reaching toward objects. *Psychological Research*, *77*(1), 31–39.

Ellis, R., and Tucker, M. (2000). Micro-affordance: The potentiation of components of action by seen objects. *British Journal of Psychology*, *91*(4), 451–471.

Ellis, R., Tucker, M., Symes, E., and Vainio, L. (2007). Does selecting one visual object from several require inhibition of the actions associated with nonselected objects? *Journal of Experimental Psychology: Human Perception and Performance*, *33*(3), 670–691.

Evans, N., and Levinson, S. C. (2009). The myth of language universals: Language diversity and its importance for cognitive science. *Behavioral and Brain Sciences*, *32*(5), 429–448.

Fadiga, L., Fogassi, L., Pavesi, G., and Rizzolatti, G. (1995). Motor facilitation during action observation: A magnetic stimulation study. *Journal of neurophysiology*, *73*(6), 2608–2611.

Fazio, P., Cantagallo, A., Craighero, L., D'Ausilio, A., Roy, A. C., Pozzo, T., Fadiga, L., and others (2009). Encoding of human action in Broca's area. *Brain*, *132*(7), 1980–1988.

Fedorenko, E., Duncan, J., and Kanwisher, N. (2012). Language-selective and domain-general regions lie side by side within Broca's area. *Current Biology*, *22*(21), 2059–2062.

Fischer, M. H., and Zwaan, R. A. (2008). Embodied language: A review of the role of the motor system in language comprehension. *Quarterly Journal of Experimental Psychology*, *61*(6), 825–850.

Fodor, J. A. (1975). *The Language of Thought*. Cambridge, MA: Harvard University Press.

Fodor, J. A., and Pylyshyn, Z. W. (1981). How direct is visual perception?: Some reflections on Gibson's 'ecological approach'. *Cognition*, *9*(2), 139–196.

Fogassi, L., Ferrari, P. F., Gesierich, B., Rozzi, S., Chersi, F., and Rizzolatti, G. (2005). Parietal lobe: From action organization to intention understanding. *Science*, *308*(5722), 662–667.

Frey, S. H. (2007). What puts the how in where? Tool use and the divided visual streams hypothesis. *Cortex*, *43*(3), 368–375.

Freyd, J. J., and Finke, R. A. (1984). Representational momentum. *Journal of Experimental Psychology: Learning, Memory, and Cognition*, *10*(1), 126.

Friston, K. (2005). A theory of cortical responses. *Philosophical Transactions of the Royal Society of London B: Biological Sciences*, *360*(1456), 815–836.

(2009). The free-energy principle: A rough guide to the brain? *Trends in Cognitive Sciences, 13*(7), 293–301.

(2010). The free-energy principle: A unified brain theory? *Nature Reviews Neuroscience, 11*(2), 127–138.

(2011). What is optimal about motor control? *Neuron, 72*(3), 488–498.

Friston, K., Daunizeau, J., Kilner, J. and Kiebel, S.J. (2010). Action and behavior: A free-energy formulation. *Biological cybernetics, 102*(3), 227–260.

Friston, K., Kilner, J., and Harrison, L. (2006). A free energy principle for the brain. *Journal of Physiology-Paris, 100*(1), 70–87.

Friston, K., Shiner, T., FitzGerald, T., Galea, J. M., Adams, R., Brown, H., Dolan, R. J., Moran, R., Stephan, K. E. and Bestmann, S. (2012). Dopamine, affordance and active inference. *PLoS Comput Biol, 8*(1), e1002327.

Fuentes, A. (2015). Integrative anthropology and the human niche: Toward a contemporary approach to human evolution. *American Anthropologist, 117* (2), 302–315.

Gallagher, S., and Zahavi, D. (2013). *The Phenomenological Mind.* Oxford: Routledge.

Gallese, V., Fadiga, L., Fogassi, L., and Rizzolatti, G. (1996). Action recognition in the premotor cortex. *Brain, 119*(2), 593–610.

Gamble, C. (2007). *Origins and Revolutions: Human Identity in Earliest Prehistory.* Cambridge: Cambridge University Press.

Gamble, C., Gowlett, J., and Dunbar, R. (2011). The social brain and the shape of the Palaeolithic. *Cambridge Archaeological Journal, 21*(01), 115–136.

Garrod, S., and Pickering, M. J. (2009). Joint action, interactive alignment, and dialog. *Topics in Cognitive Science, 1*(2), 292–304.

Gell, A. (1992). The technology of enchantment and the enchantment of technology. In J. Coote and A. Shelton (eds.), *Anthropology, Art and Aesthetics* (pp. 40–63). Oxford: Clarendon Press.

(1998). *Art and Agency: An Anthropological Theory.* Oxford: Oxford University Press.

Georgiou, I., Becchio, C., Glover, S., and Castiello, U. (2007). Different action patterns for cooperative and competitive behaviour. *Cognition, 102*(3), 415–433.

Gerbault, P., Liebert, A., Itan, Y., Powell, A., Currat, M., Burger, J., Thomas, M. G., and others (2011). Evolution of lactase persistence: An example of human niche construction. *Philosophical Transactions of the Royal Society of London B: Biological Sciences, 366*(1566), 863–877.

Geschwind, N. (1970). The organization of language and the brain. *Science,* 170 (3961), 940–944.

Gibson, J. J. (2014). *The Ecological Approach to Visual Perception: Classic Edition.* New York and Hove: Psychology Press.

Gibson, K. R., Gibson, K. R., and Ingold, T. (1994). *Tools, Language and Cognition in Human Evolution.* Cambridge: Cambridge University Press.

Gindrat, A.-D., Chytiris, M., Balerna, M., Rouiller, E. M., and Ghosh, A. (2015). Use-dependent cortical processing from fingertips in touchscreen phone users. *Current Biology, 25*(1), 109–116.

Gislén, A., Dacke, M., Kröger, R. H. H., Abrahamsson, M., Nisson, D. and Warrant, E. J. (2003). Superior underwater vision in a human population of sea gypsies. *Current Biology*, *13*(10), 833–836.

Glenberg, A. M., and Kaschak, M. P. (2002). Grounding language in action. *Psychonomic Bulletin and Review*, *9*(3), 558–565.

Godfrey-Smith, P. (2017). Senders, receivers, and symbolic artifacts. *Biological Theory*, *12*(4), 275–286.

Goldenberg, G., Hermsdörfer, J., Glindemann, R., Rorden, C., and Karnath, H.-O. (2007). Pantomime of tool use depends on integrity of left inferior frontal cortex. *Cerebral Cortex*, *17*(12), 2769–2776.

Goldin-Meadow, S. (2005). *Hearing Gesture: How Our Hands Help Us Think*. Cambridge, MA: Harvard University Press.

Gonçalves, B., Perra, N., and Vespignani, A. (2011). Modeling users' activity on twitter networks: Validation of Dunbar's number. *PloS One*, *6*(8), e22656.

González-Perilli, F., and Ellis, R. (2015). I don't get you: Action observation effects inverted by kinematic variation. *Acta Psychologica*, *157*, 114–121.

Goodale, M. A., and Graves, J. A. (1982). Retinal locus as a factor in interocular transfer in the pigeon. In D. J. Ingle, M. A. Goodale, and R. J. W. Mansfield (eds.), *Analysis of Visual Behavior* (pp. 211–240). Cambridge, MA: MIT Press.

Goodale, M. A., and Humphrey, G. K. (1998). The objects of action and perception. *Cognition*, *67*(1–2), 181–207.

Goodale, M. A., Milner, A. D., Jakobson, L. S., and Carey, D. P. (1991). A neurological dissociation between perceiving objects and grasping them. *Nature*, *349*, 154–156.

Goslin, J., Dixon, T., Fischer, M. H., Cangelosi, A., and Ellis, R. (2012). Electrophysiological examination of embodiment in vision and action. *Psychological Science*, *23*(2), 152–157.

Gould, S. J., and Vrba, E. S. (1982). Exaptation – A missing term in the science of form. *Paleobiology*, *8*(01), 4–15.

Grafton, S. T. (2010). The cognitive neuroscience of prehension: Recent developments. *Experimental Brain Research*, *204*(4), 475–491.

Greenfield, P., Andreae, J., Ryan, S., Pepperbert, I., Westergaaard, G., and Pinon, P (1994). Language, tools, and brain: The ontogeny and phylogeny of hierarchically organized sequential behavior. *Behavioral and Brain Sciences*, *17*(2), 357–365.

Greenfield, P. M. (1991). From hand to mouth. *Behavioral and Brain Sciences*, *14*(04), 577–595.

(1998). Language, tools, and brain revisited. *Behavioral and Brain Sciences*, *21*(01), 159–163.

Grèzes, J., Costes, N., and Decety, J. (1998). Top down effect of strategy on the perception of human biological motion: A PET investigation. *Cognitive Neuropsychology*, *15*(6–8), 553–582.

Guan, C. Q., Meng, W., Yao, R., and Glenberg, A. M. (2013). The motor system contributes to comprehension of abstract language. *PloS One*, *8*(9), e75183.

Guiard, Y. (1987). Asymmetric division of labor in human skilled bimanual action: The kinematic chain as a model. *Journal of Motor Behavior*, *19*(4), 486–517.

Hagoort, P. (2005). On Broca, brain, and binding: A new framework. *Trends in Cognitive Sciences*, *9*(9), 416–423.

Halligan, P. W., Fink, G. R., Marshall, J. C., and Vallar, G. (2003). Spatial cognition: Evidence from visual neglect. *Trends in Cognitive Sciences*, *7*(3), 125–133.

Halligan, P. W., and Marshall, J. C. (1991). Left neglect for near but not far space in man. *Nature*, *350*(6318), 498–500.

Handy, T. C., and Mangun, G. R. (2000). Attention and spatial selection: Electrophysiological evidence for modulation by perceptual load. *Perception and Psychophysics*, 62, 175–186.

Hauser, M. D., Chomsky, N., and Fitch, W. T. (2002). The faculty of language: What is it, who has it, and how did it evolve? *Science*, *298*(5598), 1569–1579.

Hecht, E. E., Gutman, D. A., Khreisheh, N., Taylor, S. V., Kilner, J., Faisal, A. A., Bradley, B. A., Chaminade, T., and Stout, D. B. (2014). Acquisition of Paleolithic toolmaking abilities involves structural remodeling to inferior frontoparietal regions. *Brain Structure and Function*, 220, 2315–2331.

Heft, H. (2003). Affordances, dynamic experience, and the challenge of reification. *Ecological Psychology*, *15*(2), 149–180.

Heidegger, M. (1962 [1927]). *Being and Time*. Trans. John Macquarrie and Edward Robinson. New York: Harper.

Helmholtz, H. von. (1860). Theorie der Luftschwingungen in Röhren mit offenen Enden. *Journal Für Die Reine Und Angewandte Mathematik*, *57*, 1–72.

Henrich, J., Heine, S. J., and Norenzayan, A. (2010). The weirdest people in the world? *Behavioral and Brain Sciences*, *33*(2–3), 61–83.

Hinton, G. (2014). Where do features come from? *Cognitive Science*, *38*(6), 1078–1101.

Hinton, G. E., Dayan, P., Frey, B. J., and Neal, R. M. (1995). The 'wake–sleep' algorithm for unsupervised neural networks. *Science*, *268*(5214), 1158–1161.

Hinton, G. E., and Nowlan, S. J. (1987). How learning can guide evolution. *Complex Systems*, *1*(3), 495–502.

Hinton, G. E., Osindero, S., and Teh, Y.-W. (2006). A fast learning algorithm for deep belief nets. *Neural Computation*, *18*(7), 1527–1554.

Hinton, G. E., and Sejnowski, T. J. (1986). Learning and relearning in Boltzmann machines. In D. E. Rumelhart and J. L. McClelland (eds.), *Parallel Distributed Processing: Explorations in Microstructures of Cognition* (pp. 282–317). Cambridge, MA: MIT Press.

Hiscock, P. (2014). Learning in lithic landscapes: A reconsideration of the hominid 'toolmaking' niche. *Biological Theory*, *9*(1), 27–41.

Hohwy, J. (2007). Functional Integration and the mind. *Synthese*, *159*(3), 315–328.

(2013). *The Predictive Mind*. Oxford: Oxford University Press.

Hommel, B., Colzato, L. S., and Van Den Wildenberg, W. P. (2009). How social are task representations? *Psychological Science*, *20*(7), 794–798.

Hudson, M., Nicholson, T., Ellis, R., and Bach, P. (2015). I see what you say: Prior knowledge of others' goals automatically biases the perception of their actions. *Cognition, 146*, 245–250.

Hudson, M., Nicholson, T., Simpson, W. A., Ellis, R., and Bach, P. (2016). One step ahead: The perceived kinematics of others' actions are biased toward expected goals. *Journal of Experimental Psychology: General, 145*(1), 1.

Hufendiek, R. (2016). *Embodied Emotions: A Naturalist Approach to a Normative Phenomenon*. New York: Routledge.

Humphrey, N. K. (1974). Vision in a monkey without striate cortex: A case study. *Perception, 3*(3), 241–255.

Humphrey, N. K. and Weiskrantz, L. (1967). Vision in monkeys after removal of the striate cortex. *Nature, 215*, 595–597.

Humphreys, G. W., and Riddoch, J. R. (2001). Detection by action: Neuropsychological evidence for action-defined templates in search. *Nature Neuroscience, 4*(1), 84–88.

Humphreys, G. W., Yoon, E. Y., Kumar, S., Lestou, V., Kitadono, K., Roberts, K. L., and Riddoch, M. J. (2010). The interaction of attention and action: From seeing action to acting on perception. *British Journal of Psychology, 101*(2), 185–206.

Hurley, S., and Chater, N. (eds.) (2005). *Imitation, Human Development and Culture (Vol. 2)*. Cambridge, MA: MIT Press.

Hutchins, E. (1995). *Cognition in the Wild*. Cambridge, MA: MIT Press.

Iacoboni, M., Molnar-Szakacs, I., Gallese, V., Buccino, G., Mazziotta, J. C., Rizzolatti, G., and others. (2005). Grasping the intentions of others with one's own mirror neuron system. *PLoS Biol, 3*(3), e79.

Iacoboni, M., Woods, R. P., Brass, M., Bekkering, H., Mazziotta, J. C., and Rizzolatti, G. (1999). Cortical mechanisms of human imitation. *Science, 286* (5449), 2526–2528.

Ingold, T. (2000). *The Perception of the Environment: Essays on Livelihood, Dwelling and Skill*. London and New York: Routledge.

  (2013). *Making: Anthropology, Archaeology, Art and Architecture*. London and New York: Routledge.

Iriki, A., Tanaka, M., and Iwamura, Y. (1996). Coding of modified body schema during tool use by macaque postcentral neurones. *Neuroreport, 7*(14), 2325–2330.

Jakobson, L. S., Archibald, Y. M., Carey, D. P., and Goodale, M. A. (1991). A kinematic analysis of reaching and grasping movements in a patient recovering from optic ataxia. *Neuropsychologia, 29*(8), 803–809.

Jeannerod, M. (1981). Intersegmental coordination during reaching at natural visual objects. *Attention and Performance IX, 9*, 153–168.

  (1988) *The Neural and Behavioral Organization of Goal-Directed Movements*. Oxford: Clarendon Press.

Kahneman, D. (2012). *Thinking, Fast and Slow*. New York: Penguin.

Kendal, J., Tehrani, J. J., and Odling-Smee, J. (2011). Human niche construction in interdisciplinary focus. *Philosophical Transactions of the Royal Society B, 366*, 785–792.

Kilner, J. M., Friston, K. J., and Frith, C. D. (2007). The mirror-neuron system: A Bayesian perspective. *Neuroreport*, *18*(6), 619–623.

Kirkpatrick, S., Gelatt, C. D., and Vecchi, M. P. (1983). Optimization by simulated annealing. *Science*, *220*(4598), 671–680.

Kita, S. (2009). Cross-cultural variation of speech-accompanying gesture: A review. *Language and Cognitive Processes*, *24*(2), 145–167.

Kivell, T. L., Kibii, J. M., Churchill, S. E., Schmid, P., and Berger, L. R. (2011). Australopithecus sediba hand demonstrates mosaic evolution of locomotor and manipulative abilities. *Science*, *333*(6048), 1411–1417.

Kiverstein, J., and Wheeler, M. (2012). *Heidegger and Cognitive Science*. New York: Palgrave Macmillan.

Koechlin, E., and Jubault, T. (2006). Broca's area and the hierarchical organization of human behavior. *Neuron*, *50*(6), 963–974.

Kohler, E., Keysers, C., Umilta, M. A., Fogassi, L., Gallese, V., and Rizzolatti, G. (2002). Hearing sounds, understanding actions: Action representation in mirror neurons. *Science*, *297*(5582), 846–848.

Kohler, I. (1963). The formation and transformation of the perceptual world. *Psychological Issues*, *3*(4,Monogr. No. 12), 1–173.

Kripke, S. A. (1980). *Naming and Necessity*. Oxford: Blackwell.

Króliczak, G., and Frey, S. H. (2009). A common network in the left cerebral hemisphere represents planning of tool use pantomimes and familiar intransitive gestures at the hand-independent level. *Cerebral Cortex*, *19*(10), 2396–2410.

Kuzawa, C. W., and Bragg, J. M. (2012). Plasticity in human life history strategy: Implications for contemporary human variation and the evolution of genus Homo. *Current Anthropology*, *53*(S6), S369–S382.

Lakatos, I. (1978). *The Methodology of Scientific Research Programmes*. London and New York: Cambridge University Press.

Lakoff, G., and Johnson, M. (1980). The metaphorical structure of the human conceptual system. *Cognitive Science*, *4*(2), 195–208.

Laland, K. N., Uller, T., Feldman, M. W., Sterelny, K., Müller, G. B., Moczek, A., Jablonka, E. and Odling-Smee, J. (2015). The extended evolutionary synthesis: Its structure, assumptions and predictions. *Proceedings of the Royal Society B*, *282*, http://rspb.royalsocietypublishing.org/content/282/1813/20151019

Laland, K., Uller, T., Feldman, M., Sterelny, K., Müller, G. B., Moczek, A., Jablonka, E., Odling-Smee, J., Wray, G. A., Hoekstra, H. E., Futuyma, D. J., Lenski, R. E., Mackay, T. F., Schluter, D., and Strassmann, J. E. (2014). Does evolutionary theory need a rethink? *Nature*, *514*(7521), 161.

Latour, B. (1999). *Pandora's Hope: Essays on the Reality of Science Studies*. Cambridge, MA: Harvard University Press.

(2005). *Reassembling the Social: An Introduction to Actor-Network-Theory*. Oxford: Oxford university press.

(2007). Can we get our materialism back, please? *Isis*, *98*(1), 138–142.

Leakey, M. D. (1971). *Olduvai Gorge, vol. 3*. Cambridge: Cambridge University Press.

Leavens, D. A., and Hopkins, W. D. (2005). Multimodal concomitants of manual gesture by chimpanzees (*Pan troglodytes*): Influence of food size and distance. *Gesture, 5*(1), 75–90.

Leroi-Gourhan, A. (1993). *Gesture and Speech*. Cambridge, MA: MIT Press.

Levin, T. L., and Simons, D. J. (1997). Failure to detect changes to attended objects in motion pictures. *Psychonomic Bulletin and Review, 4*(4), 501–506.

Leyton, A. S., and Sherrington, C. S. (1917). Observations on the excitable cortex of the chimpanzee, orang-utan and gorilla. *Quarterly Journal of Experimental Physiology, 11*(2), 135–222.

Liberman, A. M., and Mattingly, I. G. (1985). The motor theory of speech perception revised. *Cognition, 21*(1), 1–36.

Linell, P. (2004). *The Written Language Bias in Linguistics: Its Nature, Origins and Transformations*. London and New York: Routledge.

Liszkowski, U., Carpenter, M., Striano, T., and Tomasello, M. (2006). 12- and 18-month-olds point to provide information for others. *Journal of Cognition and Development, 7*(2), 173–187.

Lotto, A. J., Hickok, G. S., and Holt, L. L. (2009). Reflections on mirror neurons and speech perception. *Trends in Cognitive Sciences, 13*(4), 110–114.

McBride, J., Sumner, P., Jackson, S. R., Bajaj, N., and Husain, M. (2013). Exaggerated object affordance and absent automatic inhibition in alien hand syndrome. *Cortex, 49*(8), 2040–2054.

McConkie, G. W., and Currie, C. B. (1996). Visual stability across saccades while viewing complex pictures. *Journal of Experimental Psychology: Human Perception and Performance, 22*(3), 563.

McLeod, P., Plunkett, K., and Rolls, E. T. (1998). *Introduction to Connectionist Modelling of Cognitive Processes*. Oxford: Oxford University Press.

MacGregor, N. (2011). *A History of the World in 100 Objects*. New York: Penguin.

McNair, N. A., Behrens, A. D., and Harris, I. M. (2017). Automatic recruitment of the motor system by undetected graspable objects: A motor-evoked potential study. *Journal of Cognitive Neuroscience, 29*(11), 1918–1931.

Malafouris, L., and Renfrew, C. (2010). *The Cognitive Life of Things: Recasting the Boundaries of the Mind*. Cambridge: McDonald Institute for Archaeological Research.

Manera, V., Becchio, C., Cavallo, A., Sartori, L., and Castiello, U. (2011). Cooperation or competition? Discriminating between social intentions by observing prehensile movements. *Experimental Brain Research, 211*(3–4), 547–556.

Mangun, G. R., and Hillyard, S. A. (1995). Mechanisms and models of selective attention. In M. D. Rugg and M. G. H. Coles (eds.), *Electrophysiology of Mind: Event-related Brain Potentials and Cognition* (pp. 40–85). New York: Oxford University Press.

Mark, L. S. (1987). Eyeheight-scaled information about affordances: A study of sitting and stair climbing. *Journal of Experimental Psychology: Human Perception and Performance, 13*(3), 361–370.

Marr, D. (1982). *Vision: A Computational Investigation into the Human Representation and Processing of Visual Information*. San Francisco: WH Freeman.

Marteniuk, R. G., MacKenzie, C. L., Jeannerod, M., Athenes, S., and Dugas, C. (1987). Constraints on human arm movement trajectories. *Canadian Journal of Psychology/Revue canadienne de psychologie, 41*(3), 365.

Marx, K., and Engels, F. (1970. *The German Ideology.* London: Lawrence & Wishart.

Marzke, M. W. (2013). Tool making, hand morphology and fossil hominins. *Philosophical Transactions of the Royal Society of London B: Biological Sciences, 368*(1630), https://europepmc.org/abstract/med/24101624

Marzke, M. W., and Shackley, M. S. (1986). Hominid hand use in the Pliocene and Pleistocene: Evidence from experimental archaeology and comparative morphology. *Journal of Human Evolution, 15*(6), 439–460.

Mauss, M. (2006). *Techniques, Technology and Civilization.* Oxford: Berghahn.

Meltzoff, A. N. (1988). Infant imitation after a 1-week delay: Long-term memory for novel acts and multiple stimuli. *Developmental Psychology, 24*(4), 470.

(1990). Foundations for developing a concept of self: The role of imitation in relating self to other and the value of social mirroring, social modeling, and self practice in infancy. In D. Cicchetti and M. Beeghly (eds.), *The John D. and Catherine T. MacArthur Foundation Series on Mental Health and Development. The Self in Transition: Infancy to Childhood* (pp. 139–164). Chicago: University of Chicago Press.

(2005). Imitation and other minds: The 'like me' hypothesis. *Perspectives on Imitation: From Neuroscience to Social Science, 2*, 55–77.

Meltzoff, A. N., and Moore, M. K. (1977). Imitation of facial and manual gestures by human neonates. *Science, 198*(4312), 75–78.

Merleau-Ponty, M. (1967). *The Structure of Behavior.* Boston, MA: Beacon Press.

(1968). *The Visible and the Invisible.* Evanston, IL: Northwestern University Press.

(2002). *Phenomenology of Perception.* London and New York: Routledge.

Messud, C. (2017). Matisse: The joy of things. *New York Review of Books,* 20 June, www.nybooks.com/daily/2017/06/20/matisse-the-joy-of-things

Michaels, C. F. (2003). Affordances: Four points of debate. *Ecological Psychology, 15*(2), 135–148.

Miller, D. (1987). *Material Culture and Mass Consumption.* New York: Basil Blackwell.

(2005). *Materiality.* Durham, NC: Duke University Press.

Milner, D., and Goodale, M. (2006). *The Visual Brain in Action.* Oxford: Oxford University Press.

Mishkin, M., Ungerleider, L. G., and Macko, K. A. (1983). Object vision and spatial vision: Two cortical pathways. *Trends in Neurosciences, 6*, 414–417.

Molenberghs, P., Cunnington, R., and Mattingley, J. B. (2012). Brain regions with mirror properties: A meta-analysis of 125 human fMRI studies. *Neuroscience and Biobehavioral Reviews, 36*(1), 341–349.

Moll, H., Richter, N., Carpenter, M., and Tomasello, M. (2008). Fourteen-month-olds know what 'we' have shared in a special way. *Infancy, 13*(1), 90–101.

Moll, H., and Tomasello, M. (2007). Cooperation and human cognition: The Vygotskian intelligence hypothesis. *Philosophical Transactions of the Royal Society of London B: Biological Sciences*, *362*(1480), 639–648.

Morgan, T. J. H., Uomini, N. T., Rendell, L. E., Chouinard-Thuly, L., Street, S. E., Lewis, H. M., Cross, C. P., Evans, C., Kearney, I., de la Torre, A., Whiten, A., and Laland, K. N. (2015). Experimental evidence for the co-evolution of hominin tool-making teaching and language. *Nature Communications*, *6*, 6029.

Mukamel, R., Ekstrom, A. D., Kaplan, J., Iacoboni, M., and Fried, I. (2010). Single-neuron responses in humans during execution and observation of actions. *Current Biology*, *20*(8), 750–756.

Murata, A., Fadiga, L., Fogassi, L., Gallese, V., Raos, V., and Rizzolatti, G. (1997). Object representation in the ventral premotor cortex (area F5) of the monkey. *Journal of Neurophysiology*, *78*(4), 2226–2230.

Nagell, K., Olguin, R., and Tomasello, M. (1993). Processes of social-learning in the tool use of chimpanzees (*Pan troglodytes*) and human children (*Homo sapiens*). *Journal of Comparative Psychology*, *107*(2), 174–186.

Naish, K. R., Reader, A. T., Houston-Price, C., Bremner, A. J., and Holmes, N. P. (2013). To eat or not to eat? Kinematics and muscle activity of reach-to-grasp movements are influenced by the action goal, but observers do not detect these differences. *Experimental Brain Research*, *225*(2), 261–275.

Napier, J. R., and Tuttle, R. (1993). *Hands*. Princeton, NJ: Princeton University Press.

Neidle, C. J. (2000). *The Syntax of American Sign Language: Functional Categories and Hierarchical Structure*. Cambridge, MA: MIT Press.

Neisser, U. (1994). Multiple systems: A new approach to cognitive theory. *European Journal of Cognitive Psychology*, 6, 225–241.

Newell, A. (1980). Physical symbol systems. *Cognitive Science*, *4*(2), 135–183.

Newman-Norlund, R. D., van Schie, H. T., van Zuijlen, A. M., and Bekkering, H. (2007). The mirror neuron system is more active during complementary compared with imitative action. *Nature Neuroscience*, *10*(7), 817–818.

Newman-Norlund, R. D., Bosga, J., Meulenbroek, R. G. J., and Bekkering, H. (2008). Anatomical substrates of cooperative joint-action in a continuous motor task: Virtual lifting and balancing. *Neuroimage*, *41*(1), 169–177.

Nisbett, R. E., and Masuda, T. (2003). Culture and point of view. *Proceedings of the National Academy of Sciences*, *100*(19), 11163–11170.

Nisbett, R. E., Peng, K., Choi, I., and Norenzayan, A. (2001). Culture and systems of thought: Holistic versus analytic cognition. *Psychological Review*, *108*(2), 291.

Noë, A. (2004). *Action in Perception*. Cambridge, MA: MIT Press.
  (2010). Vision without representation. In N. Gangopadhyay, M. Madary and F. Spicer (eds.), *Perception, Action, and Consciousness: Sensorimotor Dynamics and Two Visual Systems* (pp. 245–256). Oxford and New York: Oxford University Press.

Norman, J. (2002). Two visual systems and two theories of perception: An attempt to reconcile the constructivist and ecological approaches. *Behavioral and Brain Sciences*, 25(01), 73–96.

O'Connell, J. F., Hawkes, K., and Jones, N. B. (1999). Grandmothering and the evolution of Homo erectus. *Journal of Human Evolution*, 36(5), 461–485.

Odling-Smee, F. J., Laland, K. N., and Feldman, M. W. (2003). *Niche Construction: The Neglected Process in Evolution*. Princeton, NJ: Princeton University Press.

Orban, G. A., Claeys, K., Nelissen, K., Smans, R., Sunaert, S., Todd, J. T., Wardak, C., Durand, J., and Vanduffel, W. (2006). Mapping the parietal cortex of human and non-human primates. *Neuropsychologia*, 44(13), 2647–2667.

O'Regan, J. K., and Noë, A. (2001). A sensorimotor account of vision and visual consciousness. *Behavioral and Brain Sciences*, 24(05), 939–973.

O'Regan, J. K., Rensink, R. A., and Clark, J. J. (1999). Change-blindness as a result of 'mudsplashes'. *Nature*, 398, 34–34.

Özçalışkan, Ş., Lucero, C., and Goldin-Meadow, S. (2016). Is seeing gesture necessary to gesture like a native speaker? *Psychological Science*, 27, 737–747.

Pascual-Leone, A., Amedi, A., Fregni, F., and Merabet, L. B. (2005). The plastic human brain cortex. *Annual Review of Neuroscience*, 28, 377–401.

Pelegrin, J. (2005). Remarks about archaeological techniques and methods of knapping: Elements of a cognitive approach to stone knapping. *Stone Knapping: The Necessary Condition for a Uniquely Hominid Behaviour*, 23–33.

Pellegrino, G. di, Fadiga, L., Fogassi, L., Gallese, V., and Rizzolatti, G. (1992). Understanding motor events: A neurophysiological study. *Experimental Brain Research*, 91(1), 176–180.

Penfield, W., and Boldrey, E. (1937). Somatic motor and sensory representation in the cerebral cortex of man as studied by electrical stimulation. *Brain*, 60 (4), 389–443.

Perenin, M.-T., and Vighetto, A. (1988). Optic ataxia: A specific disruption in visuomotor mechanisms. *Brain*, 111(3), 643–674.

Perry, C. J., Amarasooriya, P., and Fallah, M. (2016). An eye in the palm of your hand: Alterations in visual processing near the hand, a mini-review. *Frontiers in Computational Neuroscience*, 10, 37.

Pinker, S. (1995). *The Language Instinct: The New Science of Language and Mind*. London: Penguin.

Pinker, S., and Jackendoff, R. (2005). The faculty of language: What's special about it? *Cognition*, 95(20), 201–236.

Poldrack, R. A. (2006). Can cognitive processes be inferred from neuroimaging data? *Trends in Cognitive Science*, 10(2), 59–63.

Previc, F. H. (1990). Functional specialization in the lower and upper visual fields in humans: Its ecological origins and neurophysiological implications. *Behavioral and Brain Sciences*, 13(03), 519–542.

Pulvermüller, F. (2005). Brain mechanisms linking language and action. *Nature Reviews Neuroscience*, 6(7), 576–582.

Pulvermüller, F., and Fadiga, L. (2010). Active perception: sensorimotor circuits as a cortical basis for language. *Nature Reviews Neuroscience*, 11(5), 351–360.

Ramenzoni, V. C., and Liszkowski, U. (2016). The social reach 8-month-olds reach for unobtainable objects in the presence of another person. *Psychological Science*, *27*(9), 1278–1285.

Rao, R. P. N., and Ballard, D. H. (1999). Predictive coding in the visual cortex: A functional interpretation of some extra-classical receptive field effects. *Nature Neuroscience*, *2*(1), 79–87.

Reed, E. S. (1996). *Encountering the World: Toward an Ecological Psychology*. New York: Oxford University Press.

Renfrew, C. (1996). The sapient behaviour paradox: how to test for potential. *Modelling the Early Human Mind*, 11–14.

(2008). Neuroscience, evolution and the sapient paradox: The factuality of value and of the sacred. *Philosophical Transactions of the Royal Society B: Biological Sciences*, *363*(1499), 2041–2047.

Rensink, R. A., O'Regan, J. K., and Clark, J. L. 1997). To see or not to see: The need for attention to perceive changes in scenes. *Psychological Science, 8* (5), 368–373.

Riddoch, M. J., Edwards, M. G., Humphreys, G. W., West, R., and Heafield, T. (1998). Visual affordances direct action: Neuropsychological evidence from manual interference. *Cognitive Neuropsychology*, *15*(6–8), 645–683.

Rizzolatti, G., and Arbib, M. A. (1998). Language within our grasp. *Trends in Neurosciences*, *21*(5), 188–194.

Rizzolatti, G., and Craighero, L. (2004). The mirror-neuron system. *Annual Review of Neuroscience*, *27*, 169–192.

Rizzolatti, G., Fadiga, L., Gallese, V., and Fogassi, L. (1996). Premotor cortex and the recognition of motor actions. *Cognitive Brain Research*, *3*(2), 131–141.

Rizzolatti, G., Fadiga, L., Matelli, M., Bettinardi, V., Paulesu, E., Perani, D., and Fazio, F. (1996). Localization of grasp representations in humans by PET: 1. Observation versus execution. *Experimental Brain Research*, *111* (2), 246–252.

Rizzolatti, G., Gentilucci, M., and Matelli, M. (1985). Selective spatial attention: One center, one circuit or many circuits? In M. Posner and O. S. M. Marin (eds.), *Attention and Performance XI* (pp. 251–265). Hillsdale, NJ: Earlsbaum.

Rizzolatti, G., and Matelli, M. (2003). Two different streams form the dorsal visual system: Anatomy and functions. *Experimental Brain Research*, *153*(2), 146–157.

Rizzolatti, G., Matelli, M., and Pavesi, G. (1983). Deficits in attention and movement following the removal of postarcuate (area 6) and prearcuate (area 8) cortex in macaque monkeys. *Brain, 106*(3), 655–673.

Rizzolatti, G., Scandolara, C., Matelli, M., and Gentilucci, M. (1981). Afferent properties of periarcuate neurons in macaque monkeys. II. Visual responses. *Behavioural Brain Research*, *2*(2), 147–163.

Rizzolatti, G., and Sinigaglia, C. (2008). *Mirrors in the Brain*. Oxford: Oxford University Press.

(2010). The functional role of the parieto-frontal mirror circuit: Interpretations and misinterpretations. *Nature Reviews Neuroscience*, *11*(4), 264–274.

Rochat, P., Goubet, N., and Senders, S. J. (1999). To reach or not to reach? Perception of body effectivities by young infants. *Infant and Child Development*, 8(3), 129–148.

Rosenbaum, D. A., Vaughan, J., Barnes, H. J., and Jorgensen, M. J. (1992). Time course of movement planning: Selection of handgrips for object manipulation. *Journal of Experimental Psychology: Learning, Memory, and Cognition*, 18(5), 1058.

Rumelhart, D. E., Smolensky, P., McClelland, J. L., and Hinton, G. E. (1986). Schemata and sequential thought processes in PDP models. In *Parallel Distributed Processing: Explorations in the Microstructure, Vol. 2: Psychological and Biological Models* (ch. 14). Cambridge, MA: MIT Press.

Sampaio, M., and Bach-y-Rita, P. (2001). Brain plasticity: 'Visual' acuity of blind persons via the tongue. *Brain Research*, 908, 204–207.

Sartori, L., Becchio, C., and Castiello, U. (2011). Cues to intention: The role of movement information. *Cognition*, 119(2), 242–252.

Schick, K. D., Toth, N., Garufi, G., Savage-Rumbaugh, E. S., Rumbaugh, D., and Sevcik, R. (1999). Continuing investigations into the stone tool-making and tool-using capabilities of a bonobo (*Pan paniscus*). *Journal of Archaeological Science*, 26(7), 821–832.

Schmidt, R. C., Carello, C., and Turvey, M. T. (1990). Phase transitions and critical fluctuations in the visual coordination of rhythmic movements between people. *Journal of Experimental Psychology: Human Perception and Performance*, 16(2), 227.

Schnall, S., Zadra, J. R., and Proffitt, D. R. (2010). Direct evidence for the economy of action: Glucose and the perception of geographical slant. *Perception*, 39(4), 464–482.

Schütz-Bosbach, S., Haggard, P., Fadiga, L., and Craighero, L. (2008). Motor cognition: TMS studies of action generation. In C. M. Epstein, E. M. Wassermann, and U. Ziemann (eds.), *Oxford Handbook of Transcranial Stimulation* (pp. 463–478). Oxford: Oxford University Press.

Searle, J. (1980). Minds, brains and programs. *Behavioral and brain sciences*, 3, 417–424.

(1989). Artificial intelligence and the Chinese room: An exchange. *New York Review of Books*, 36, 2.

Sebanz, N., Knoblich, G., and Prinz, W. (2003). Representing others' actions: Just like one's own? *Cognition*, 88(3), B11–B21.

Sebanz, N., Knoblich, G., Prinz, W., and Wascher, E. (2006). Twin peaks: An ERP study of action planning and control in coacting individuals. *Journal of Cognitive Neuroscience*, 18(5), 859–870.

Senior, C., Ward, J., and David, A. S. (2002). Representational momentum and the brain: An investigation into the functional necessity of V5/MT. *Visual Cognition*, 9(1–2), 81–92.

Shapiro, K. L., Raymond, J. E., and Arnell, K. M. (1997). The attentional blink. *Trends in Cognitive Science*, 1(8), 291–296.

Shockley, K., Santana, M.-V., and Fowler, C. A. (2003). Mutual interpersonal postural constraints are involved in cooperative conversation. *Journal of Experimental Psychology: Human Perception and Performance*, 29(2), 326.

Simons, D. J., and Levin, T. L. (1997). Change blindness. *Trends in Cognitive Science*, 7(1), 261–267.

Simons, D. J., and Rensink, R. A. (2005). Change blindness: Past, present and future. *Trends in Cognitive Science*, 9(1), 16–20.

Smith, B. H., and Tompkins, R. L. (1995). Toward a life history of the Hominidae. *Annual Review of Anthropology*, 24(1), 257–279.

Smith, L. B., and Thelen, E. (2003). Development as a dynamic system. *Trends in Cognitive Sciences*, 7(8), 343–348.

Spence, C., Pavani, F., Maravita, A., and Holmes, N. (2004). Multisensory contributions to the 3-D representation of visuotactile peripersonal space in humans: Evidence from the crossmodal congruency task. *Journal of Physiology-Paris*, 98(1), 171–189.

Spivey, M., Tyler, M., Richardson, D., and Young, E. (2000). Eye movements during comprehension of spoken scene descriptions. In *Proceedings of the 22nd Annual Conference of the Cognitive Science Society*. https://escholarship.org/uc/item/7z34j8zw

Sporns, O., and Edelman, G. M. (1993). Solving Bernstein's problem: A proposal for the development of coordinated movement by selection. *Child Development*, 64(4), 960–981.

Steele, J., and Uomini, N. (2005). Humans, tools and handedness. In V. Roux and B. Bril (eds.), *Stone Knapping: The Necessary Conditions for a Uniquely Hominin Behaviour* (pp. 217–239). Cambridge: McDonald Institute for Archaeological Research.

Sterelny, K. (2011). From hominins to humans: How sapiens became behaviourally modern. *Philosophical Transactions of the Royal Society of London B: Biological Sciences*, 366(1566), 809–822.

Sterelny, K., and Hiscock, P. (2014). Symbols, signals, and the archaeological record. *Biological Theory*, 9(1), 1–3.

Stokoe, W. C. (2001). *Language in Hand: Why Sign Came before Speech*. Washington, DC: Gallaudet University Press.

   (2005). Sign language structure: An outline of the visual communication systems of the American deaf. *Journal of Deaf Studies and Deaf Education*, 10(1), 3–37.

Stout, D. (2011). Stone toolmaking and the evolution of human culture and cognition. *Philosophical Transactions of the Royal Society B: Biological Sciences*, 366(1567), 1050–1059.

Stout, D., and Chaminade, T. (2007). The evolutionary neuroscience of tool making. *Neuropsychologia*, 45(5), 1091–1100.

Stout, D., Toth, N., Schick, K., and Chaminade, T. (2008). Neural correlates of Early Stone Age toolmaking: Technology, language and cognition in human evolution. *Philosophical Transactions of the Royal Society of London B: Biological Sciences*, 363(1499), 1939–1949.

Strogatz, S. H., Abrams, D. M., McRobie, A., Eckhardt, B., and Ott, E. (2005). Theoretical mechanics: Crowd synchrony on the Millennium Bridge. *Nature*, 438(7064), 43–44.

Symes, E., Tucker, M., Ellis, R., Vainio, L., and Ottoboni, G. (2008). Grasp preparation improves change detection for congruent objects.

Journal of Experimental Psychology: Human Perception and Performance, 34 (4), 854.

Tarr, B., Launay, J., Cohen, E., and Dunbar, R. (2015). Synchrony and exertion during dance independently raise pain threshold and encourage social bonding. *Biology Letters, 11*(10), 20150767.

Tennie, C., Call, J., and Tomasello, M. (2009). Ratcheting up the ratchet: On the evolution of cumulative culture. *Philosophical Transactions of the Royal Society B: Biological Sciences, 364*(1528), 2405–2415.

Thomas, L. E. (2013). Grasp posture modulates attentional prioritization of space near the hands. *Frontiers in Psychology, 4*, 312.

Thomsen, M.-L. (1984). *The Sumerian Language: An Introduction to Its History and Grammatical Structure* (vol. 10). Copenhagen: Akademisk forlag.

Tomasello, M. (1996). Do apes ape? In C. M. Heyes and B. J. Galef (eds.), *Social Learning in Animals: The Roots of Culture* (pp. 319–346). London: Academic Press.

Tomasello, M. and Carpenter, M. (2007). Shared intentionality. *Developmental Science, 10*(1), 121–125.

Tomasello, M., Carpenter, M., Call, J., Behne, T., and Moll, H. (2005). Understanding and sharing intentions: The origins of cultural cognition. *Behavioral and Brain Sciences, 28*(05), 675–691.

Tomasello, M., and Haberl, K. (2003). Understanding attention: 12- and 18-month-olds know what is new for other persons. *Developmental Psychology, 39*(5), 906.

Tomasello, M., Kruger, A. C., and Ratner, H. H. (1993). Cultural learning. *Behavioral and Brain Sciences, 16*(03), 495–511.

Toth, N. (1985). Archaeological evidence for preferential right-handedness in the Lower and Middle Pleistocene, and its possible implications. *Journal of Human Evolution, 14*(6), 607–614.

Trevarthen, C. B. (1968). Two mechanisms of vision in primates. *Psychologische Forschung, 31*(4), 299–337.

Triesch, J., Ballard, D. H., Hayhoe, M. M., and Sullivan, B. T. (2003). What you see is what you need. *Journal of Vision, 3*(9), 86–94.

Tucker, M., and Ellis, R. (1998). On the relations between seen objects and components of potential actions. *Journal of Experimental Psychology: Human Perception and Performance, 24*(3), 830–846.

(2004). Action priming by briefly presented objects. *Acta Psychologica, 116* (2),185–203.

Turvey, M. T. (1992). Affordances and prospective control: An outline of the ontology. *Ecological Psychology, 4*(3), 173–187.

Turvey, M. T., Shaw, R. E., Reed, E. S., and Mace, W. M. (1981). Ecological laws of perceiving and acting: In reply to Fodor and Pylyshyn (1981). *Cognition, 9*(3), 237–304.

Ungerleider, L. G., and Mishkin, M. (1982). Two cortical visual systems. In D. J. Ingle, M. A. Goodale, and R. J. W. Mansfield (eds.), *Analysis of Visual Behavior* (pp. 549–586). Cambridge, MA: MIT Press.

Ullman, S. (1980). Against direct perception. *Behavioral and Brain Sciences, 3*, 378–381.

Umilta, M.A., Kohler, E., Gallese, V., Fogassi, L., Fadiga, L., Keysers, C., and Rizzolatti, G. (2001). I know what you are doing: A neurophysiological study. *Neuron, 31*(10, 155–165.

Uskul, A. K., Kitayama, S., and Nisbett, R. E. (2008). Ecocultural basis of cognition: Farmers and fishermen are more holistic than herders. *Proceedings of the National Academy of Sciences, 105*(25), 8552–8556.

Vainio, L., Symes, E., Ellis, R., Tucker, M., and Ottoboni, G. (2008). On the relations between action planning, object identification, and motor representations of observed actions and objects. *Cognition, 108*(2), 444–465.

Vainio, L., Tiainen, M., Tiippana, K., Komeilipoor, N., and Vainio, M. (2015). Interaction in planning movement direction for articulatory gestures and manual actions. *Experimental Brain Research, 233*(10), 2951–2959.

Vainio, L., Schulman, M., Tiippana, K., and Vainio, M. (2013). Effect of syllable articulation on precision and power grip performance. *PLOS one.* http://journals.plos.org/plosone/article?id=10.1371/journal.pone.0053061

Varela, F. J., Rosch, E., and Thompson, E. (1992). *The Embodied Mind: Cognitive Science and Human Experience.* Cambridge, MA: MIT Press.

Vuilleumier, P., Valenza, N., Mayer, E., Reverdin, A., and Landis, T. (1998). Near and far visual space in unilateral neglect. *Annals of Neurology, 43*(3), 406–410.

Vygotsky, L. S. (1967). Play and its role in the mental development of the child. *Soviet Psychology, 5*(3), 6–18.

(2012). *Thought and Language.* Cambridge, MA: MIT Press.

Warneken, F., Chen, F., and Tomasello, M. (2006). Cooperative activities in young children and chimpanzees. *Child Development, 77*(3), 640–663.

Warneken, F., and Tomasello, M. (2006). Altruistic helping in human infants and young chimpanzees. *Science, 311*(5765), 1301–1303.

Warren, W.H. (1984). Perceiving affordances: Visual guidance of stair climbing. *Journal of Experimental Psychology: Human Perception and Performance, 10*(5), 683–703.

Warren, Jr., W. H., and Whang, S. (1987). Visual guidance of walking through apertures: Body-scaled information for affordances. *Journal of Experimental Psychology: Human Perception and Performance, 13*(3), 371–383.

Waxman, S. R., Fu, X., Ferguson, B., Geraghty, K., Leddon, E., Liang, J., and Zhao, M.-F. (2016). How early is infants' attention to objects and actions shaped by culture? New evidence from 24-month-olds raised in the US and China. *Cultural Psychology,* 97. https://doi.org/10.3389/fpsyg.2016.00097

Weiskrantz, L. (2009). *Blindsight: A Case Study Spanning 35 Years and New Developments.* Oxford: Oxford University Press.

Weiskrantz, L., Warrington, E. K., Sanders, M. D., and Marshall, J. (1974). Visual capacity in the hemianopic field following a restricted occipital ablation. *Brain, 97*(4), 709–728.

Weiss, P. H., Marshall, J. C., Wunderlich, G., Tellmann, L., Halligan, P. W., Freund, H., Zilles, and Fink, G. R. (2000). Neural consequences of acting in near versus far space: A physiological basis for clinical dissociations. *Brain, 123*(12), 2531–2541.

Wheeler, M. (2013). Science friction: Phenomenology, naturalism and cognitive science. *Royal Institute of Philosophy Supplement, 72,* 135–167.

Whiten, A., Horner, V., and De Waal, F. B. (2005). Conformity to cultural norms of tool use in chimpanzees. *Nature, 437*(7059), 737–740.

Whiten, A., McGuigan, N., Marshall-Pescini, S., and Hopper, L.M. (2009). Emulation, imitation, over-imitation and the scope of culture for child and chimpanzee, *364*(1528), 2417–2428.

Wikman, P. A., Vainio, L., and Rinne, T. (2015). The effect of precision and power grips on activations in human auditory cortex, *Frontiers in Neuroscience, 9,* 378.

Wilson, B., Kikuchi, Y., Sun, L., Hunter, D., Dick, F., Smith, K., Thiele, A., Griffiths, T. D., Marslen-Wilson, W. D., and Petkov, C. I. (2015). Auditory sequence processing reveals evolutionarily conserved regions of frontal cortex in macaques and humans. *Nature Communications, 6,* 8901.

Wilson, F. R. (2010). *The Hand: How Its Use Shapes The Brain, Language, and Human Culture.* New York: Pantheon.

Wilson, M. (2002). Six views of embodied cognition. *Psychonomic Bulletin and Review, 9*(4), 625–636.

Wilson, M., and Knoblich, G. (2005). The case for motor involvement in perceiving conspecifics. *Psychological Bulletin, 131*(3), 460.

Witt, J. K. (2011). Action's effect on perception. *Current Directions in Psychological Science, 20*(3), 201–206.

Witt, J. K., Proffitt, D. R., and Epstein, W. (2005). Tool use affects perceived distance, but only when you intend to use it. *Journal of Experimental Psychology. Human Perception and Performance, 31*(5), 880–888.

Zahavi, D. (2003). *Husserl's Phenomenology.* Stanford, CA: Stanford University Press.

(2004). Phenomenology and the project of naturalization. *Phenomenology and the Cognitive Sciences, 3*(4), 331–347.

Index

accelerated evolution, 129–131
Acheulean epoch
  language use during, 149–150
  material cultures during, 125–127
  tool manufacturing during, 73
Acheulean Industrial Complex, tool use
  and, 67
action. *See also* cooperation in joint action
    on objects; joint action hypothesis
  higher-level cognition and, 4
  joint, 111–112, 163–164
  MNS and, 110–116
    joint activity, 111–112
    through shared toolspace, 114
    synchronous activity, 114–115
  perception and, 4, 15, 35
  physical, 100
  taxonomy of, 171, 172
  vision and, 35
  visual attention and, 61–62
action understanding, 85–87
Actor-Network Theory (ANT), 135–136
adaptations. *See* plastic adaptations
affective cognition, 19
affordances, 32, 43–53
  AHS and, 47–48, 52
  associative memory and, 45
  in body-centred space, 44
  canonical, 52
  criticisms of, 34, 51
  hand-object, 52
  imitation and, 96
  learning and, 50–51
  MEPs and, 47
  microaffordances, 47–49
  MNS and, 95–96
    imitation and, 96
  paradoxes in, 49–50
  stable, 52
  TMS and, 47
  toolspace and, 75–76
  variable, 52

whole body, 51
agency, 123–127
  in ANT, 135–136
agent–object distinction, 126–127
alien hand syndrome (AHS), 47–48, 52
ambient visual systems, 36–38, 39
American Sign Language (ASL), 139–140
ANT. *See* Actor-Network Theory
apprentice learning, 132
artefacts
  in joint activities, 2
  language as, 155–156
  as objects, 124
artificial intelligence, 18
artificial neural networks, 103
ASL. *See* American Sign Language
associative learning, 97–99
associative memory, 45
attention, visual, 53–60
  action and, 61–62
  modulation of, 59–60
attention biases, 123

biases. *See* attention biases
blindsight, 38
Boltzmann machines, 104–105, 106
Bourdieu, Pierre, 121
brachiating, 63–64
brain development, 21. *See also* mirror
    neurone system; sensorimotor brain
    networks
  artificial neural networks, 103
  Broca's area, 87–88
    language use and, 141, 143–145,
    147–149
  cortical functions, 9
  exocerebrum, 169
  language use and
    in mirror hypothesis, 141, 143–145
    in toolmaker hypothesis, 147–149
  neural plasticity and, 23, 164–167, 173
  tool use and, 73–78

CPSIA information can be obtained
at www.ICGtesting.com
Printed in the USA
LVHW081701311020
670371LV00007B/89